AN URBAN ODYSSEY

Also by Sam Hall Kaplan:

LA Follies: Design and Other Diversions in a Fractured Metropolis
LA Lost and Found: An Architectural History of Los Angeles

As Samuel Kaplan:

The Dream Deferred: People, Politics and Planning In Suburbia
(with Gilbert Tauber) *The New York City Handbook*

ABOUT THE COVER

The view is the urban scene at the convergence of Broadway and Fifth Avenue; on the street, the purposeful pedestrians and impatient traffic, and above, the iconic Flatiron Building. A local and national landmark, celebrated as one of New York City's first skyscrapers, it was designed by the renowned architect Daniel Burnham, and completed in 1902. At first, the 22-story, steel-framed, limestone and ornate terracotta-clad structure, was scorned as a folly, but soon after, embraced for its ornate Beaux-Arts style and distinctive triangular shape, alluding to a flat clothes iron. This prompted the label of the building at 23rd Street and the surrounding neighborhood: the Flatiron District.

On a personal note, I lived for a time in the mid-1970s in the neighborhood, a few blocks east on 24th Street and Third Avenue. The apartment was a block from New York's singular public school for the hearing impaired, "47," including an addition of classrooms with a residential tower above. It was then being built by the city's Educational Construction Fund when I was its director of development.

To the far west of the district in Chelsea is the High Line, which, before it became a much-lauded linear park, was a raw elevated train track for refrigerated cars of produce going to the city's market in the nearby Meat District. There in the summers of the late 50s I prowled nights on the tracks checking produce for the Railroad Perishable Inspection Agency. Days I hustled chess games for pocket money south of the district in Greenwich Village's Washington Square Park. These urban experiences informed my fledgling journalism.

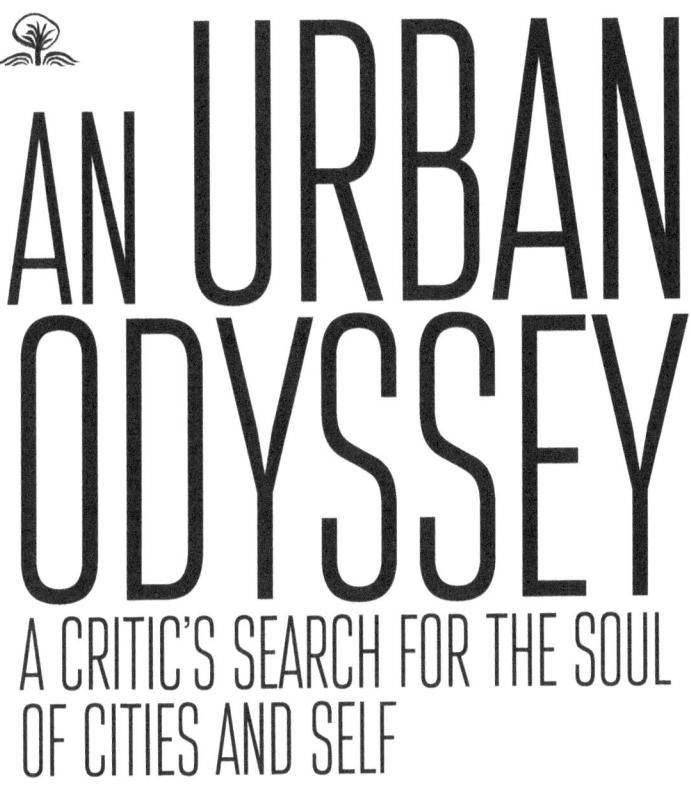

AN URBAN ODYSSEY

A CRITIC'S SEARCH FOR THE SOUL OF CITIES AND SELF

SAM HALL KAPLAN

CHERRY ORCHARD BOOKS
2025

Library of Congress Cataloging-in-Publication Data

Names: Kaplan, Sam Hall, author.
Title: An urban odyssey : a critic's search for the soul of cities and self / Sam Hall Kaplan.
Description: Boston : Cherry Orchard Books, 2024.
Identifiers: LCCN 2024021970 (print) | LCCN 2024021971 (ebook) | ISBN 9798887195476 (hardback) | ISBN 9798887195483 (paperback) | ISBN 9798887195490 (adobe pdf) | ISBN 9798887195506 (epub)
Subjects: LCSH: Kaplan, Sam Hall. | Journalists—United States—Biography. | Critics—United States—Biography.
Classification: LCC PN4874.K3425 A3 2024 (print) | LCC PN4874.K3425 (ebook) | DDC 070.92 [B]—dc23/eng/20240604
LC record available at https://lccn.loc.gov/2024021970
LC ebook record available at https://lccn.loc.gov/2024021971

Copyright © 2024, Academic Studies Press
All rights reserved. Second, revised edition, 2025.

ISBN 9798887195476 (hardback)
ISBN 9798887195483 (paperback)
ISBN 9798887195490 (adobe pdf)
ISBN 9798887195506 (epub)

Book design by Dina Nemirovsky
Cover design by Ivan Grave

Published by Cherry Orchard Books, an imprint of Academic Studies Press
1577 Beacon Street
Brookline, MA 02446, USA
press@academicstudiespress.com
www.academicstudiespress.com

Dedicated to My Loving Family:

Wife: Peggy
Children: Alison, Mike, Josef, and Kyle
Grandchildren: Zoe, Anna, and Mara
Siblings: Rose, Saul, Manny, and Fran
Sister-in-law: Lucette
Brother-in-law: Jerry
Daughters-in-law: Vic and Bridget
And the memory of my parents, Sadie and Joe

With special thanks to the Academic Studies Press editorial team of Alessandra Anzani, Stuart Allen, Becca Kearns, Matthew Charlton, and Kira Nemirovsky, and my abiding friends George Malko, Lance Brown, Judi Goldstein, Jose Rios, Bill Wood, Julie Taylor, Cory Buckner, Anne Zimmerman, Marc Haefele, and Katherine and Joe Highcove, and bones to my faithful standard Poodles, Lucy and Luna, for their patience.

"WHAT IS THE CITY BUT THE PEOPLE."

— William Shakespeare
Coriolanus, Act 3, Scene 1

CONTENTS

Introduction	xi
The Stoop, and City Beyond	1
Jobs and Bosses	11
Wide-Eyed and Bushy-Tailed	22
City Desk Diversions	31
Saint Jane of Planning	39
Good Times, Bad Times	49
Reality Bites	62
Dreams Deferred	74
Jumping Rock to Rock	86
Los Angeles Beckons	97
Welcome to the Land of Sunshine and Shadows	107
"L.A.'s The Place"	118
Persevering Preservation	129
Planning, for Better or Worse	138
The Art and Angst of Architecture	151
Moving On	162
Disney Hall and Its Discontents	172
Critic at Bay	184
Tough Love Urbanism	196
Teaching as a Delight	211
Ever the Iconoclast	223
Community Planning Challenged	234
Critic Unbound	248

Reading Architecture	258
Misanthropic Malibu	267
The Fire and the Aftermath	282
Democracy's Soft Underbelly	290
Going Forward	295
Afterthoughts	301
Index	302
About the Author	303

INTRODUCTION

As a critic unbound, the search for a sense of place has been for me a compelling, fragmented urban odyssey. Recalled in memory and measured in experience, the odyssey cannot be summed up in a simple narrative of engrossing events and observations, deftly woven together.

A life as an odyssey is not really like that—certainly mine hasn't been. I view it as a puzzle of peopled events and deeply felt emotions, in a disturbing chaotic and cruel political climate and an alarming, threatened environment, scattered with embers of glittering hope. In retrospect, it is to me, personally, both rational and absurd, a contradiction, yet absorbing, a life in bits and pieces, fits and starts, to be recorded, candidly.

Though I occasionally had written personal reflections, my founding had been in pragmatic journalism, to report impartially, without fear or favor, and even in my years as a critic and commentator, to be sure when offering an opinion, at least trying to be dispassionate and fair. These were the posts that I grabbed onto and that guided me as I jumped from assignment to assignment, rock to rock, in the swift stream of writing.

Having authored several books, with some critical success and financial reward, I was encouraged by family and friends to write yet another, though this time a more personal chronicle. But I had deferred for various reasons, among them, frankly, not getting any foundation grants to subsidize my writing or any reasonable advance on royalties, both of which I received when younger, credentialed as I was by the *New York Times* and later the *Los Angeles Times*, and enjoying the exposure of radio and television, and an evolving social media.

To be sure, intellectual properties are problematical. And publishing has been sadly on the wane, in the rising competition for the disposable dollar in the vast bubbling multimedia and entertainment cauldron.

There is also my age to consider, at this writing eight-seven, and that I'm comfortably retired, still scribbling to be sure, but at leisure—an occasional book review and commentaries on the internet's social media where I have had a responsive following. And while reveling in reciting some of my varied adventures to family and friends, the thought of another book was off-putting. Writing is enjoyable, though also work.

But no surprise, I also have an ego, and I weakened when two of my children, one a recognized poet and the other an accomplished scholar, joined together on Father's Day, 2022, in a touching e-mail and addressed the issue of my writing a memoir of sorts, declaring that doing so would "be a beautiful way to preserve the power of your voice and the unique shape and content of your life for posterity, so your kids, grandkids, great grandkids (at some point) will have a window into your life and mind." My other two learned children, a professor and a lawyer, echoed the appeal, and so did my wife, Peggy.

Touched, I of course accepted the challenge, and began culling my scattered clippings selectively saved in portfolios, in books reviewed and authored and in a few magazines and newsletters collecting dust on shelves. And thank heaven for Wikipedia. All I had needed to get me started, really, was the heartfelt assignment, especially from my family, to whom

I have dedicated this book. Without their prodding, I wouldn't have initiated this writing.

To be sure, in my years as a writer for print or broadcast, be it a newspaper, periodical, or book, a radio or television script, daily news or short- or long-form documentaries, a speech or a lecture, I also rarely turned down an assignment. My dictum had been to most always say yes, and then worry about doing it; for if I said no, that would be final, and then I wouldn't even have a chance to attempt it and might never be called again. I especially liked assignments with deadlines, leaving no time for dreaded writer's block, which I never have suffered, but still fear, especially in my older years.

In retrospect, I had been hardwired to be a deadline-driven writer, from my very beginnings as a journeyman journalist. Indeed, my first paid assignment, in 1952, fifteen dollars a submission, was compiling the Queens Teen column for the Sunday *Long Island Daily Press*, and getting it to its office in by 5:00 p.m. on Thursdays, on 168th Street, south of Jamaica Avenue, rain or shine. Then there was being news writer and editor of WQXR, the radio station of the *New York Times*, where I had to produce a five-minute pithy script "every hour, on the hour." The job also included writing on occasion the news crawl of flashing honed headlines encircling the Forty-Second Street Times Square Tower, to be updated hourly.

Among my memories is writing "HAPPY NEW YEAR, 1960," and then having to elbow my way through milling crowds to the tower and up three flights to where the sign's typist perched, handing my script into eager hands, then going out into a teeming Times Square crowd, elbowing my way to Broadway and Forty-Third Street, and in the crush of cheering multitudes, glimpse the flashing bulletins and my words. Fleeting but satisfying.

Quickening the pace and pulse a few years later were the deadlines of night rewrite at the *Times*, with an editor hovering over me, and the rumble of the presses below as I banged away two and three fingered on a typewriter, to update for the next edition a breaking story, be it an earthquake (Alaska), a five-alarm fire (New York City), an election (wherever of import), the Academy Awards (Hollywood), or a political assassination and bloody coup (then Vietnam).

There also was no time for a coffee break, having to type three editorials to fill the news hole on the opinion page of the *New York Post* on days when its editorial editor would pass out drunk at his typewriter, impossible to wake as the deadline loomed. Or worse, he did wake, albeit wasted, to tap out an incomprehensible column, which had to be fact-checked and rewritten by me, while witnessing a once honored editor stumble through the tragic third act of his demise, while on deadline.

At the more tranquil *Los Angeles Times*, deadlines were problematical, depending on the story, and the writing more relaxed. If there was pressure, it was self-generated, for there was no want of planning and design issues in what I described as an adolescent city in the throes of a growth spurt. I enjoyed the time it tendered, writing a book, compiling another, and in the world beyond, being a husband and parent.

Then later into my sixties more demanding were the sporadic deadlines of television, whether the scheduled nightly broadcast or breaking news, a camera in the studio or in the field, be it in front of an angry mob, a raging firestorm, or an in-house director, its uncovered lens focused on me, up tight, a red light flashing above, the operator pointing a finger at me, telling me that I was "live," and to start reporting, and let's not have any dead air, please—never. But it was for me only a three-days-a-week job, leaving more time for freelancing and the family.

My book reviews and essays at the time sharply focused on the drift planning, design, and development, which had been stirring up a personal following, and I began assembling them as the grist for another book. Tentatively entitled "Searching for the Soul of Cities," it attracted interest, and despite my age, then seventy-five, I was primed to proceed, but then was stricken with cancer, and had to drop the project and put aside my notes. Thanks to UCLA Medical's oncology department and experimental treatments, the cancer was conquered, but left me weak.

The thought of a book lingered, less journalistic and more biographical, to document my critical writings and adventures in planning, design, and development. Then there was my family's history, which had roused my interest when researching a review in 2007 for the *Jewish Journal* on the planned National Museum of Jewish History in Philadelphia.

Aside from the architecture, the museum's programming interested me, that the planned featured exhibition would "seek to tell the dynamic story" of Jewish migration and adaptation to America. Resonating with me was the theme "It's Going to Be Your Story," for I had been trying for some time to get my mother, Sadie, who lived alone in an apartment in Rockaway, Queens, to talk about the roots of our large, loquacious family.

Though 104 years old in 2007, her memory was as sharp as ever, which not coincidentally had made her the subject of a longevity study of 150 or so select Jewish seniors being conducted by the Institute for Aging Research at Albert Einstein College of Medicine in the Bronx. She apparently was blessed, and possibly her children, myself included, with something that has been labeled the "Ashkenazi gene" (a designated protein CETPVVW) that may aid mental function and extend life.

But my mother preferred not to recall the stories she had once regaled me with, now dismissing them as *bubbemeises*, grandmother tales, that long ago crossed over the line from fact to fiction, and back again.

Was my great-great paternal grandfather really a sergeant in the French army, who when left behind as Napoleon retreated from Moscow, in 1812, deserted south into Ukraine, married a Jewess, and spent the rest of his life under the whip of the czar? My cousin Alan Cheuse, then the NPR book critic, believed it, and so included the item in his book *Fall Out of Heaven* (Peregrine Smith, 1987), a loose biography of his father, my Uncle Fishel, my father's younger brother. He had been a captain in the Soviet air force during the 1930s, who my father in time sponsored to come to the United States.

Or is this a story my father invented to ingratiate himself when he lived in Paris in the 1920s? He had gone to France as a coal miner after he spurned joining the Red Army in the Russian Civil War, and that after having been forced to serve in World War I and the Russian Revolution. In his later years he spoke French better than English, and would not speak Russian, except when spitting on the floor at the mention of the czar, Stalin, or Hitler. Yiddish was reserved for my mother and his surviving siblings.

And what about my mother's blood relatives who, after booking passage to America with their last penny at the turn of the nineteenth century, were instead dropped off ailing at a dock in Cork, Ireland? Some eventually made it to America, some didn't. One of my sons, Josef, a poet who spent a year at Trinity College in Dublin, has embraced this, as has my part Irish, Oregon-rooted wife, Margaret Mary.

It should be added that Josef was named after my father, who we believed was a "Joseph." But a few years after his passing, we were told by my mother that my father actually had been anointed that at Rikers Island by an immigration inspector who thought the name Joseph would serve him better as an "American" than his birth name, Shiah, in Yiddish meaning a girl or boy with the promise of perseverance and curiosity.

Who on my mother's side also were the ones left behind, to be driven down to the blue Danube by Hungarian fascists at the end of World War II, shot and thrown into the river that turned red with their blood; or who on my father's side were herded out of Kyiv by the occupying Nazis in 1941 to be slaughtered at Babyn Yar? Kyiv also was where an uncle reportedly had been put to death during the purges of 1938 by order of Stalin. Could it be that he complained too loudly about the famine that devastated Ukraine, or was linked somehow to Fanny Kaplan, who had shot Lenin?

We do know from my father that he was drafted into the czar's army at fourteen and fought in World War I. He claimed to have deserted three times and been caught twice, once being dragged out of his house and lined up to be shot. Except the execution was stopped by a priest, allowing my father time to slip away, kiss my grandmother goodbye, jump out a rear window, and run, literally for his life. Or at least so goes the story. "Thank God the window was facing west," he told me.

The stories continue about how he walked from town to town, picking up odd jobs, eventually signing up in Poland to be a coal miner in France, and put on a train going west. But instead of getting off the train as directed in the Saar mining district, he bribed the conductor and stayed on until Paris. There, with the help in that city's small Jewish community, he became a tailor and supposedly romanced countless French women widowed by the Great War. He talked fondly of this time when I taped him shortly before his death in 1980. My mother would not comment.

Was it Uncle Zalman, no longer fighting for the communists in Ukraine but a bartender in south Philly, who wrote him to come to the "Goldene Medina," the golden land, of America? He eventually did, on a purloined passport, to settle in Brooklyn. There he became a peddler in the era of tough Jews, *shtarkers*, then knowing how to sew, an upholsterer, and, finally, an interior decorator, furnishing the model apartments on Coney Island for, among others, developer Fred Trump, the father of the Donald. I did have some contact with that schmuck years later when he was hustling real estate in New York City, but it came to nothing.

So why was first cousin Alan a Cheuse, while me and most of my extended family are Kaplans? In his book, Alan writes that his father, Fishel, changed his name to Phil and the family name to Cheuse, which had had been my maternal grandmother's maiden name. He apparently did so to throw off the KGB, which he thought was hunting him down after his plane crashed in the Sea of Japan and he deserted the Soviet air force, to later end up in Shanghai and fly airmail for the Chinese nationalists. It is hard to make up these stories.

Or was it because Uncle Fishel hated his father, my paternal grandfather, for going to America after some pogrom or other and leaving behind the family in Ukraine, including my father, never to send for them as promised? Abandoning them. While they eventually made it to America, others did not, to die in World War II or to continue as what was described to me as the living dead in the ruins of Mother Russia.

"What is there to believe?" I asked my mother.

"You believe what you want to believe," she replied. "Some may be true, some may not. What difference does it make? You are who you are. Be happy." Then she added her daily counsel, and "be good, do good."

With these thoughts echoing, I soon was back writing, a gift of sorts to my large and loving family, friends and acquaintances, and whomever will find engaging the bits and pieces of my life, remembered, the fragments persisting and pertinent. Enjoy it.

THE STOOP, AND CITY BEYOND

Whether the stoop we shared as one of six families in the two-story, attached row house on East Eighth Street in the Flatbush section of Brooklyn was a public space or not was never broached when I grew up there during the Depression and World War ll.

However labeled, the stoop was, technically, a collective private space, used publicly for the immediate families living there and invited others. That included what relatives and neighbors might also want to *plotz,* sit with a sigh, there, as was the custom in the modest Jewish and Italian neighborhood; someone living in the 'hood was in effect family, anyone else from anywhere else, family or not, "landsman" or "familiga," was treated with suspicion.

Sitting on the concrete steps or the low sidewalls, or a faded foldout beach chair taken from an apartment, a grandstand was formed of the exterior steps, a stage set of sorts, offering views of the interminable gabbing, lounging residents and the passing parade of characters on the sidewalk, or to make room for a stoopball game, to watch, cheer, and bet on. I can sometimes hear the echo of my father saying, "I putta dime on Sammy," which of course spurred me to up my game. A dime was a lot in those days. That's what a heaping ice cream sugar cone cost in the nearby corner candy store on Coney Island Avenue; with sprinkles, a penny more.

Then as a youth and much later as a critic, I was curious to know just how these prime places in our urban sprawl came to be, and how they were shared with neighbors and, beyond Brooklyn, with the disparate masses. These man-made places and spaces included sidewalks and streets, squares, parks, and playgrounds, as well as the varied vestigial scenes, such as the iconic local stoops, a remnant of Amsterdam. To me, they were, and continue to be, the existential life of the city, its "genius loci."

These are the places that people experience and take pride in. Varying in form from city to city, layered with local tradition, past, present, and evolving. These places are what lend a city and its people that evanescent quality of soul. And as I ventured beyond Brooklyn and experienced the world, I found this ill-defined essence fascinating, be it in diverse urban and suburban neighborhoods and singular settings, including the streets of New York City and Paris, the commons of Boston, the beaches of Southern California, the night markets of Thailand, and the piazzas of Italy.

There was a housing shortage in Brooklyn back then, as there always seems to be, the East Eighth Street apartments I recall were overcrowded with large families—some with two. That is, if you counted the daughter with a child living with her parents during the war while her husband served abroad in the armed forces. The six, soon to be seven, in our family were crammed into a two-bedroom flat, my parents sleeping in the combined living and dining room. So, in all but the worst weather, the stoop was our real living room—private, but shared. And if necessary, we could always get a sweater or umbrella.

Everyone knew that my family—the occupants of 1460's big, walk-through, first-floor railroad flat apartment—was the landlord, as well as the super, and owned the building up to the center crack of the stoop. The other half belonged to the landlord of 1458, who lived in one of the apartments upstairs, preferring to rent out the lucrative large, first-floor owner's unit.

The crack was in the center off the stoop ball court, which encompassed the concrete apron from the sidewalk to the steps that led up to four doors—two doors for the downstairs flats and two for the four upstairs flats. The coarse concrete and brick amphitheater it created was my first experience of a public space, a playground where stoop ball dominated. But first it was my playpen of sorts, where I learned to crawl and stand, and then a performance area where I took my first steps.

The territorial imperative of the stoop collective expanded to the sidewalk and the street itself. The activity would continue there: hopscotch on a court of linear squares chalked on the sidewalk; intense games of marbles on the dirt median between the sidewalk and the curb; and finally, when we were big kids, stickball on the street.

Traffic was light, as the street was secondary and driving was limited by wartime gas rationing. And anything that did come down the street tended to go slow because one of the many urban legends in Flatbush told of how cars that sped got pelted with rocks and those that parked were stripped.

If, heaven forbid, someone playing outside tripped and got injured, no one was going to sue anyone, at least not in our neighborhood of shtarkers and wise guys. Justice was simple, swift and, being among neighbors, rare, thankfully. But if someone wanted to, they could sweep or hose down the stoops or sidewalk. And if they had an extension cord, they could bring a radio out and listen to a ballgame, fight, or, on one occasion, an opera.

The adults shared glasses of iced tea and chilled bottles of beer, along with gossip about what was then a close-knit working class neighborhood. Everybody knew each other's business, legal or not; and whether the men who left every morning with their lunch boxes were union or not, toiled standing up, or were big shots, that is, worked sitting down.

As for us kids, the 'hood was our world, where you could run free and far, as long as you could hear your mother's voice summoning you for supper. And you always obeyed because a neighbor was always watching, ready to kick your ass home. You didn't risk having to be told twice; you kicked the can down a sewer, if not into oblivion, and pocket the Spalding rubber ball.

As a young teenager in high school, the after-hours public place for us was the school yard. If the gate was locked, we could get in, that is, if someone had a wire cutter. And someone always did, so we'd squeeze through a hole in the chain link fence. It was even easier for those who could climb up and over the fence. There, we played whatever, and when it got too dark for a game, we would just hang out and "shoot the shit."

On weekends, when older and adventurous, and now living in Jamaica, Queens, I would hop a subway to Greenwich Village, try to look cool hanging out in Washington Square Park, maybe hustle a chess game for some pocket change, or just listen to the guitar and bongo drum players, while checking out the social scene, the action. And perhaps get lucky, score a date for a movie, preferably with an M&A (High School of Music & Art) girl, maybe go dutch on a cheap meal, or go back to her place to eat and listen to music. But only if she was "GD," geographically desirable, and did not live in, say, the Bronx, which would take me an hour to get home from.

I never thought about it back then, but I felt comfortable in public places. When I later lived on Manhattan's West Side, it was Riverside and Central Parks; when settled in East Harlem, it was Junior High School 117's playground, where I played in pick-up basketball and softball games. Less welcoming were the vacant lots, most of them trashed, such as the one I remember on a forlorn East One Hundredth St., a few blocks from my apartment on 106th St. I shied away from that one, until with some effort, while serving on the local planning board, we turned it into a community garden and a social space.

I subsequently wrote about the sweat labor endeavor for the *New York Times*, where I was a cub reporter, having been hired, I was told, for my New York City "street smarts." My article won an award from the city's council for parks and playgrounds, and me a tip of the crushed fedora favored by the city editor. He wore it indoors at his desk, I presume to avoid the stares of staff, and also as an eyeshade to avoid the glaring lights of City Room, which had become my second home in my twenties. As for the council's award, there was no cash, but a potted plant, which I planted in the garden, and a plaque, which I still have.

Then there was the historic New Haven Green, where in 1966 a team headed by the landscape architect Dan Kiley redesigned the sixteen-acre city center landmark, based in part on the user interviews I conducted as a fledgling planner.

And as I went on to direct the development of public schools in multiuse structures for the New York City Educational Construction Fund, my identifying the user became more pronounced, be it a student, teacher, janitor, a visiting parent, or a person passing on the street or living nearby—whomever might be affected by the places and spaces being created. I considered them my prime clients, and the architects to take heed if they hoped to get another commission from the fund.

Credit this stratagem to architectural educator Bernard Spring, who had mentored me at Princeton's Center for Environmental Studies, which I attended in 1967 and '68 while working as a housing consultant to the state of New Jersey. Bernie a year later moved on to the City College of University of New York, to become dean of its school of architecture. This prompted me to consider enrolling there and pursuing a degree in architecture, attending part time because it was determined I only needed a few credits for a degree. However, Bernie rejected the idea and, citing my varied experiences, hired me as an adjunct full professor instead, where overseeing student thesis projects I assumed the role as a user advocate.

It was a perspective I further refined with an earnest thanks to a grant from the National Endowment of the Arts to study public plazas as a socializing element. To my delight, they flourished where I had always yearned to visit—Italy. I went and viewed many, but focused in on Rome and the more modest Piazza de Santa Maria in Trastevere. There, in addition to its design, I diligently noted its varying uses—as a farmer's market, a soccer field, an arts and crafts venue, an antiques fair, a political arena for rallies and protests, the *passeggiataa*, trysting, and prostitution—sometimes all in a single day, and at varying times, twenty-four seven, for a varied demographic, from the neighborhood and beyond. It was unquestionably one of the most enjoyable experiences in my maverick education.

The resulting user advocacy was a perspective that was ingrained in all my future planning projects and critical critiques, and for which I was to be known when the design critic for the *Los Angeles Times*, and later as an urban affairs commentator for broadcast and print. That is, except in my East Harlem, where I would not call them "users," but rather "homies." And at Disney Imagineering, where for a few years I was master planning parks as a senior creative consultant, but mostly concerned with the public spaces between the venues, and the infamous queuing for the more popular rides. In this case, users were labeled, more appropriately, as guests, and respected as such.

I liked that; it was a sentiment I always thought was needed in the planning and use of public and private places, and too often disdained by the design profession.

I continued to advocate for public places, even a few decades ago when gaggles of planning and design critics and pandering politicians were bemoaning its death, a victim of municipal neglect, overt commercialism, and media disinterest. It seems we then had surrendered the weaving of our urban fabric to an unholy alliance of traffic engineers, duplicitous developers, disingenuous elected officials, and undiscerning pedants.

As designers of singular structures for a predominately private and public elite, the self-absorbed design professionals were mostly condescending or worse, indifferent to the unadulterated urban condition. Streets were shunned, sidewalk gatherings suspect, and parks avoided. Pervading all except perhaps a policed shopping mall or a monitored amusement park was a fog of civic unease.

Post-pandemic, in a notable change of personal perception and popular fortune, a growing number of urbanists is now celebrating the design and care of public spaces as a harbinger of a more open and inviting city, a place where people can come out of their crowded apartments and from behind their computer screens to experience a rare sense of community, however fleeting. Add to this chorus of the mostly comfortable are the ubiquitous tourists, their communal ardor feeding local coffers and conceits.

As for the architects, there seems to be a new awareness for context and community, the purpose and potential of public space, and a need to hone the cryptic craft of placemaking. If prompted by the ever-increasing competition for new clients, or whatever, architects have immodestly taken on the more magnanimous mantle of urban designer, landscape architect, and planner. As a play on a popular witticism suggests, you can call architects anything, but do not call them late for lunch. Give them a canvas, they will paint; clay, they will sculpt; or a plot of land, they'll design.

There is no denying a manifest rising design consciousness in the shaping of public spaces. This is most welcome to anyone who has ever looked for a place to sit in a park, rather than in a coffee house where you have to pay for the privilege with a cup of something. For New Yorkers, who, because of convenience and price, eat off of a street cart or roach coach, a nearby ledge can be a public amenity. A blessing too, if herding a child in whatever city, is finding a fenced playground where you can let go of their hand so they can romp at will.

That has to be one of the liberating joys of city life, played out as only it can be in an accessible public space.

The fact is that public space has always distinguished human settlements, from the first days of the Sumerian city of Ur, fabled Pompeii, to an evocative Paris and evolving New York City. Architectural icons might be interesting to examine from a distance; envision the Empire State Building in New York City. But it and singular others are just backdrops in a city, heedlessly providing edges to the adjacent streets, at best as an afterthought.

The real city envelops. For me in my youth it was the stoops of Flatbush that served our family and neighbors as a living room, then in my arrested adolescence the Central Park dog run for my loving Lab, and in my later years "kibitzing" with other "alte kockers" in Bennett Park in Washington Heights, identified also as Upstate Manhattan, by the denizens among whom I occasionally belonged, when for a time I was bi-coastal.

Los Angeles, where I now bask in my dotage, also has special public places for me. These include the beaches of Santa Monica and Malibu that are in effect joyous, sand-covered piazzas, hosting the city's multicultural throngs—if they can find parking and access, that is. Then, for strolling, there's the Venice boardwalk and the inviting trails in the Santa Monica mountains and, yes, in upscale Beverly Hills, with their ebb and flow of idiosyncratic crowds. But these are disembodied locales; for despite the city's welcoming and benign weather, its public places are frail and fractured, due in part to an irresolute populace and politic.

Less so New York City. Whether uptown or downtown, a park or a street corner, the select spaces are gathering places, in effect, where people make eye contact, bump buttocks, and rub shoulders, feeding commerce, socialization, and collective memories. On occasion, they're also historic stages for both protests and play. Whether a thirty-year war or some other conflict or plague was raging, despot or religious fanatic ranting, these places persevered. They were, and are, the soul of cities, and as our metropolises and populations grow, the need for such places becomes paramount.

Working nearly a half century ago as a food inspector for the Railroad Perishable Inspection Agency on a then-raw Chelsea waterfront on Manhattan's West Side, I never could have envisioned that the elevated B&O spur, where I toiled nightly, would be transformed into what is today a linear park, the High Line. But someone did, and it makes me wonder what derelict sliver of the city, what interstitial civic space, will next be turned into a people place.

The challenges to repurpose and shape spaces excite and demand a design intelligence that includes sensitivity for, and a commitment to, the user. "What is the city but the people," Shakespeare reminds us in *Coriolanus*. My memories meanwhile remain rooted in Brooklyn and the echo of my mother telling me to get out of the house and play and "Stay on the street and watch out for the cars!" Good advice then and now.

JOBS AND BOSSES

Ever hustling in a large family struggling to keep food on the table during the Great Depression of the '30s and the war and postwar years, I had in my rollicking youth many and diverse jobs and bosses. All, in time, illuminated my search for the soul of the city and sense of self.

First and unforgettable, for reasons good and bad, was my abiding taskmaster, Russian-born and shtetl ill-bred father, Joseph. He was a tough love, quick to criticize and slap, but also quick to praise and hug. Then there was his antidote, my loving and beloved mother, Sadie, ever-ready with encouragement and a treat, a favorite being a frozen Milky Way cut in half. We were a ravenous bunch.

I arbitrarily consider that the succession of my first of real jobs began at the age of fourteen, which was when I could and did get a legal work permit. To be sure, I had several ad hoc money-making gigs before then. They included delivering bagels to homes Sunday mornings—a dollar, sometimes two, for going three nonstop hours, plus a breakfast for me and a dozen free bagels for my family.

Still two years shy of being fourteen and eligible for a work permit, I worked off the books as a newspaper boy doing double duty, delivering the Jewish papers (The Yiddish *Tug* and English *Forward*) in the early morning before school, and the local *Brooklyn Eagle* in the late afternoon. Tips I remember were measly. When we later moved to Jamaica, Queens, I got my work permit and delivered the *Long Island Daily Press*. Tips were a little better, as were prospects of jobs, which included being a shlepper. Whatever the odd job would come my way, I always said "yes" and worried after if I could do it.

This included posing as a waif at the exit of the local A&P supermarket, on Hillside Ave. in Jamaica, Queens, Saturdays and asking the women leaving carrying groceries if I could help them, for which I would get tips, be it a few coins or empty bottles I could turn in for two cents apiece. I used to make enough in an hour, shorter if the weather was bad, to later that day purchase a twenty-five cent ticket to a matinee double feature, and if going to the Jamaica Theatre, five live vaudeville acts. And there also was the five cents for candy bars, for all I could hustle was mine.

When we moved from Brooklyn to Queens and I turned a teenager, my reality did not include the allowance that I learned most other kids received. They of course did not live in a house with two bedrooms and one bathroom for seven persons, behind a store, as I did; rather, they were in homes with several bathrooms for their smaller families in nearby envied Jamaica Estates. I learned early that I was on my own, begrudgingly buoyed up by my parents, under the dark cloud of the Depression and World War Two that lingered long over the family.

In the summers of my junior and senior high school years I went with my parents mixed blessing to work as an itinerant farm laborer under the auspices of a New York State program for underprivileged youth, ostensibly to get them out of the hot, dangerous city, albeit it to live with an alien family, to hay, milk, and clean the barns from dawn to dusk. My first summer was on a family dairy farm outside of Warwick, the second near Herkimer in the Mohawk Valley, the latter run by a stony, antisemitic clan.

It was a form of slave labor, but I came back toughened, if not sunburnt, to attend an overcrowded Jamaica High School, on a split session of 8:00 a.m. to noon. This allowed me to work daily 3:00 to 11:00 p.m., a forty-hour week, as a counterman and short order cook at a Walgreens in Fresh Meadows, Queens. The counter meals I made for myself were a bonus.

Delivering the daily paper to the Jamaica Estates home of an editor of the L.I. Daily Press led to another job, my first in journalism. Hearing of my hustling, he felt I had the making of a good newsman and gave me a tryout as the paper's Teens Queens columnist. For the then-goodly sum of fifteen dollars, I did a weekly wrap-up of the borough's high school social scene. Crafting a column of items submitted by already blessed obliging student stringers in various schools, it was my first taste of journalism. As an editor, it was empowering, and I liked it.

In addition, on weekends I reluctantly but dutifully delivered furniture and hung drapes for my father's interior decorating business, for tips, and occasionally with some trepidation served payment notices and summonses to his slow-to-pay and deadbeat customers. To be sure, there was no hope of tips, but the subsequent confrontations tempered me as a fledgling journalist.

Scoring decent-paying jobs was survival for me while attending Cornell University, in Ithaca, NY, where I needed to supplement the eighty-five dollars a month (upped to one hundred my junior year) I was getting from home to survive. This meant living in attics and rooms off campus, which were less expensive, but sadly less social than the dorms. I managed it by taking a variety of menial jobs, that included slaving as a lowly dishwasher, to rise to an unctuous waiter, then as a slogging pot boy, in agreeable sorority houses of chattering, flirtatious undergrads, and bartending weekends at drunken frat parties. My social life mainly consisted of befriending, with occasional favors, coeds whose dates had passed out at the parties.

Ever hustling, touting my Cornell Agricultural School enrollment, I supplemented my earnings seasonally by butchering Thanksgiving table-bound turkeys in a local frozen food processing plant. That was in the fall. In the winter I worked as a tree pruner in an apple orchard, when the trees were dormant and leafless. In the spring I tended livestock, assisting births and slaughters. Most lucrative of all, in two summers I was a fresh fruit and vegetable inspector for the Railroad Perishable Inspection Agency, checking to see if there was any spoilage or bruising in the refrigerated cars as they rolled into the Hudson Yards on Manhattan's far West Side, the produce unloaded during the night, to be delivered in the predawn hours to the city's wholesale markets. That I could help myself to the select produce to take home to the family was truly a perk.

I graduated from Cornell with a bachelor of science in biochemistry, something practical my parents thought would get me a desirable job sitting down. "How bad could it be if you work sitting down?" was a repeated comment by my father when discussing vocations. The month after graduation was rudely followed by a six-month stint in the National Guard consisting of active service in the US Army, at Fort Dix, New Jersey, and Fort Bliss, Texas. I summed up this experience at the end of my tour with an article for Cornell's undergraduate newspaper the *Daily Sun* entitled "The Unwilling, Led by the Incompetent, to Do the Unnecessary," stirring wide comment when printed. The article could be considered my first foray as a critic.

Meanwhile, I remember, it was a cold winter and I was out on the street, looking for a job while I decided whether I wanted to be a lawyer and, if so, how I could afford going back to school. So much for my rough-hewn youth. The fun would start soon enough.

Defining my first real job as the one that made me self-sufficient if not self-confident was as a coveted copyboy position with the *New York Times*, in February, 1958. Having just been discharged (honorably) from the army, and forsaking a future in biochemistry, I needed a job to tide me over until the fall, when I could enroll in a yet undetermined local law school, if that is what I chose.

Completing a forgettable week as a temporary clerk in a Doubleday Bookstore on Wall Street, and after attending the company's orientation program in its midtown offices, I wandered over to Bryant Park, at Forty-Second Street and Sixth Avenue, to make myself comfortable on a bench, enjoy the afternoon sun, and thumb through the job ads in a descarded dog-eared, *New York Times*. And there, while scanning the openings for law clerks, a prominent, boxed appeal for an office boy for the newspaper itself caught my eye.

"What the hell!" I thought; so about 2:00 p.m., I found a phone booth that hadn't been vandalized, called the *Times*, and got through to someone in employee relations, who after listening to my spiel, suggested I make an appointment to come to their office the next day for an interview. Of course,

I said yes, remembering my adage to say yes to any proposal. You can always change it to a no later, but not vice versa.

And I added that, since I was just a few blocks from the *New York Times* offices and printing plant on West Forty-Third street, I should come in that day. Why not? was the reply, which would make me the first person interviewed for the job rather than the last.

Several hour later at the *Times*, after taking a spelling and grammar test, I recall having a most pleasant interview, at the end of which I was offered the job of nightside copy boy on the spot. Apparently, what had impressed my genial interrogators more than my gratuitously disclosure that I was an avid reader of the newspaper, was that as an Ivy League graduate, born and bred in New York City, albeit it then bourgeois Brooklyn, I seemed to be street wise.

I interpreted that as looking British, thinking Yiddish, and having some actual newsroom experience at the *Long Island Daily Press*. There, in addition to my weekly teen column, I had also snared an assignment as a high school sports stringer; five dollars for each three-paragraph story, plus the box score covering the Jamaica High basketball team, the Hilltoppers.

And then there was my newspaper lineage, if it could be called that. My maternal grandfather, Samuel Martin, who had died in early 1935 and for whom I was named when born later that year, worked most of his adult life as a printer, specifically a typesetter, for the *Staats-Zeitung un Herold*, for a century the leading German-language daily newspaper in the United States. This, of course, prompted my mother, whenever explaining why I had become a "newsman," to comment that I had inherited a dab of printer's ink in my blood from my grandfather who, she added, was a kindly man with a love of books which she had inherited and hoped I would also.

So when asked if I could possibly start that evening, on the 7:30 to 3:00 a.m. shift, for which I would earn a night differential of one dollar, on top of a fifty-two dollar a week salary, and the hint of more if I could cover select church sermons as a stringer on Sundays, I enthusiastically replied yes. It seemed someone had just quit the day before, and they were short staffed. So after signing some papers and a handshake, I was escorted downstairs to the third floor and ushered into the paper's beating heart and soul, its sprawling, smoke-filled, bustling, noisy, newsroom to meet my boss. The room was love at first sight, but not so the bosses.

There were two of them, Frank S. Adams, the formidable city editor, and Sammy Solovitz, the rambunctious chief of the copy boys, whose ranks I was to join that very evening. Misters Adams and Sammy could not have been more dissimilar.

I was first introduced to Mr. Adams, who was always addressed and referred to as a mister. He rose with difficulty out of his office armchair, a stern-faced, strait-laced, stocky and compact figure of a man, who looked as if he liked his thick-cut steaks rare, aged Scotch neat, and his conversations terse. Feeling like a poor pledge before a privileged fraternity president, I answered briefly when questioned and mostly listened intently to his short, declarative comments, his talking the way I learned in good time he liked his stories written, per Strunk and White's masterly *The Elements of Style*, which he referred to several times and suggested I buy a copy. It became my guide to writing for the *Times*.

Mr. Adams was very much a proud Princeton alum, a tiger, like the school's mascot, and in a word, taciturn. He noted with a hint of disdain that though I was a Cornell graduate, and a product of the New York City public school system, he nevertheless expected me to be presentable, to dress Ivy League, I presumed as a Princeton man, and be well groomed. Above all, I distinctly remember he used the word "demure" to describe preferred behavior, a word I had seldom heard before in my previous workplaces. Most importantly, he told me he expected me to do whatever I was asked in the newsroom—running copy, of course, but also performing personals that included getting coffee and supplying aspirins. I was, in effect, going to be a lackey inside the walls of the paper and, beyond, a reserved "gentleman from the *Times*."

Then I was introduced to Sammy Solovitz, who though four foot nine, stood tall and carried himself with the swagger of a cocky drill sergeant, the newsroom his boot camp, always ready with a smart-ass answer to anyone who dared question his snap demands. No matter who you were, be it the son of a friend of the publisher, a wunderkind editor of a college paper, or a *pisher* off the New York streets who, like myself, somehow got lucky and got a job at the august *Times*, you were treated with equal derision. In self-defense, I interpreted this as affection and would hurl his gutter insults back at him, which most others could not, or were afraid to. Not me, the son of a tough Jew—a shtarker.

If my father had taught me anything, working those Saturdays delivering furniture and summonses, it was not to take any shit from anyone. Little Sammy, as I referred to him, soon realized I was a streetwise bullshitter, and we got along just fine—he, of course, being a bullshitter as well. I ran copy, got coffee, had aspirins at the ready, which I would offer to Sammy with a smile that he interpreted correctly as: don't fuck with me.

The jabbering and feigned insults continued for a year until I was promoted to news assistant on the national desk, and with it, a welcomed if worn chair to sit in and a necessary phone. ("National desk, can I help you?") Soon after, I reached the promised land, the metropolitan news staff, my namesake Sammy cheering me on with the warning not to fuck up, adding that with my promotion I now had to buy him his beers. I did so, happily. He was a cheap drunk.

I was sad to hear that Sammy retired a few years later at the paper's required age of sixty-five, which I do not doubt prompted his death a short six years later, in Houston, far away from his beloved NYC. One of the few times he confided in me, to be sure after beers in a pub the staff populated, Gough's, on Forty-Third Street, was that the *Times* was his life, the newsroom his home, the staff his family. I agreed with him; you don't argue with someone when you see tears in his eyes. But I silently thought that I certainly didn't want that to be my universe, let alone my epitaph. That night, I didn't start thinking about if I should leave the *Times*—but about when. I did not want it to be my velvet coffin.

There were no such confessions, let alone sentiments, from Mr. Adams, who rarely spoke to me after our initial meeting, though I always felt his eyes on me as I passed his desk. His were cold eyes, for me, for everyone, except maybe the publisher. You could not bullshit him, nor did you want to. And I know he read my stories, as he did other people's, even complimenting me on several occasions; and once in confidence he told me he was nominating me for a Times Publisher's Award, for which I also would get a few extra dollars in my next paycheck. It would be twenty-five dollars. But it was not about the money, though appreciated. It was the recognition: for me, mother's milk.

Mr. Adams had been with the paper since graduating from his beloved Princeton in 1925, and was only fifty-six when I met him in 1958; but I remember him as much older, and was sad when he was "promoted" upstairs to the editorial board in 1963, to make way for a very different city editor, A. M. Rosenthal. Incidentally, the "A" was not for Abe, as he was addressed, but "Asshole," as he in short order had shown himself to be. No one could write a story as well as he could, at least that is what he felt and made you feel. He was a very real put-down artist, which was no surprise. It was how he hid his limitations as an editor and human being.

As for Mr. Adams, he died at his desk a few years later, at sixty-eight, after I had moved on to not necessarily greener, but rather more open pastures, where one could loosen one's tie and be less demure.

There also was another editor at the *Times* who influenced me, though I would never consider him a "boss," as were Misters Adams and Sammy, controlling as they did my daily grind. He was Harvey Shapiro, who was an "upstairs" editor for the lofty weekly *New York Times Magazine*, for which I had presumptuously written a piece on spec about street life in teeming, vibrant East Harlem: "A Summer Walk with Carlos." It made print in the magazine on July 8, 1962.

To the surprise of many, I had moved to low-income East Harlem, from the then-middle-class Upper West Side, to the larger and cheaper apartment I needed for my growing family of wife and newborn, and frankly because I was perhaps naïvely attracted to what I considered were welcoming neighborhood vibes that reminded me of my childhood Brooklyn. It also gave me a wary glimpse of the urban poverty and pervasive violence which I wove into a rewrite of my spec piece shepherded by Harvey, ten years my senior, but seemingly older, aged. A Yale- and Columbia-educated, erudite editor with a welcome soft touch and soft voice, Harvey was for me a break from the clamorous newsroom and was very appreciated. That was Harvey's day job. At other times, he was a renowned, self-described Jewish poet. The city was very much his subject, and he once explained to me that NYC was like living in a maze, a religious trial of sorts where "a man tries to find himself and the right way to live." It was a challenge for my writing, which Harvey encouraged, using his respected relationships at *Times* to get me assigned—in addition to my day job—to write short book reviews as fillers for the then-daily book column, edited at the time by his friend, Eliot Fremont Smith, also erudite and, with me, patient and encouraging.

And so began my critical writing. It was Harvey and Eliot both who offered helpful comments about my reviews, and Harvey who prodded me to explore the city's neighborhoods for what was the beginning research for writing *The New York City Handbook* (Doubleday, 1966). Co-authored with the well-versed, amicable Gilbert Tauber, it was to become a local paperback bestseller and go through several printings.

I credited Harvey when I could for the book and was saddened by the news of his death in 2013, at age eighty-eight, having written a dozen acclaimed books of poetry and edited untold thousands of articles, no doubt gently encouraging the writers, as he did me.

WIDE-EYED AND BUSHY-TAILED

If my nearly seventy years as a journalist, part time, full time, and overtime, afforded me anything, it was a lofty perch and a perspective to view an unending parade of disparate people at their newsworthy prime, my existential accounts recorded in print, on tape, digitally, and in memory. Among those remembered in particular is Bobby Kennedy.

I still can make out the scene, however hazy in my mind's eye, years ago, in June 1965, Bobby in a rumpled blue suit that looks slept in, a wrinkled white shirt, hanging out over a belt, collar unbuttoned, a red tie loosened. He was leaning back, hands locked behind his head, propping up his bushy hair, sitting relaxed in a rear-facing bucket seat in a limousine, his leather-soled shoes, worn, but polished, their heels resting on the edge of the back car seat; he a youthful forty years old, looking intently at me, a twenty-nine-year-old.

Wide eyed and bushy tailed with excitement, I struggled to appear relaxed-yet-serious; after all, sitting on my shoulder was Mr. Adams. Trying to avoid the soles of the senator's shoe, I sat stiffly to the side of the seat, leaning forward slightly, facing him. I was a clean-shaven young reporter wearing his work clothes: a favored blue blazer from my college days, less the school logo which I had removed from the breast pocket, unbuttoned to reveal a light-blue, wing collar shirt, a conservative paisley print, a Windsor-knotted tie, pressed khaki pants, and a pair of comfortable desert boots. With notebook and ballpoint pen at the ready, and on assignment for the *New York Times*, I was accompanying the famed first-term senator from New York on a whirlwind tour, by limo and helicopter, of the five boroughs. I tried to hide my excitement.

It had a page one potential written all over it, as well as the promise of overtime, making me one happy scribe. I adhered to the journalistic adage that you are not as good as your last story, as popularly believed, but only as good as the story you are in the present working on. Tomorrow will take care of itself.

Bobby was not the principal newsmaker on the tour, which was a quick stop, look, pose for photos, and leave steeplechase of select playgrounds and small parks in the city's "underserved" communities. The leading dramatic role was to be performed by Secretary of the Interior Morris Udall, up from Washington, DC for the day to announce a new federal commitment to meet inner city recreation needs. And that would be the lead of my story, which was to appear under my byline, then Samuel Kaplan. (It became Sam Hall Kaplan years later in Los Angeles, Hall being my wife's family name. I took it in deference to her because the family had no male survivors. I also liked the way it read.)

I had been assigned the story, for I had in my first few years as a metropolitan reporter consciously cornered the parks and poverty beat, in addition to covering the housing court, to be sure by default, for these assignments were considered a local dead end by most of the paper's ever-aspiring, competitive writers. Their ardent goal was more likely to become a foreign correspondent, flying first class to be treated with deference in distant storied cities, on an expense account, witnessing momentous world events, and far away from the office politics of the paper.

The idea was to avoid becoming a metropolitan reporter who rode the city's crowded subways every day and wrote unread stories about minor events and unattractive people.

Ignoring the palpable condescension in the newsroom, I had the comfort of knowing I had made staff in the relative short time of two years since being explicitly hired as a copyboy because of my affinity for New York City. I was quite content to ride the subway to the kinds of edgy neighborhoods where I had grown up and could write about local politics and people with confidence and on deadline. I had street smarts, was a tough Jew like my father, and was durable.

The city desk also appeared to like the idea of my riding along with Bobby for most of the tour, finishing with Udall for the wrap-up. To be sure, the young senator was a surviving scion of America's royal family, and as such vulnerable, in constant danger of harassment, if not worse, and if anything did happen, it would be good to have someone at the scene. As if, as a native New Yorker, I needed to be reminded every day that there were a lot of nutcases out there, as there still are.

So typical of the mindset of *Times*'s resident news hawks, they also thought that by hanging with Bobby I could maybe establish some sort of connection with him, that the enterprising hustler could have access to exclusive stories in the future, in the same way that the Washington bureau's Anthony Lewis had done when Bobby was attorney general during his brother's administration.

Besides, Bobby was good copy and always provided a telling sound bite, especially given the tour's focus on "kick-ass" neighborhoods had been his idea; his New York office having prepared the day's demanding itinerary and accompanying script. But to get Udall to come to New York and make the announcements, Bobby agreed to defer to the interior secretary and take a supporting role, as would a host of other local and national politicians, including the placid Mayor Wagner and the affable senior senator Jacob Javits, each of whom had been assigned a limo so they could invite whomever they wanted to ride with, be it a favored donor or a cloying reporter.

Surprisingly, it seemed Bobby also wanted me serving in to ride with him and, unknown to me, had extended the invitation through the city desk. My first thought was that he did so in the hope he might get a better play in the *Times*, but it turned out he wanted to talk to me about, of all things, the East Harlem zeitgeist.

Somehow, he had learned from a staffer or someone that I lived there and was a community activist and advocate, having on my own time shed the cloak of a stolid and detached *Times*-man, eschewing the more desirable Upper East, the bourgeois West Side, or sedate suburbia, where most of the paper's people resided.

This had intrigued Bobby, apparently, for at that time his office was struggling to jump-start a redevelopment project in poverty-stricken Bedford-Stuyvesant, Brooklyn, which he wanted to become an example of bootstrap growth for other impoverished neighborhoods. The challenge was considered presumptuous and, reportedly, was vexing him. So instead of my interviewing him, he turned the meeting around and peppered me with questions, making my encounter with him quite memorable, if also flattering.

But you had to like his unassuming curiosity, willingness to admit ignorance, and his self-confidence to be open, to listen.

These qualities are rare among the many I have interviewed. Michael O'Donnell, one of his aides, observed when talking about Bobby's appeal to many that he "offered the most intoxicating of political aphrodisiacs: authenticity. He was blunt to a fault, and his favorite campaign activity was arguing with college students. To many, his idealistic opportunism was irresistible."

I was certainly a fan, and not being shy, I answered his questions at length, and enthusiastically, for I had immersed myself in the community as a challenge to my liberal leanings and also as an alternative to doing a stint in the then-praiseworthy and altruistic Peace Corps. I had thought about the latter, but rejected it because I already had a challenging and socially conscious job. Not to mention that I enjoyed being married to Sharron Walther, an avowed liberal and public school teacher, and was anticipating a family.

Also, being active in East Harlem for me was, frankly, fun. Employing my journalistic proclivities, I was publishing a monthly bilingual newspaper, the *East Harlem Independent*, for which I was the reporter, editor, and sales manager; it could be considered a hobby-and-a-half. This undoubtedly had gotten me selected for the local planning board, for which I was subsequently elected vice chairman, as the candidate to placate the rival Puerto Rican and Italian contingents. I was the white boy compromise, and a Jew no less, albeit not observant.

Bobby was very interested in my moving into Benjamin Franklin Houses, a massive 1,635-unit residential complex, originally built as a low-income project, the kind of housing with which East Harlem was studded. This made the area very much a ghetto. But thanks to the efforts of a Bill Kirk of the Union Settlement, a private social welfare agency, and other community activist, the project had been imaginatively converted into a moderate-income cooperative, Franklin Plaza, under a liberal state program called HOPE—Housing Opportunities for People.

In its appeal to moderate income families, for which I qualified, it also offered a subsidized, below market rate loan program, with a sweet equity option for those qualified to attract low income working families. This made the project refreshingly integrated and stable, and in time noticeably improved the area's admittedly below average public schools, as well as reducing the vandalism that had been a problem, and with it, crime. I was very much an advocate and had praised the project in several stories I was able to write for the circumspect *Times*. Questioning my politics, the city desk had edited my copy closely, but nevertheless recognized the stories as newsworthy, and not anything then-rival *Herald Tribune* could match.

Helping my stature in East Harlem, though a gringo, was that I was also—if I may be so immodest—a much sought-after softball pitcher, in a community where pickup games on weekends were a serious pastime and the scene of heavy betting on and off the schoolyard fields. I was known as Doc, not because I wore glasses, but because I could place a rising fast ball with surgical precision, usually up and tight on wary batters, domineering and winning most games. For this, the usual bet of twenty dollars each player on the teams had to be put up before a game; mine was surreptitiously covered by whatever team picked me. I therefore could win twenty dollars and lose nothing, except the enmity of my team, if we lost. But we rarely did.

Not incidentally, I also played softball for the *Times* in the famed Broadway League, in Central Park, the only person from the news department, which the city desk ruefully acknowledged. I didn't mention this to Bobby, though I knew he liked sports, principally touch football with some notables when he lived in Virginia. It was not my sport of choice.

My dialogue with Bobby continued for most of the morning, as the limo stopped with others at several playgrounds, then on to Central Park and the Tavern on the Green, for a pleasant free luncheon. At the senator's table, we were joined by Ada Louise Huxtable, the renowned architecture critic of the *Times,* and a congenial colleague, and Gay Talese, an aspiring feature writer recently elevated from the lowly ranks of sportswriter (and later to become a celebrated magazine writer and author). Ada was to write a sidebar to my story about the architect celebrity Philip Johnson being selected to design one of the parks (which he never did) and Gay a color story on Bobby.

After the luncheon and much self-aggrandizing by the politicians, Ada went back to the paper to write her story and an ingratiating Gay joined me in the limo, quite taken being in the presence of a Kennedy. But no sooner had we settled into our seats, the door opened and in squeezed two more persons, a winsome young woman and an urbane man. That would end my dialogue with Bobby, who immediately focused on them, with warm greetings and praise, and made my day even more memorable.

The woman was Gloria Steinem, then an ambitious writer of my age on the NBC TV satirical review *That Was the Week That Was,* though best known then for an article in which she posed in a Playboy Bunny costume and famously wrote, undercover, how the women were exploited at Hugh Hefner's Playboy

Club, especially because of the constant sexual demands. She went on, of course, to become a leading figure of second-wave feminism and cofounded the feminist magazine *MS*.

But Steinem didn't say much that afternoon, nor did she take notes, which made me assume correctly or not that she was there accompanying the man who had a reputation of being a womanizer, if anyone cared. I reasoned that they had probably spent the night together, and over breakfast had decided to spend the day as well, to attend the celebrity-studded luncheon at the Tavern on the Green, hobnob, and meet Bobby.

I recognized Saul Bellow immediately from the photos on the book jackets of his famed novels; he was fifty, fit, and basking from the raves for his most recent bestseller *Herzog*. I recall that he remarked he was there researching a profile of Bobby he was going to write for *Life*—no doubt a lucrative assignment. Steinem deferred to him, but so did everyone else in the limo, me as well as Bobby, obviously fans. I was an avid reader of Bellow's books, especially *The Adventures of Augie March*, which I consumed back in high school, identifying with the title's character, a pugnacious Jew who grows up in a poor family during the Depression and goes on to lead an exultant life.

Though I wanted to, I did not attempt to tell Bellow how much I liked the book, as no doubt countless others have told him, for I found the man off-putting. I don't remember the questions he asked Bobby, or what the answers were, or what others said. I just sat there in awe of a writer I had pretensions of perhaps becoming. My dialogue with Bobby was over, though it was to be remembered and a factor among many others in my departure from the *Times* within a year.

As for that memorable day, June 7, 1965, it ended for me back at the paper, writing my story under deadline. As anticipated, it would appear the next day, on page one, under my byline, albeit practically hidden in one column, beneath a bold banner eight column headline "2 ASTRONAUTS DOWN SAFELY AFTER 4 DAYS," and a prominent three-column headed story: "HIGH COURT BARS CURBS ON BIRTH CONTROL," with a sub-head adding, "establishing a new constitutional 'right of privacy.'"

Those were the stories that the powers-that-be in the newsroom were talking about the next day, and to my disappointment there wasn't a word on my piece about the promise of Udall to address the dearth of open space in the city's poorer neighborhoods. But I did get some overtime, and from the senator's office a coveted PT 109 tie clip the family gave out selectively, in remembrance of Bobby's older brother, John, the thirty-fifth president. Though I haven't worn a tie in decades, I treasure the clip.

CITY DESK DIVERSIONS

During the hours I spent with Bobby Kennedy that day in June1965, I thought of mentioning that I had once met his brother when he was campaigning for the presidency. But I didn't. It was not relevant to our conversation on how community efforts I was involved with in East Harlem could be applied to Bedford-Stuyvesant. To bring his hallowed brother into the conversation would have been gratuitous and, besides, our encounter was fleeting. For me, though, it was memorable.

So had been my experience with the buoyant older brother. It was the Sunday just two days before the 1960 elections, and candidate Kennedy was on a whirlwind tour of New York City; despite the freezing rain, he'd been attracting large, enthusiastic crowds. They had been so excited at some scheduled stops that they'd breached police barriers to get close to the candidate, screaming his name so as to drown out his remarks. As they surged forward, several people fell and were injured, seriously enough for ambulances to be dispatched to the scene.

It being Sunday night, and the newsroom nearly empty, I was drafted off the WQXR desk (I'd been writing the hourly five-minute news broadcasts) and sent up to Columbus Circle where Kennedy was to speak inside the convention center. The assigned writer, the venerable Harrison S. Salisbury, would be doing the lead story, dry and inside, and I would be outside, in the rain, with the overflow crowd watching the speech on a large television screen; I'd file some color, to be inserted if needed.

Thank goodness the speech was short because I was shivering on a makeshift platform overlooking the milling crowd when Kennedy exited the center and was hustled by aides and the Secret Service into a waiting motorcade. But surveying the crowd, he turned and shuffled through a gaggle of groupies to the wooden platform; climbing to the top, he stopped just a few feet from where I was standing, and with a wide grin and flailing arms shouted something inaudible to the crowd below, which screamed back at him.

I remember he then turned to the rear on the stand crowded with local politicians and media; he beamed and asked no one in particular, "What do you think?" I replied in a shout: "You're a rock star!"

I don't think he heard me because I could barely hear myself. And in a flash of light, raincoat draped over his broad shoulders, he was down the stairs, and I was back to the newsroom to turn in my brief notes (of the enthusiastic crowd ignoring the rain) to the rewrite desk handling Salisbury's copy. I then returned to the radio broadcast cubicle, happy to be out of the rain, to begin typing a story that now more than sixty years later I would guess declared, "The news, on the hour, every hour, brought to you by the *New York Times*. And in New York City today, despite a steady rain, Senator John Kennedy..."

I never was in the presence of John Kennedy again in the three short years he was to serve as president, nor Bobby Kennedy, as he went a few years later onto his fateful bid for the presidency; but I still think how the nation and world would have been so much better if they had lived. The thought and scenes haunt me.

Several months after Kennedy narrowly defeated Richard Nixon, to be sworn in on January 20, 1961, with few people in the newsroom one night, I was again drafted by the city desk off the broadcast desk. Ironically, this time, it was to go to LaGuardia Airport and interview the former vice president flying commercially from Washington, DC, to New York City, where he was to join the prominent law firm of Mudge Rose Guthrie Alexander & Ferdon. I was the only reporter there to meet him; that is what comes with working for a paper of record.

I don't remember much about the interview, other than Nixon looking dour and not stopping walking as I peppered him with the obvious questions: how he felt and whether he wanted to share further thoughts about the election. Accompanied by several Secret Service agents, he made his way to an awaiting limousine, answering my questions monosyllabically, if at all, and was driven off. As it turned out, John Mitchell was also in the law firm; he became attorney general when Nixon was elected president in 1968; Mitchell was involved in the Watergate scandals, too, for which he was convicted and jailed for nineteen months, the only AG ever to be so.

To add to the irony, when wearing a very different hat than that of a reporter, I met Mitchell in the mid-'60s when he was a senior partner in the firm, which subsequently had added Nixon to its name. Mitchell was a leading municipal bond specialist, and retained by the New York City Educational Construction Fund, for which for several years I was the director of development, involved in the planning and financing of public schools in mixed-use projects. I never mentioned to Mitchell when reviewing the draft bond issues with him that I'd had a brief interaction with the former president, now his partner. It was all business.

Also among the future or past presidents I met was Harry S. Truman. To be sure, when he was retired and walking briskly in midtown Manhattan, on what he called his "constitutional." He was staying in the presidential suite at the Waldorf Astoria Hotel, on Park Avenue, and visiting several blocks away his daughter, Margaret, her husband, Clifton Daniel Jr., and oldest grandson, also named Clifton, which, I feel, says something about his father's pretensions. It being Sunday morning with few reporters in the newsroom, I had once again been drafted off the broadcast desk to accompany the former president and write a brief item.

But unlike Nixon, Truman was talkative and friendly, so much so that it was hard for me to keep up with him and his accompanying Secret Service agent. What I remember of the interview is the thirty-third president asking me what I and others at the *Times* thought of his son-in-law, who was notably the paper's august managing editor and no doubt why the city desk had assigned me to accompany Truman.

To be sure, I was discreet, replying that he was fair-minded and meticulous, and did not add that I found the British accent he layered over his native North Carolina drawl and the Savile Row suit he wore from his days as a correspondent in London completely affected. His son-in-law was, I felt, very different than the plain-speaking Truman, and wondered what he thought, though I did not ask him. The item turned out to be short, three paragraphs, noting that Truman was in New York to see his daughter and family, and had taken his customary "constitutional" under a clear sky, to be recognized by startled pedestrians. The city desk was pleased.

Another memorable politician I enjoyed over time was Dick Lee, the long-serving, popular mayor of New Haven.

When I was writing an article about the city's redevelopment program in 1965, he beguiled me to eventually leave the *Times* to become the city's downtown renewal director. It was not as presumptuous and hasty as family and friends thought at the time. They described my career change as someone jumping from one rock to another in a quick flowing river.

I was charmed by the mayor, who was very much a loquacious and charismatic character, who did not let you forget was from a local working-class Irish family. I liked him from the moment I met him, laughing in his office in city hall, on Church Street, overlooking the historic green and Yale University beyond. Preferring to be addressed as Dick, and not mayor, his frankness and humor were in sharp contrast to the self-conscious tenor of the *Times*, and at the end of a long afternoon his offer of learning about city planning on-the-job as a redevelopment administrator was enticing, drawing as it did upon my experiences in East Harlem and my desire to do something about improving a city instead of just writing about it. I returned smitten to New York, wrote the article (*NYT*, Sept. 7, 1965) lauding the city's initiatives and the mayor's dynamism, and pondered his offer.

Another mayor that I remember fondly was Ed Koch, who I had known from his early, more subdued years as a fledgling politician in Greenwich Village. He had lost an election for the Democratic nomination for a New York State Assembly seat in 1962, and doggedly ran again the next year for district leader against the community's long-time political boss, Carmine DeSapio, and unexpectedly won. I recall going to a celebratory dinner with him and others at a Chinese restaurant, where he proceeded to open everyone's fortune cookie, until he found one he liked, and laughingly claimed it. He also told jokes—badly.

Ed was irrepressible, describing himself as a "Jewy Jew," which to the embarrassment of some he wore on his sleeve, along with a chip on his shoulder. We fell out of touch when I left the paper, and he became an indefatigable and increasingly loud congressman in Washington, although his heart was in New York City, and he ran for mayor in 1973, only to drop out before the primary. I sent my condolences, which were acknowledged.

But in 1977 he was running for mayor again, and I was chief editorial writer for the tabloid *New York Post*, which had recently been bought by an upstart from Australia, Rupert Murdoch, who was a very hands-on publisher, and at least then, politically a populist. I liked him, if only for being up-front with his opinions, stabbing me with them in my chest, rather than in the back, as they did at the *Times*.

Anxious about making a mark on his adopted New York City, Rupert wanted to show his mettle, and with me interviewed the mayoral candidates, which in a runoff was down to Koch and Mario Cuomo, then in a virtual tie. Koch, perhaps seeing me, was relaxed, funny, and, as expected, verbose, while Cuomo was serious and studied.

Conferring after, I remember saying to Rupert that I felt more comfortable with Koch because he was a New Yorker and "a mensch." I didn't know at the time if Rupert knew what a mensch was, but he replied that he thought Koch would make better copy for the paper and certainly would be friendlier to the *Post*, more than the stolid Cuomo. "And also he is your friend," Rupert added, and with that told me to write a strong endorsement for Koch, to run boldly bannered on page one.

The next day I heard from Ed, who thanking me, suggested we celebrate with—what else?—a Chinese dinner; and to show his appreciation he'd make the rare exception and pick up the check. We never had that meal.

Memorable also was a city desk assignment in 1963 to cover an NBC Sunday morning talk show on which the acclaimed Black author James Baldwin was to appear with the Black Muslim firebrand Malcolm X. For several years they had been debating each other on campuses over the politics of the rising Civil Rights Movement, both agreeing with the goals of African-Americans acquiring strength and confidence, but Baldwin adding that the endgame should be coexistence with whites and Malcolm X separation. It was a fundamental difference to an emotional and controversial issue.

I listened with rapt attention, reporting that the back-and-forth dialogue was articulate and cordial, ended with a warm handshake and a hug, and that they continued to banter as they left the studio. I did not add that, when leaving, Malcolm X noted that all the media present was white, singling out the *Times*, which at that time embarrassingly did not have a writer of color. But I had been quite happy to get the assignment, even though I recognized that most likely I had been painted at the *Times* as a liberal living in East Harlem, and that the innately prejudiced city desk, not knowing the dominant minority there was Puerto Rican, not Black, or more shocking to me, that it didn't make a difference. It wasn't white.

As a footnote, that very evening I was having dinner in a small West Village restaurant when in walked Baldwin, with a white companion, and seeing me, came over smiling to say hello and ask what I thought of the debate. All I could blurt out that it was "great," wanting to but not adding that I loved his coming-of-age book *Go Tell It on the Mountain*. So much for my brush with someone I considered a literary luminary.

I also saw Malcolm X once more, sitting in the passenger seat of a car that pulled aside me on a bridge exiting Harlem, rolling the window down, and laughing at me, "What are you doing up here, whitey?" He pulled away before I could answer, laughing to his driver, leaving me nonplussed.

It was just two years later, when I'd been sent by the city desk uptown to 168th street, to the Audubon Auditorium off Broadway, that there was a report Malcolm X had been shot. He had, and the scene there was chaotic. He was to die hours later at nearby Columbia Presbyterian Hospital, another reporter doing the obit (*NYT*, Feb. 22,1965), as I covered the firebombing of a Muslim Temple on 116th Street (*NYT*, Feb. 23,1965). It was a long night for me in a nervous Harlem.

SAINT JANE OF PLANNING

If there is one person of all the notables and characters l met when toiling at the *Times* and traversing New York City in the early '60s that influenced my writing and stirred my urban discontents, it was Jane Jacobs. Before being anointed the Saint Jane of planning and acclaimed as the author of *The Death and Life of Great American Cities* (Random House, 1961), she was an abiding friend when living in Greenwich Village and later from a distant Canada, never shying away from offering opinions and advice that still linger decades after her passing.

The Jane I knew back in her New York in the early '60s was an unapologetic populist and a heartfelt humanist. Frankly homely, and awkward, yet radiant and endearing, she was a sometime journalist and a steadfast community activist. As for me, I was a fledgling metro reporter for the *Times* who also surreptitiously wrote for the *Village Voice* and haunted her West Village neighborhood.

The Village had been my stomping grounds as a teenager, hanging out in Washington Square Park with the guitar playing crowd from Music & Art High School, and during my college summers when I hustled chess games during the day and worked on the nearby Hudson River waterfront at night, as an inspector of produce filled refrigerator cars, on what is now the High Line. Fast-forward to a few years later and I was writing about the park and local politics for the *Times*, but unable to afford Village rents and pretensions, was living in an affable East Harlem and paying $113 a month for a three bedroom apartment.

Jane had written disparagingly about East Harlem and the concentration of cookie-cutter housing projects where I lived; how they had replaced vibrant streets of small businesses and a social network—but, from my perspective, also a rat's nest of decrepit slum tenements and grubby streets that were not so friendly during the day and threatening at night.

But to Jane's credit, she nonetheless praised my efforts and those of others to convert one of the dreary high-rise, low-income buildings to a moderate-income cooperative, to stabilize the community and hopefully generate a pride of place. She also cheered my publishing a local newspaper there, the *East Harlem Independent*, and serving on the local planning board.

There's no doubt a factor in our friendship was my working at the *Times* and I could be a valued contact for her community activism. But that could work both ways. She was a presence in the politicized Greenwich Village and would be more so as her book gained traction. So we became friends, and among other things shared our disdain for city planners and others shortchanging communities.

She also was a kindred soul, measuring the swirling city around us not by its commercial or architectural conceits, but by the livability afforded its residents; that as William Shakespeare wrote in *Coriolanus*, act 3, scene 1, "What is the city but the people?" With that quote we would clink our beer mugs in our then favored tavern, the White Horse, not incidentally a former haunt of the poet Dylan Thomas, where we and some select nefarious others hung out, a few wobbling steps from her second-floor apartment on Hudson Street.

Self-taught and staunchly street savvy, she reveled in the daily drama of her adopted New York, beguiling an entourage, me and other writers included, with a plainspoken honesty that questioned the city planning dogma of the day and the powers that be. It made for good copy and good company.

Jane's appreciation of cities was visceral, not abstractions viewed from an upper-floor boardroom, or from the back seat of a cab, or as a site plan in an architect's office. Rather, cities were to be experienced on the sidewalk, moveable feasts appealing to the five senses. She ate like ignoble, native New Yorkers, standing up at curbside hot dog stands and storefront pizza stalls, and sitting down at family tables in communal Italian restaurants or to have a beer at bars that smelled of spilt beer.

Jane's book, published in 1961, had become in short time a classic treatise, challenging the planning establishment's portentous practice of slum clearance with a wealth of trenchant observations about the vitality of neighborhoods and the benefits of density and diversity. Reading it had a profound influence on me, prompting a better appreciation of the joys of the city, while lending a perspective to my writings and raising questions as to how I might better pursue my innate urbanism.

Meanwhile, her planning precepts were to influence generations of other planners, city administrators, and architects, despite sporadically being misapplied by sham urbanists shamelessly shilling for private real estate interests pushing bloated developments and deficient designs. Her pleas to preserve particular neighborhoods have also been attacked as "nimbyism," and she's been accused of racism—these accusations whispered by avaricious realtors who had targeted the area for blockbusting, to which she would reply: "Bullshit."

Whether cheered or castigated, Jane's theories continued beyond the '60s to be central to any discussions of city planning and the future of cities. In a poll a few years ago by the planning and development website Planetizen, ranking "the most important urban thinkers of all time," she was number one. This homeschooled, self-styled urban economist won by a nearly two to one margin over the nearest nominees that included both current and past luminaries, such as park designer Frederick Law Olmsted.

The curmudgeon that she was no doubt would have enjoyed the fact that her nemesis in a series of pitched community battles that forever changed the way planning and development is pursued in cities, the autocrat Robert Moses, was a distant twenty-second. And this despite being championed of late by neocon commentators bemoaning not having such bullying bureaucrats as Moses around anymore to bulldoze away the opposition to their favored over-indulgent design. She would consider them elitists and not have kind words for them; nor would she appreciate those who try to codify her axioms.

Disdainful of plodding planners, pandering politicians, and tedious academics, most of whom Jacobs considered feckless, if alive and kicking today, probably would have ignored the accolade with a quip that such polls tend to be blatant promotional ploys and to hell with them, and downing a beer, if one was near at hand.

But these sentiments, echoing in academic seminars and eulogies upon her death that extolled her life, to be sure would also have amused the Jane I knew as a self-styled community activist and idiosyncratic author, who though very much the celebrity in her later years remained plain spoken as she was plain dressed; utterly and charmingly unpretentious. That the book had been written by an untutored urbanist, with no academic credentials or professional conceits, made it more salient.

Though it should be noted, she was mentored by the social critic William H. Whyte, who had written the classic *The Organization Man* (Simon & Shuster,1956) and was a respected editor at *Fortune*. An inveterate city dweller, living in a booklined brownstone on East Ninety-Fourth Street on the Upper East Side when I knew him, Whyte had hired Jane in the early '50s as an assistant, despite her modest credentials of previously writing for trade publications.

Becoming in time alert to her off-hours activism in the then-gritty West Village, aware of her knowledge of design picked up from her husband, Bob, an architect, and recognizing her aptitude, Whyte, known to all as Holly and as a progressive, assigned Jane to write an article on urban downtowns for the prestigious magazine. "It was the best assignment I ever made," he once mentioned to me over coffee in Los Angeles years later, also thanking me for proposing him for a MacArthur Fellowship, the so-called "Genius Award," specifically for his studies of street life in cities. He was not given the honor, perhaps, I thought, because he was too old and not affiliated with any prestigious universities, the MacArthur having its prejudices. He died in 1999, at eighty-one years.

The *Fortune* magazine article subsequently stirred up interest and debate in both academic and civic circles, for Jane sharply questioned the then-accepted slum clearance approach to urban redevelopment, which was to bulldoze swaths of a community and sell the land at a discount to politically connected, covetous developers, who would erect a commercial or residential cash cow, to sell to speculators for a guaranteed profit. Wiped from the neighborhood would be whatever sense of place and community might have existed—and the people who lived there.

Reprinted in a thin tome called *The Exploding Metropolis* (Anchor, 1958), the article now with the cachet of being included in the book, not incidentally edited by Whyte, became the basis for a grant from the Rockefeller Foundation for the neophyte Jacobs to research and write what was to become *Death and Life* (1961). Criticized at first by academics and the planning profession, "jealous guardians of their own credentials," noted a reviewer in retrospect, the book in contrast was lauded by community activists, outlier urbanists and, in time, if not by professors, by their planning students.

When, following the publication, she was interviewed by the press, Jane would inevitably comment how critical it was for the media to raise the public consciousness of what makes cities special and the need to protect them from the outrages of Olympian plans flaunted by petty tyrants fronting for the greedy design and development community. It became her mantra, and the book a prop of sorts to her continuing community activism, which after all had been the seed for *Death and Life*.

"I guess I should thank Bob Moses," she once ruefully said to me, for it was his proposal to extend Fifth Avenue south through Washington Square Park that had triggered her activism and also got her thinking about what she and her family loved about the city and made it livable. And that did not include having her favorite park being sliced and diced to give a redevelopment project to the south that Moses had promoted a more marketable Fifth Avenue address.

Jane spearheaded the incipient uprising to stop the roadway and save the park, thwarting the imperious Moses, a man of many municipal hats and powerful friends, both public and private, who rarely, if ever, had been denied a locality's rubber stamp for a pet project, be it a building, a bridge, parkway, or park.

The rest is history. She and her neighbors stopped the roadway, the book was published, and she became famous, if not notorious. This in turn helped her a few years later to win yet another battle with the fading Moses, burying a plan to have a fourteen-block expanse of the then-gritty but vibrant and viable West Village declared a slum so it could be replaced by a pricey residential redevelopment scheme.

In part motivating Jacobs to kill the proposed "slum" clearance project was that it included the demolition among thousands of buildings, the modest walk-up she and her husband had painstakingly renovated for themselves and three children. Located on a heavy truck traveled commercial street, Hudson, Jane had romanticized as an inviting neighborly retail strip, they had purchased the property in the early '50s for seven thousand dollars (equal to about a month's rent today), very much in the tenacious spirit of early urban pioneers. The plan to lay waste the West Village was defeated.

This was followed with another ignominious defeat for Moses—of an ambitious plan under the banners of slum clearance and highway construction, the demolition of a broad strip of lower Manhattan to make way for an elevated cross-town highway. Typical of a Moses plan, it showed little regard for the tens of thousands of residents and businesses that would have had to be rudely relocated, as had occurred in the South Bronx to make way for that infamous cross county expressway. But with Jane and cohorts packing the city hall chambers, the city council yielded and killed the project.

To the dismay, then of the New York establishment, and in defiance of how things were done back in the bad old days of bulldozing and building, the resident Village neighborhood, with author Jacobs its champion, tangentially succeeded in rendering the heretofore heroic public works overlord toothless and tottering. The battles exposed Moses as a despotic bureaucrat, who up until then had been an acclaimed master builder in the mold of a Baron Hausman and a self-anointed savior of the city. It became obvious he had stayed too long at the party, and in time he was stripped of his various local, regional, and state jurisdictions.

Hastening his demise was Moses's penchant for impolitic put-downs, prompted by Jacobs's goading, such as when he dismissed her and a group of protesters of being impertinent housewives. This was a particularly ill-timed remark, coming as it did at the dawning of the feminist rights movement. Even now, more than a half century later, the battle pitting Jacobs against Moses is an inspiring story.

By then, the Vietnam War was heating up, and prodded by her husband, Jacobs and family moved to Toronto, principally to protect their sons from the draft, according to our private conversation. Meanwhile, I had left the *Times* to try my hand at urban planning, a move she also encouraged. We kept in touch, as she continued to write books with urban themes.

When I returned to daily journalism, first as an editor at the *New York Post* and later as the design critic for the *Los Angeles Times*, Jane kindly wrote notes of good luck and a blurb for my book *LA Lost & Found*, calling the sprawling metropolis "an improbable city" and praising me for taking it on. She really didn't like or understand LA and urged me to move back to New York ("it needs you") or even to Toronto ("it is a city"), as she had encouraged others to do.

While I told her I had come to love LA as she had Toronto, there was no question that New York had been our crucible. For me, Jane was first a good story and then, in time and foremost, a friend and mentor, as she was for a generation of urban planners.

True to form, Jane became very much involved in Canadian politics from her venerated perspective, debunking grand planning theories and championing the concept of community, her arguments emotional and persuasive. She riled against "bigness" in her *Economy of Cities* (Vintage, 1970) and in a book supporting Quebec's vain struggle to break away from Canada *The Question of Separatism* (Vintage, 1981).

I wrote in a review of the latter in the *Los Angeles Times* that Jane based her belief that regions with cultures as distinct as Quebec's would be economically healthier and politically happier if not constantly pressured to be more "Canadian," she observed wryly, "in the name of a greater nationalism." If anything, Jane to the end was a true warrior in the defense of local autonomy.

Jacobs sadly passed in 2006; and while her teachings live on, I'm sure she would acknowledge her West Village and the White Horse Tavern have changed.

I have gone back to the tavern several times over the past years to find it no longer a gathering spot for journalists and would-be revolutionaries, writers, and poets; nor is the neighborhood a gritty mix of incomes and trades edging a rough waterfront, as extolled by Jane, and where I once worked the ominous nightshift.

Instead, there are pricey boutiques and higher priced housing catering to the Wall Street, the Hollywood-on-the-Hudson crowds, and moneyed millennials. Cabs now prowl the streets where once they never dared venture.

There has to be a certain irony that the West Village neighborhood Jane helped save by blocking its designation as a slum, recently had its 10014 zip code cited in Forbes magazine as the most expensive in the gilded Manhattan galaxy. Not too far down the list was 10012, SoHo, which the Lower Manhattan Expressway would have taken out.

GOOD TIMES, BAD TIMES

Etched in bold type over the archways leading from the lobby to the elevator bank of the former *New York Times* building on West Forty-Third Street was the adage "EVERY DAY THE WORLD REBORN." For me that was a challenge, and I would read it and smile as I passed under it for nearly a decade when I worked there.

After advancing from copyboy to news assistant and to staff in two short years, I truly thought I would be a lifer, to never leave. My press pass was a free ticket to an orchestra seat in the twenty-four seven theater that was New York City, featuring a daily parade of surprise comedies, dramas, and vaudeville acts. I reveled in it.

"So why did you ever leave?" asked family and friends when it appeared my job there as a metropolitan reporter was secure and I was seemingly happy. I had been getting more prime assignments, and the book I had co-authored, *The New York City Handbook* (Doubleday,1966) had just been published, reviewed well, and was selling. This had spurred my freelancing that included a monthly script for NBCTV's *New York Illustrated*, for which I was generously paid. On the home front, I had just become a father, a second child was planned, a co-op on the upper West Side of Manhattan where we had a deposit on a four-bedroom unit was under construction, and in addition had purchased a barn that had been converted into a small house in the rural Berkshires, where we were enjoying weekends and holidays. Life by any measure was good.

But nagging me was no less than the drift of my New York City, its shaping and misshaping, exacerbated by insensitive planning, rapacious redevelopment, gross income disparity, and innate racism. And me not doing anything about it except to expose it by writing, and that with increasing difficulty because of the politics and prejudices then of the *Times*. This played on my conscience, which had already been prodded by the day I spent with Bobby Kennedy, my continuing dialogues with Jane Jacobs, Holly Whyte, and a very supportive wife at the time, Sharron, an avowed liberal, who had been an inspired schoolteacher in Harlem, and my own involvement in the formative years of the Franklin Plaza cooperative in East Harlem.

Also very much a presence in my life then was Bill Kirk, the self-described "head worker" of East Harlem's Union Settlement and, before that, an ordained Episcopal minister. With the countenance of his former calling, Bill questioned my commitment to social change, urging me to go beyond writing about it, to instead get involved. "Don't tell me, show me," he intoned in his homey office on East 104th St., throwing back at me the template for writing for television I had once mentioned to him.

Bill had been refreshingly direct ever since he called me out of the blue one day at the *Times* when I was a news assistant doing innocuous items on sermons I attended on assignment at the more prominent city churches on Sundays, principally to show my mettle and earn a few extra dollars. He suggested I should some Sunday go to the East Harlem Protestant Parish, located on the infamous gang-infested, East One Hundredth Street, between First and Second avenues, to sit among the poverty-stricken parishioners and listen to a bilingual sermon.

He called the church "a baptized settlement house," a phrase I liked, so I pitched it to the religion editor for inclusion in the weekly sermons column to which I was contributing. "Interesting," he said, a reply that at the *Times* was almost always followed with a "thank you, but no." I had tried.

I nevertheless accepted the amiable Bill's invitation to East Harlem, not to listen to a sermon, but to learn more about how he and other community activists were struggling to integrate the area by trying to convert a sprawling, stereotypical low-income housing project to a moderate-income co-op—that is, to bluntly attract bourgeoise white families, like mine, and break the mold of the area's predominately Puerto Rican ghetto projects.

Impressed, I wrote the story, and shortly brimming with good intentions, and wife Sharron agreeing, moved into the co-op with our growing family. It was to be both our personal versions of the Peace Corp, albeit in an ailing Third World neighborhood in New York City.

And with Bill as an inspirational cheerleader, within a few years I was duly appointed to the local community planning board, and soon after launched the *East Harlem Independent*, a bilingual monthly newspaper. This raised some eyebrows at the *Times*, along with disapproving murmurs of my obvious social concerns, which were felt would compromise my reporting.

But I turned my questioned community involvement to an advantage, writing on spec an evocative article for the *Times Sunday Magazine* about youths adrift in East Harlem (July 8, 1962). Thanks to the enthusiasm and editing of Harvey Shapiro, the article to my delight made it into print, with me identified as a *Times* reporter "living in the area he describes." Countering as it did a current criticism of the paper having a limited, elitist view of its host city, upper management praised the magazine's editors for publishing the article and me for my initiative. I in turn thanked Bill for introducing me to East Harlem. Living there, playing softball in the school yards, talking to neighbors, generated several other "exclusive" articles for the *Times*, mention in the paper's inhouse newsletter, "Winners and Sinners," and kudos from colleagues and readers.

Bill, not coincidentally, was also a friend and resource for Jane Jacobs, having also taken her as he did me on tours of his vibrant East Harlem. Indeed, it was Bill that nudged me to become friendlier with her as a resource for my writing about the city, despite her initial distrust of the paper for its editorial support of Bob Moses and his array of public projects. But we shared our fondness for Bill, who Jane in the introduction to her classic *Death and Life* credits him for helping her begin to understand "the intricate social and economic order under the seemingly disorder of cities," adding that "by showing me East Harlem, [he] showed me a way of seeing other neighborhoods, and downtowns too."

So it was for me, too, and at a critical time, for with an increased sensitivity to the urban condition inherent in my now living in East Harlem came the challenge to be more engaged in its disposition, as Bill had urged, not just sitting on the sidelines, albeit with a good seat. And this happening at an optimistic time when being launched and promoted by an enlightened if naive federal government were the promises of the Model Cities and Great Society programs, the War on Poverty and the Peace Corp.

But here I was, not yet thirty years old, and feeling the existential challenges and enthusiasms of the "awakening"

'60s slowly fading; that the *Times* in its posture and conceits was indeed the civil service of journalism, as someone once described it to me; that there was more to life than the nightly rumbling of its presses and the thud on the pavements of bundles of newspapers with your story on page one. The thought nagged at me.

Then there was the experience of the city's prolonged newspaper strike, which ran from December 8, 1962 to March 31, 1963—114 days. This too weakened my ties to the *Times*, which in a sweetheart agreement with the other city papers locked out its employees. Though given the contracts with the newspaper association and the unions, it really had no choice.

Be that as it may, the action dealt a telling blow to the myth that the *Times* was more than a corporation, that it was family, and in return for your loyalty you'd be taken under its wing in time of economic depression, war, or whatever. Instead, we found ourselves on the street, dependent on a modest stipend from the union and savings. But for me not too long.

My family's survival ethic was emerging. Soon I was doing a neighborhood news segment several times a week as an on-air reporter for WNBC'S *Late Afternoon News*, a similar bit for CBS's *Sunday Morning* news show, freelance articles for weekly community and trade papers, and in addition had gotten a modest advance with a self-made city historian, Gilbert Tauber, to begin research on *The New York City Handbook* under contract with Doubleday.

By the time the strike ended, the issues of automation and wages resolved, and the doors on West Forty-Third Street opened for our return, I was making more than I had before and what I was going to get as a raise back at my desk.

I returned, of course, but with the knowledge I could make a good living elsewhere doing whatever, which had the effect of further weakening my ties to the paper. I was not going to be a lifer, as so many others there had resolved themselves to be.

Though I did not know it at the time, hastening my eventual departure was that after the strike ended the stolid Mr. Adams was promoted to the editorial board on an upper dusty floor, to be replaced as city editor by A. M Rosenthal. A Pulitzer Prize winning foreign correspondent, Rosenthal was known for both his initiative and abrasive attitudes. He was most definitely not a Princeton man, as Mr. Adams was, but rather was in the misanthropic mold of the Bronx, where he was born, and the proletariat City College, where he had gone to school and been the *Times* campus correspondent.

Having, with other aspiring reporters in the newsroom, looked forward to his tenure, assuming change would be for the better, we were soon disabused by his red-faced angry outbursts and his playing petty office politics and favorites. It was like being back in a churlish high school.

While Abe was both unctuous and unpleasant with me, he encouraged me to take the initiative and generate disparate stories. This I liked. But when I turned them in, and though accepted, he made it clear to me they were not as good as if he'd written them. That might have been true, but he said it as a put-down and not to be constructive.

The stories of his mismanagement and rants soon became newsroom legend; and prodded by Dan Wolfe, the editor of the *Village Voice*, I wrote an article that, if it didn't mention the mercurial and temperamental Abe by name, was clearly an expose of a *Times* in turmoil. Played prominently and headlined "All the Pap That's Fit to Print," with no byline, it ran November 19, 1964:

> The New York Times, depended upon for a century by citizens, civic groups, and government to reliably report the news of the day, has abandoned its traditional role and responsibility in the metropolitan area. The Times's city staff no longer produces news. It has become passive, waiting for someone to tell it what is going on. Times reporters who once kept a watchful eye on the doings and not of the numerous agencies supposedly serving the public are now scampering about the city on so-called non-stories, such as features and long background and mood pieces.

"While these stories are easier to read and more pleasant reading, there is less reason to read them. The mood and the flavor of the city is being conveyed, but not its activities, be they a city hall hearing or a Brooklyn Heights protest rally. The Times local news coverage is cute, but not very informative," I wrote, nervously to be sure, knowing that I was being disloyal to the *Times*, but with the hope that it would prod the publisher to reign in Abe. The article continued:

> No longer do we have the "Timesman" availing himself to malcontents in city agencies, studiously following up leads, paying unexpected call on officials, and developing a reputation that readers can depend upon and to whom tipsters can feed

stories. To be sure, news events are covered—but never uncovered. The Times still gives its special brand of exhaustive coverage to "spot" news, such as an air crash or the arrival of a President. And it pays homage to the press releases, sorting them out, rewriting them, putting them into perspective."

Maybe, I thought this should get the lordly Sulzbergers' attention, especially my citing in detail and identifying reporters, and how the once gifted beat staffs had been decimated and that several of the stalwart were looking to leave. I concluded, sadly, that the *Times* could no longer be relied upon, that the old grey lady was, in effect, showing signs of institutional dementia.

As could be expected, hesitantly handed a copy of the *Voice* article by his sycophantic deputy, Arthur Gelb, as several reporters surreptitiously looked on, Abe threw a temper tantrum, literally screaming, vowing he would find out who wrote the story "and cut his balls off." When he eventually calmed down, he assigned a favored investigative reporter, Bob Alden, to take as much time as he needed and find out who had written what he considered blasphemy.

Alden pestered the *Voice*, beleaguering for weeks his contacts there, but Wolfe had told no one, not even his co-publisher, the writer Norman Mailer, and remained silent. I remained nervous, knowing that by attempting to light a fire under the old grey lady, I'd also burned my bridges to the *Times* and that undoubtedly, someday, it would haunt me. If anything, the article, to the applause of the media, did expose Rosenthal's arrogance, as in retrospect it did mine.

The piece was indeed a coup for the *Voice*, then a respected, feared, and widely read weekly. Though not then, or ever, identified as the author, I was undoubtedly suspected by Abe, who never directly asked me. Tyrants, I have found tend to be cowards. And me being a bad liar, I frankly don't know what I would have answered. Fourteen months later, I resigned. My only true regret was that by putting a year more in at the *Times* I would have vested for a modest pension at sixty-five, which the strike of '62-'63 had improved.

But I did continue to write book reviews for the *Times* and the *Village Voice*, among other publications, about the *Times*, not surprisingly given my short, sweet, and sour stint there. In particular was a review I wrote of Turner Catledge's *My Life and The Times* (Harper and Row,1971) published in the *Voice* on July 15, 1971, titled "INVOLVEMENT IS A DIRTY WORD": "Whether we like it or not, The New York Times is our primary source of news, or what passes as news," I observed in my portentous lead sentence:

> Plunking down 15 cents or picking it up free on a subway seat we are compelled to read it. The Times is a habit, and we depend on it. It is the bookmark of the city, if not the world, and all our favorite weeklies, this one included, magazines, periodicals and reviews just do not have the comprehensiveness we demand in order to know. The Times has established itself over the years as the public arbitrator of events and as an institution and asks us to accept it as such.

But I continued that "our experience and knowledge bear out the sad fact that the Times again and again is incomplete, and worse, in error. The distortions and omissions in the Times have been explained by some as duplicity—that the Times is a member of the 'establishment,' consciously acting to withhold news as part of a sinister national plot."

To be fair, I added that its publication of the Pentagon Papers dispelled that theory, but still did not answer the question as to "Why had the Times not aggressively sought the story out when it was happening in the septic conference rooms of the decision makers in Washington and Santa Monica?"

I dutifully answered my own question:

> [M]y experience as a reporter for the Times and the experience of others, including apparently, Turner Catledge, is that the Times simply has a very difficult time keeping up with the times, that it is a settled, secure institution and, as a result, smug and not easily changed, despite the efforts of some within it desperate for change. It is not duplicity that causes the distortions and omissions, but rather ignorance and insularity.

I noted that the resulting corporate and editorial battles within its hallowed walls were dramatized in Gay Talese's popular epic *The Kingdom and the Power* (New American Library-World, 1969), which I also had reviewed for the *Voice* (July 31, 1969).

It entertainingly revealed much about the personalities struggling to direct the paper, but little about what they stood for and hoped to accomplish, other than just to grab power.

I added that Catledge answers some journalistic "whys" raised in Talese's book, writing frankly about the smugness and insularity he found at the paper, whose editors were content "to do things today the way we had done them yesterday and not to worry about tomorrow."

The petty politics among editors and "desks" and the omnipresent paternalistic publisher, the Sulzbergers, described by Talese, I noted in my review were put into sharper, less personal, but more perceptive focus by Catledge. "Working with a double-edged scalpel, Catledge cuts up Times men with a fine surgeon's hand. In particular, he gives a fascinating first-hand view of the maneuverings of the Times' top management."

But as well intentioned as he might have been, I added that it was apparent Catledge tended to avoid the constant confrontations over content, to enjoy his prestige and good life as the paper's top news executive, hoping in the meantime his modest maneuverings would allow the paper to keep pace with the changes outside its walls. "Catledge, and the Times, are evidently sensitive to these changes, which keep accelerating, paced by the social, technological, and political revolution about us," I observed, quoting him that "we are all caught up in a time of political passion. Our newspapers have contributed to the intensity. We have reported in detail America's social explosions—the riots, the shoot-outs, the demonstrations— but have we been so alert and so bold and thorough in reporting the conditions that led to them?"

Good question, which Catledge answers by declaring "that social conflict arises because people are uninformed,' the responsibility of which he contends lies uncomfortably close to our newsrooms; he therefore urges that papers must continue to strive for objectivity and impartiality. But in doing so, they must seek more than objectivity, I argued: "We must have a new dimension to our journalism. We must give society a deeper, truer picture of itself." To which I added in my review of a half century ago: "The problem is translating this concern into a commitment, a commitment by editors and reporters to dig deeper, to better understand the machinery of change and to gain and give perspective."

But to achieve this goal, I continued, "takes commitment and commitment is involvement and knowledge, something the Times does not display much of. Of course, other papers and the media in general suffer from these failings, but it is the Times that purports to tell it all and tell it best." I wrote: "Involvement is a dirty word at the Times, which has contended that it destroys impartiality, the paper's hallmark." This was not necessarily true then, as it is not now. In fact, my experience has been that the more you become "involved" in an area the more its complexities are revealed and the better able you are to put it in perspective and explain it.

For example, I believed I was a better "housing and planning" reporter for the *Times* because I lived at the time in gritty East Harlem and was vice chairman of its planning board. I was involved. But I could also put in perspective the nonsense being spouted by city hall. Admittedly, it also makes you more cantankerous because the problems seem more urgent; and just because they haven't been blessed by a press release, they are viewed with suspicion.

I contended in the review that "reporters and editors are trained and programmed to write what other people tell them, not what they know, because knowledge takes an effort most reporters do not want to, or are not allowed to, expend. This is further complicated by the insularity of the news business," which, I added, drives reporters and editors into their own world, supposedly to keep their independence and objectivity, but really to keep them isolated from reality and to keep them feeding off one another's ego. I continued:

> The values of the business are such that the goal is to be assigned to a hot story that keeps one's byline on page one and places one in good company where the action is, not off following a complex thread through the old bureaucracy or new technocracy, which would take researching and time.

That was the essence of the new journalism that Catledge so eloquently called for, and which, I added, the *Times* failed to deliver, as it persisted in conveying "to us for the most part canned news, garnered second hand, with perhaps a little new flavoring. It certainly is easier on all of us, for the Times to print and for us to read

On I went, castigating the paper's coverage, which I felt was aggravating the "tenuous connection between the growing alienated population and its distant political and technical masters." The scorching intention was to throw another log on the fire that would in the distant future burn down my bridge back to the *Times*. But as a daily journalist I was not thinking of the future, but the present, and the story in hand.

REALITY BITES

Emancipated from the stolid *Times* and the parochialism of New York City, feeling the rush of new beginnings, off I went, family in tow, to New Haven in early spring 1966. As I had written in the article in the *Times* the year before, in its proffering "the American Dream of a Slumless City," New Haven had become respected nationally in the mid-'60s for its imaginative pursuit of a livable city, labeled a "model city" and a paradigm for other municipalities to emulate.

Among the lessons both good and bad I was to learn in my brief tenure in New Haven was a variation on the truism for public figures—that they should not believe their own publicity. For newspersons, it should be: "Don't necessarily believe something you might have written." To my embarrassment, copies of the article were included in the PR package the city handed out when hosting a steady stream of visiting officials wanting to learn how New Haven had become that model city I had described, however naïvely.

Guided by a lauded team of urbanists reorienting public services to better serve minorities and the poor, the small New England city, to the delight of Washington, was reinforcing faith in the federal government's urban renewal and anti-poverty programs. Paper proposals were being turned into real projects, improving the lives of people beyond the usual sycophantic bureaucrats, or so it seemed. You wanted to believe the hype.

It was all good; a government by the people, and for the people, with the city not incidentally becoming well adept in raking in federal funds and foundation grants to attract the likes of me and other well-intentioned reformers and liberals, "sailing to Byzantium."

Nevertheless, I had left the *Times*, and feeling confident because of my hardheaded experiences in East Harlem and what I'd observed in the rising community consciousness of the West Village, I was looking forward to my on-the-job mastering of urban planning. That was what Mayor Dick Lee had dangled in luring me to New Haven, though he added that my writing skills would be appreciated now and then, to be sure, for grant applications, but assured me not public relations, of which he was a master.

There was also the promise of introductions to Yale's respected architecture and planning programs, and the possibility of my pursuing an advanced degree, or given my experiences, maybe becoming a part-time lecturer.

To underline his proposal, the mayor appointed me not to his staff, where I might be wrongly identified as his new public relations aide, but citing my practical planning experiences, as the city's downtown renewal director. And further to emphasize my position, my office would not be in city hall, but on State Street, several blocks away, in an area scheduled for renewal. In fact, at my suggestion, it would not be an office, but a storefront, its door open to all, and with a window display of its renderings of the street's proposed redevelopment.

If there had been a lesson I learned at the *Times* as a reporter, it was the importance of listening; and once settled into the storefront, what I heard from the occasional drop-ins who sensed I was approachable, was a litany of complaints about how the city's downtown redevelopment programs were failing the very people they were supposed to help: the small businesses.

The reality I was learning, to my increasing dismay, was that however affable Dick Lee was as a mayor, and however well intentioned were the renewal efforts, the city's problems persisted. And it was not just the decaying downtown, which ostensibly was my prime focus, but a city pockmarked by poverty and poor housing, which revealed itself to me on foot and by bike off hours and at weekends. To be sure, this was not on the tour I had been given months before when, as a visiting newsman, I was shown a frankly impressive selection of well-designed and welcomed projects for which the city was famed. But reality had bitten.

There had obviously been some successes in the renewal program, spurring many in the city government to assiduously strive for more, hiring some architects, generating imaginative plans, initiating new programs, crafting budgets, and padding staff. The process was a municipal merry-go-round of urban planners and administrators who were happy to climb on and prosper.

Unfortunately, I concluded that unaware of the lesson I had learned—not to believe what I had written—the development denizens believed what was being said about them. That is, what a good job they were doing. They forgot that much of it was public relations calculated to help the city garner yet more money, public and private. What they also forgot was for whom this supposedly a major public undertaking was to serve—the people, notably the poor. All they could do was watch the merry-go-round continue turning, for it could not stop, for if it did a lot of people would fall off.

So what if those imaginative plans by renowned architects for which all involved would be praised required swaths of the city to be bulldozed, the rationale being that a few eggs had to be broken for the promised architectural omelets. The result was a particularly insensitive relocation program, in the mold of a Robert Moses, and disingenuous community programs. I subsequently learned after some discreet inquiries that some eight hundred businesses had been bulldozed in the first downtown project, Church Street, and a total of twenty-two hundred businesses and eight thousand people were "lost" across the city through the years of renewal programs. That was a big number in a small city.

As for redevelopment staff I had thought to be enlightened, having enjoyed the best possible public relations, they were disinclined to hear my reports of the complaints about the relocation program they deemed necessary to achieve their vision of a vibrant New Haven. I suggested perhaps pursuing a more modest redevelopment effort, spot renewal, that would preserve select businesses, to lend the area a continuity and an identity. The effect it had was like asking the agency administrators to take a cut in pay and pride. To no one's surprise, it was to no avail. Cutting back in addition to cutting budgets and jobs, would also diminish reputations, and lessen the opportunities for staff to move to other cities up the redevelopment ladder for more pay.

My popularity waned, and soon I was not being notified about agency planning sessions, though I was still welcomed on its softball team. But as I had hoped in coming to New Haven,

I was still soaking up the basics of urban planning and, for better or worse, an aptitude for bureaucratic management. Yes, I could bullshit with the best of them, thanks again to Cornell for grooming me to look preppy. It did get me some invites to select Yale architectural seminars and planning workshops.

These benefits, and Sharron and myself as new parents in a comfortable house, and liking New Haven, were cited by Mayor Lee when he tried to counter my disappointments with the redevelopment program and my suggestions about how it might be improved. This pointedly included for the city to pursue less bulldozing and more preservation. He said he would think about it, which was his way of saying thanks, but no thanks. He also didn't want to hear my warning that people, his constituents, fearing relocation, were angry, and that their protests might become open and embarrassing to him and the city. I had seen this type of anger grow into a riot in Harlem in 1964, and it was ugly. He looked at me as if I was from Mars, pointing out "there is no Harlem in New Haven."

That conversation was taking place in the fall of 1966. Nine months later in August 1967, riots erupted in New Haven. To be sure, there were neither fatalities nor extensive property damage. Some called it a "disturbance," and it was, if comparing it to what would happen that summer in Detroit, Los Angeles, and Newark. Nevertheless, in a few short days the "disturbance" destroyed the image of a "model city" that had taken New Haven years to build, and left the local and federal bureaucracies, and the urban establishment that feeds on them, dazed and defensive.

But that day was still months in the future, and Dick Lee was of good cheer for the present, and countered my concerns with the suggestion I join his reelection team, for which I could earn a few extra dollars producing a TV commercial for him, aware of my experience in New York City for which I had earned a local Emmy nomination. That of course broke the understanding we'd had when I accepted the job, but Lee reassured me that it would be an exception and that, after he won, I would continue as a redevelopment administrator. I didn't believe him, but I did the commercial, shooting it in New Haven but editing it back in New York City, where I could also look for a new job.

Not wanting to go back to daily journalism at that time, I rather preferred to continue with urban planning, possibly consulting at a public agency, while ideally having time to do freelance articles and reviews, and maybe write another book. Putting out some feelers, I figured I could wait until the spring of 1967, which would be a more pleasant time to move than in winter, as well as meaning I had spent more than a respectable year in New Haven.

Having discovered that when thinking positively, positive things happened, which was the case in the spring, once again I uprooted my growing family. This time it was to move to Princeton, New Jersey, to become a housing consultant to the state's newly constituted Department of Community Affairs, headed by Dr. Paul Ylvisaker. With a PhD in government from Harvard and the reputation of a Ford Foundation shaker and doer, Ylvisaker was as peripatetic as me and very open to creative ideas. I liked him.

Unfortunately, the department almost immediately came under pressure to perform when the state's largest city, Newark, erupted into a ruinous riot which left twenty-six dead and millions of dollars in damages. There were lots of emergency meetings, with Ylvisaker asking me to pursue in Newark a program similar to the East Harlem one I had been involved with—converting low-income housing to a moderate-income co-op and empowering residents.

The problem was that New Jersey did not have the necessary public financing New York had, and getting the state legislature to create it turned out to be a frustrating dead end. My tenure was brief, as was Ylvisaker's. He in short time returned to academia, and me in less than a year to New York City in a focused job that I could sink my teeth into—site-specific projects, building innovative public schools in mixed-use projects.

It was administratively complicated and architecturally challenging. But there was funding, and for me a desirable, boots-on-the-ground appointment, in a freshly minted public benefit corporation, the New York City Educational Construction Fund, ECF, for which I would be its first development director. And not incidentally moving again, from Princeton to Port Washington, NY, in an uncommon house swap.

Once I took the job with the ECF, it was felt we should move, if not back to New York City, at least to closer housing in its suburbs, with more space for our now family of four. Scouring the real estate section of the local Princeton weekly paper in July 1968, I came across a classified ad by someone who wanted to swap their "Pre-Revolutionary War Five bedroom Home on a half-acre overlooking Manhasset Bay in Port Washington" for a house in Princeton, where he was being transferred by his company.

Also appealing to us was that Port Washington was where wife Sharron had grown up, still had friends, and where her personable mother, Dwaine, lived, making them both happy to be near each other. The landmark house would certainly be a challenge to restore, taxing my emerging design and construction skills; but the community was appealing, the commute reasonable, the congenial mother-in-law a willing babysitter, and the public school the children would attend just a block away. And so we moved, again.

Commuting now to downtown Manhattan, my bureaucratic education would also continue: the lesson I had learned in New Haven—not necessarily to believe what I might write—was followed in New Jersey with the harsh truism that if you want to build anything, have money and be site- and plan- specific, or else it is all talk.

And at the ECF under Executive Director Daniel Nelson, the task was to complete the agency's innovative projects on time and budget, and, importantly, let the affable director take credit and have the limelight. I would be essentially free to write and whatever. "Do your job, and your time is your own," I remember him saying.

When in New Jersey during my stint as a housing consultant, I engaged several architects who also were on the faculty of Princeton University and associated with the think tank I was involved with, the Center for Urban and Environmental Studies. After participating in a few seminars there, I had been subsequentially invited to become an adjunct, which I accepted and found collegial and beneficent.

Given the flexibility promised me at the ECF, I thought that with my practical knowledge of development I could perhaps continue my education and selectively attend classes to complete a degree in architecture, to go with my science degree in biochemistry from Cornell.

But after meeting with the City College School of Architecture's design faculty, a few of whom I hand known at Princeton, including the dean, Bernard Spring, I was instead given an adjunct (full) professorship. Specifically, I was to guide the school's architecture thesis program, which, Bernie assured me, did not require a degree. My qualification was my experience.

This would be on my own time, of course, like the freelance articles and book reviews I was writing that, since reality had bitten me in my attempts at urban planning, had become controversial and in demand. There is nothing better than being informed by experience if you want to add perspective, perhaps poetry, to one's critical conceits.

"Once again a book has been written about the city all but ignoring the reasons for the city's existence, its problem and its hopes—people," I declared in a review in the *Village Voice* (Dec. 21, 1967) of *Cities in the Race for Time*, by Jeanne Lowe (Random House):

> They are categorized as relocation loads, target populations, work forces, the unemployed, welfare cases, occupants of substandard dwellings and belligerents. In effect, Lowe, has reduced them—us—to pieces in a messy game of megapolis monopoly being played by what can best be described as the urban renewal establishment: key federal officials, city administrators, mayors, redevelopment agencies, housing authorities, foundations, banks and private developers.

The book had been hailed by most reviewers as a definitive study of urban redevelopment. But not by me. I labeled it

> a cautious, informed apology for the establishment... a sales job for more of the same, with some promised improvements, and more studies.... It is apparent she never forgets she was a public relations manager for an organization now called Urban America, a lobbyist and resources group that never knows where its next contribution is coming from.

In another review, this of *The Last Landscape* (Doubleday, 1969), by William H. Whyte, also in the *Village Voice* (Feb. 13, 1969), I wrote that

> Despite the planning profession's reams of maps, elaborate charts, floods of graphics, fancy schematics, endless extrapolations and studies, upon studies, upon studies, usually recommending more studies, presented at weekly, monthly, annual conferences, clinics, seminars and workshops, fees tax deductible, including lunches and tours of the nearest New Town, our cities continue to decay.

To be sure, I went on to praise the book and my mentor, Holly. But I could not pass on putting it into my prejudiced perspective of our ailing urban environment. If anything, I had become a curmudgeonly critic, on call to book review editors, ever-ready to provoke. Even if I admired the author, as I did Bernard Rudofsky, in the review of his *Streets for People* (Doubleday,

1969) for the *Village Voice* (Jan. 22, 1970, I was compelled to go off the rails and rant.

So before faintly praising the book in the review, I declared in yet another opening run-on sentence that

> In the inevitable ecological revolution hopefully soon to come, a major battle must be an attempt to reclaim the central streets of our cities for use and enjoyment, to rid them of noise and air pollution; to ban and restrict vehicular traffic; to encourage public art and landscaping; to replace parking meters with flower pots and benches; to widen, decorate and clean the sidewalks, to restore them for the pleasure of all.

I labeled the book "an excellent primer for reconstruction," but added that reading it was pure frustration, and recommended it for masochistic architects, planners, and city dwellers: "with a prickly prejudice Rudofsky rubs the nose of the reader into the ugliness, filth, crime and carbon monoxide that mark and mar our streets, with a particular bile for New York City."

During this time the bile was also building in me—over my disheartenment with the planning and design profession toadying up to real estate interests and their pandering politicians, and all but ignoring democracy's dream of crafting livable communities. This was not only happening in the struggling inner cities, but surreptitiously also in suburbia too, where I was living now. I saw that a critical book could be written about it.

So as I commuted daily between New York City and Port Washington, riding the Long Island Railroad, becoming involved in local politics, I began my research. I soon found a publisher, Seabury Press, and a kindred editor there, Michael Roloff, who blessed the book with a title I liked: *The Dream Deferred: People, Politics and Planning in Suburbia* (Seabury, 1976).

Not incidentally, the title was from a poem by Langston Hughes, who had recently passed, and that I felt was apt to the suburban world I was living in at the time:

What happens to a dream deferred?

Does it dry up
Like a raisin in the sun?
Or fester like a sore—
And then run?
Does it stink like rotten meat?
Or crust and sugar over—
Like a syrupy sweet?

Maybe it just sags
Like a heavy load.

Or does it explode?

DREAMS DEFERRED

Finding myself by choice in suburbia was an anomaly for me, and an adjustment, having been thoroughly engaged in New York City for most of my young life as a metropolitan reporter, community activist, aspiring urbanist, and now employed developing high-density, city projects. But the requisites of a growing family, and the demands of restoring a landmark home, attracted us to settle in a welcoming Port Washington, Long Island, where we also would have roots.

After spending an exhausting day moving in, we gratefully accepted an invitation to bring the children over and have dinner from a couple my wife knew. Another couple was also invited, ostensibly to greet us, and after dinner and a few drinks the conversation turned to our new common interest, the community. The two wives were quite involved in a variety of local issues, and as the discussion became more animated it reminded me of meetings I had attended in East Harlem. As I would write in *The Dream Deferred* several years later, the broad issues were the same: schools, housing, ethnic politics, economic disparity, zoning, and planning. Only this was suburbia, supposedly the enclave of the bored bourgeois, the uncommitted, not an inner city neighborhood in the throes of a constant crisis.

As the evening wore on, and the wine flowed, I was drawn into debating the latest community crisis, the public review of a draft master plan for the town of North Hempstead, of which unincorporated Port Washington was part, and which one of the women, Wini Freund, was representing as a member of the local League of Women Voters. An astute Wellesley College grad, she was both reasonable and rational in her review, so much so that I remarked she was probably being pressured by the entrenched self-interested politicians, no doubt Republicans and property rights advocates, and their questionable planning professionals. The evening ended with the suggestion that I join the review committee, given my planning experience, if not prejudices.

Several weeks later, despite being new to the community, I was appointed to the Port Washington Citizens Advisory Committee on the master plan. This in time became my introduction to suburbia and its convoluted politics and corrupt planning practices. Suburbia, as the American dream attracting a growing migration from then ailing cities nationally, was a hot topic, debated politically, and studied by think tanks, the subject of scholarly study. And I was at ground zero.

In my various readings I found the most interesting descriptions of suburbia not in the general surveys, but in the microstudies of individual communities, such as the portrait of Park Forest, Illinois, in *The Organization Man*, by William H. Whyte Jr. (Simon & Shuster, 1956). Yes, it was Holly, who not incidentally had been my and Jane Jacobs's mentor, having among other things introduced me to Jane and also to Sam Vaughan of Doubleday Publishers. Sam was to become my editor for *The New York City Handbook*, and like Harvey Shapiro of the *Times*, encouraged my writing.

I spent sixteen months exhorting the advisory committee, summing up my recommendations in what I considered a reasoned report, declaring that "the town at present is a patchwork of zoning variances and uncoordinated growth, at best ignoring its assets and, at worse, abusing them." I added that a master plan could help correct these ills, but that the proposed plan did not, suggesting the consultants be dropped. The blunt recommendations were politely received by the committee, in keeping with what I had labeled suburbia's cult of amiability and filed away. But not by me; and when I assumed that the committee was not going to do anything, I turned to my writing skills.

The article I sold to Long Island's respected *Newsday* was not on the master plan, which I knew would turn off readers, but on how I thought home rule was failing suburbia. Entitled "Will the Real Port Washington Stand Up?" (Feb. 7, 1970), I described a jumble of self-serving jurisdictions, and then with some license declared that "when the polite rhetoric of the workshops and meetings of the League of Women Voters, the Chamber of Commerce and civic associations in Port Washington is carefully considered, the summary is the same: home rule is not working; there is taxation without representation; participatory democracy in suburbia is a sham."

In addition to allowing me to vent my politics, the article touched some responsive chords, and I received some friendly calls. I also received, as I have through the years, some crank and cowardly threatening calls. It was clear in the months ahead that I had destroyed my credibility within the town power structure, especially when I subsequently joined the fledgling local Democratic club.

Though already overcommitted working, teaching, and writing, I was in due course elected club president and selected as an alternative delegate, supporting Senator McGovern, and sent to the 1972 Democratic Nominating Convention in Miami.

There, in a blur of optimism, caucusing, and carousing, I joined a cabal of planning and development avatars who drafted a housing program plank, and cheered its adoption into the Democratic platform and McGovern's nomination. I returned to Long Island to campaign for the ticket, in vain and, if not surprised, was saddened by McGovern's inglorious defeat by Nixon. The planning platform including the reforms I had championed, specifically community outreach and user advocacy, was filed away, in time to be lost.

Meanwhile, ensconced as a professed liberal in Port Washington, I was viewed as a snake on a well-manicured suburban lawn and labeled the local scold. And that is what I would be in the next several years, demonstrating against the Vietnam War and shaming all those I could through my writings.

There were articles in *Newsday*, and nationally, and several major book reviews in the *New York Times*. These included the *Housing Crisis U.S.A.*, by Joseph P. Fried (Praeger, 1971) and *Defensible Space: Crime Prevention through Urban Design*, by Oscar Newman (MacMillan, 1972). I wrote that, pathetically and as a nation, we just continued to talk about these nagging challenges while sadly doing little to translate the words into actual projects and programs to solve them.

The inaction riles me now, as it did then, in the early '70s, when I had assumed the mantle of a New Left critic. I took the designation to heart and like to think I did not disappoint in my reviews, particularly the ones that appeared in the *Washington Post*'s Book

World, where I had become a regular contributor, and pleased to know I was being read by the nation's resident decision makers. And this when developing innovative public schools in mixed-use projects in New York City, while the recalcitrant Republicans held sway in the White House.

With the *Post*'s political readership very much in mind, I declared (April 23, 1972) in a favorable review of *A Populist Manifesto: The Making of a New Majority* (Praeger, 1972), by Jack Newfield and Jeff Greenfield, that "the saving grace of democracy is that even in these dark days it seems to offer a glimmer of hope to the disenchanted and disenfranchised that the glaring and growing inequities of the system somehow, can be peacefully and politically redressed." The book, I added optimistically, was a case in point as well as a plan for action: With its sweeping style and simple, occasionally too simple, solutions, the Manifesto should in this election year replace Reich's ramblings, Tolkien's trilogy, song books and other romantic and escapists tracts on college bookshelves. It also should touch off some heated debates between students and parents, and speechwriters and candidates." I continued that the fight against a concentrated minority of people and institutions controlling too much wealth and power and using it to corrupt the political process and protect themselves from desperately needed changes: "The fight against this concentration of privilege—open and covert, legal and illegal—is, we believe, the most important political question of this decade."

And I was still banging away at the political farce that was Port Washington. In *Harper's* (Oct. 1971), I wrote that "while the North Shore (Long Island) suburbanites may be unhappy with the status quo, they are fearful of change, particularly the effort and hard feelings that would have to borne and bared to bring it about . . . seemingly content to be governed by a political system that is suited, at best, to the problems and conditions of a generation ago." And concluded with the observation that "The politicians and political scientists continue to swear unswerving allegiance to home rule, filling the newspapers with their rhetoric. It reads well, but the reality is that at the end of the commuter line, the newspapers—and their stories on home rule—will be discarded, to be collected by a scavenger, sold and recycled."

If anything was being recycled, it was my rhetoric, which became grist for my *The Dream Deferred*, which I had been working on for several years. The book would be a personal summary of my eight years in suburbia, and I feel that it is still relevant to the convoluted politics of today and the resultant anomie weakening our democracy.

It was widely reviewed and generously praised, with two full length reviews in the *New York Times* and its Sunday supplement. It called the book "a shrewd work on the suburban phenomenon." The *Los Angeles Times*, my future employer, hailed it as "one of the toughest summaries of what's wrong with suburban America."

And my mentor, William H. Whyte, declared it "a splendidly hard-headed analysis of suburbia and the political problems it now poses." It was also a modest commercial success; it went through several printings as a paperback and onto reading lists at planning schools.

I did have one victory of sorts, in suburbia, as reported in the *New York Times*: the trustees of the village I lived in, Baxter

Estate, voted to give one thousand dollars, 20 percent of their modest revenue-sharing funds, to the local anti-poverty agency for social services. Not much, but it was a gesture that I had lobbied for as the town scold and also as the conscientious owner of the landmark house for which the town was named.

After the vote, one of the village trustees said to me that the majority, him included, felt that the grant amount was cheap enough just to keep me from attending meetings. I happily approved, which was noted in the short, sweet article by the *Times* reporter, George Vecsey, who not incidentally was a family friend and lived in Port Washington (*NYT*, April 2, 1973).

Meanwhile, I was also having victories in my job at the ECF—obtaining needed community and government approvals, zoning and financing, and marshalling the design and development of some challenging projects. Easing the way was the simple fact that almost everybody benefited from the projects—in particular, the city's board of education, which lacked the funds to build desperately needed new schools.

Then there was the always needy New York City housing market, especially for the moderate-income developments we were constructing. As for the commercial real estate consortiums, they were naturally hungry for sites that they could lease without going through the difficulty and time of assembling parcels. And the city's construction industry and building trade unions were always in need, ever desperate for projects and jobs.

Also pleased was the ECF's amenable director, Dan Nelson, who graciously took the credit for the successes, while I obligingly stayed in the background, putting in my hours, to be sure, but also teaching and writing as I had hoped. He sadly passed in 2016, widely praised for the innovative program.

The arrangement was good for eight productive years. By the time Nelson left for the private sector, with me following soon after, the ECF had completed some thirteen projects, including three high schools, imaginatively combined with about four thousand units of housing and nearly a million square feet of commercial space. Another dozen was in planning, but soon stalled after we left, as the agency's bureaucratic arteries hardened. Nothing like success to stiffen the status quo. My reward was my name as development director on bronze plaques in several of the schools and knowing that as an urban planner I actually had improved the lives of others, rather than just my own.

Having to orchestrate an ensemble of divergent and, at times, discordant interests was not always easy, as I wrote later in retrospect in an article for *Oculus* magazine (Fall 2007), a publication of the New York City chapter of the A. I. A., boldly entitled, "BLOOD, BACKSTABBING AND OTHER INCONVENIENT TRUTHS ABOUT COLLABORATION:

> So you think an animal trainer in a cage with half dozen tigers and lions has it tough? Consider a conclave of design firms and consultants confronting a gaggle of clients and a chorus of lawyers and bean counters, while the cash-flow clock ticks off the hours and dollars. Then open the door to a puerile local politician, a petulant neighborhood organizer, and a petty planning director, and try to explain the collaborative construct to an indolent media.

> Or conversely, consider this entrepreneurial morass an emerging concert of wills in selfless pursuit of a singular vision of a manmade space or place-a triumph, if you will, of hope and hubris.
>
> The art and science of collaboration is indeed fraught with contradictions in this day-and-age when profit and personalities often dominate and ultimately degrade the already shaky process of design and development. To be sure, there are examples of abiding partnerships, true love, and marriages of convenience where everybody walks away from the table feeling justly rewarded, monetarily as well as emotionally. No need to call the avaricious lawyers to pick over the partnerships and profits.

In theory, I wrote, collaborations in the pursuit of architecture makes sense, given the complexities of projects that necessitate an encyclopedic knowledge of the refinements of design, the stamina to survive a demanding development process, and the ability to tolerate the strong personalities involved. I noted that such collaborations are legend, with firms forging partnerships with each other to mold their diverse teams or joining with other firms when necessary to satisfy the always insistent public client or the often imperious private client.

I added that while these provisional unions appear to be increasingly necessary, they are increasingly difficult too, at least from my perspective of forty years of involvement in almost every form and folly of collaboration. This has included being a principal, an independent contractor, a facilitator, an evaluator, and, a few times at the behest of clients, a provocateur.

> At least I have always known my role, I declared: Others, however, often confuse the process by assuming the expertise and mantle of other collaborators, so you might have, say, an architect answering legal questions while a lawyer weighs in on a design issue. And so for the dialogue and action during these collaborative sessions, they can match the bloodiest, most bitchy scenes out of a movie-of-the-week: lots of artifice, poisonings, and back stabbings.

I continued: "It really doesn't make much difference, for ultimately the final recommendations almost always seem to affirm those advanced by whomever approves the invoices. This ever surprised me, being a child during World War II when collaborators meant those who consorted with the occupying regimes." I concluded that I believed "certain design and development situations need collaboration, and when asked to join a team to respond to an RFP or whatever, I usually don't hesitate to sign on. There is always the hope that the experience will be the exception, if not a diversion."

All this was grist for my teaching as an adjunct professor to a succession of senior classes of architects at City College, where I stressed that if they wanted to participate in the design decision-making process, maybe even hopefully revitalize it, as practicing professionals they needed to advocate for a heightened awareness of human needs and the environment.

Architects needed credibility. As I wrote in a review of *With Man in Mind* (MIT Press, 1971), by Constance Perin, "Intuition and sensitivity today just do not have the credence they once had in the days of gentleman architects and gentleman builders now that we are in the age of the new Technocracy, with its deity of computers, CPM charts, cash flows and cost analyses." That appeared in the December 1970 issue of *Architect* magazine, of which I was a member of its board of contributors.

It was another arrow in my quiver, along with my day job at ECF, my teaching twice a week in the evenings, my spasmodic reviewing and writing for other publications, and appearing regularly as urban commentator on the television news program *The World at Ten* on New York's local PBS Thirteen. That on-air experience was to serve me well later in Los Angeles.

Just reflecting on that frenetic period of my life is exhausting, and not unexpectedly this overachieving eventually took a toll on my home life. My wife and I became estranged, and when I finished *The Dream Deferred* in the fall of 1975, my dream of a comfortable and comforting suburbia was also deferred. The children, Alison and Mike, were entering their independent teens, wife Sharron, a feminist, as was wont in those consciousness-raising days, had gone back to school to become a psychotherapist, and my faithful and loving Labrador Retriever, Cinders, was nearing the end of her days. And so was my marriage, evidently, as it seems at the time were so many others in our demographic. Sharron and I separated shortly before I turned forty.

There was no contested divorce or nasty custody battle. She got the children, the landmark house I had attempted to restore, the keys to an aging station wagon, the dwindling remains of the modest bank account and investments, the sympathy of old friends, and the advice of a lawyer. I got my independence and the chance to pack my bags, take my share of books and records, and move back to the New York City I knew and loved, to frankly enjoy an adolescence I never had, a forty-year-old going on sixteen.

The job was ending at the ECF, as was the teaching at City College, the book was about to be published, the nation's bicentennial year was approaching, reasonable apartments were proffered by colleagues, assorted opportunities were on the horizon, and I was very open to new challenges, once again wide-eyed and bushy-tailed.

As for nagging questions about planning and design, the need for affordable housing, the curse of income disparities, debates on politics, the environment, and racial segregation—issues then coming to the fore in suburbia—I concluded that to have any veracity they needed to be related to people and places. This perspective in my critical thinking and writing, learned in New York City and underscored in Port Washington, in time was to become deep rooted in Los Angeles and beyond.

JUMPING ROCK TO ROCK

I don't remember how I ended up on a coarse sandy beach in Vancouver walking carefully, stepping over scattered milled logs, that misty morning in early June of 1976, a chatty Canadian Broadcasting Company reporter at my side, whose name I can't recall, or if we had had breakfast yet. I would have recollected that, for I liked a good breakfast to start a day, especially if on an assignment where I did not know where it could take me, or for how long, and when I would be at leisure to eat again.

I really shouldn't have been on the beach, but coffee in hand, preferably, at one of the sessions scheduled that morning at Habitat, the United Nations Conference on Human Settlement, in Vancouver. I was attending the conference as a credentialed correspondent, thanks to the *Village Voice* and the *New Republic*. Travel expenses were covered in part by a grant awarded me by the International Aspen Design Conference, which I would be attending next to edit a newsletter, and maybe write an article for *Architect* magazine. Whatever, I was jumping from rock to rock now in the converging currents of contract writing and planning consultancy, and feeling confident, at least for the moment.

Neither do I recall any details about the night before in Vancouver, nor the room assigned to me in a University of British Columbia dorm, other than that the campus was studded with a collection of striking totem poles, carved by,

I assumed, put-upon Indigenous people of the Northwest. As for the companionable broadcast reporter, I never saw her again after that morning, though months later would receive a letter from her relating that she had left the CBC to go live with a beekeeper on a farm in New Zealand, was planning on getting married, and wished me well. There was no return address. It had all been casual and congenial—very '70s.

But that morning on the beach, there I was, with the unnamed radio reporter, in a hospitable Vancouver, far from an unfettered New York City and further from a domestic Port Washington, and not looking back. That was the immutable advice of my mother, Sadie, to me, my four siblings, and randomly to any survivor of any trauma, personal or public, physical, mental or spiritual. "There is nothing you can do to correct the past, so why bother letting it worry you," she would say, usually while sipping sugared black tea from a glass at the kitchen table. And if present, whatever the occasion, my father would add, "Try to enjoy yourself!" I did not know if this exit line was a curse or a blessing, but I took it as a blessing.

To be sure, I was feeling blessed in Vancouver, flitting in and out of sessions, where intense speakers and passionate panelists expounded on the problems of the world's poor, hungry, and homeless in an era of rapid urbanization and environmental decay. Almost all apparently agreed that the problems fed off each other, and were rising at an alarming rate, though disagreeing what that rate was and what would be the consequences, politically and militarily, that is, peaceful or violent. The discussion and debates continued after the sessions, wherever attendees gathered, in restaurants, bars, and beaches, heightened by attending luminaries that included a testy Mother Theresa, an ebullient Buckminster Fuller, and an engagingly plain-spoken Margaret Mead. All mingled with the crowd, creating a memorably congenial scene.

It was exhilarating and involving, to a degree that thoughts of my pending divorce were subsumed by the intense attendees, as I had hoped. And I loved it, for I was a very sympathetic listener to the litany of the world's woes, though knowing it was all talk and that whatever recommendations came out of Habitat most likely would get filed away and forgotten. And this is what I wrote, though I'm sure my articles suffered the same fate at best.

Nevertheless, the urgency of the portraits and precepts concerning the poor communicated at Habitat haunted me and, whenever I could, I would echo entreaties for some sort of redress. With this my mindset, I gave full bore in a review in the *New Republic* of *The Vast Majority: A Journey to the World's Poor* (Simon & Shuster, 1977), by Michael Harrington, who had written the classic *The Other America* (Penguin, 1968) years before and had been a habituate at the White Horse when I had hung out there. In the book that I praised, Harrington, a professed socialist, calls for a "modest" voluntary redistribution of the world's wealth to relieve the abject poverty overtaking the planet, sustained by "a commonwealth of humanity," based on a new international economic and political order. His argument was moral and reasonable, if naïve.

In contrast, there are no such appeals to the politics of altruism in *Poor People's Movements: Studies from the Contemporary United States* (Random House, 1977), by Frances Fox Piven and Richard A. Cloward, which I also reviewed post-Habitat, also for the *New Republic*. They compellingly contended, and

I dutifully wrote, "that the only way the poor will gain meaningful social and economic reforms is through extended protests and mass disruptions"; that these were the only way to needed change; that if the efforts turned to polite organizational and electoral politics, the movements would fail; that only true crises would work. It was a radical observation, then as now, cynical and sadly apt, as nearly a half century of half measures has proven, the homeless crisis being but one example.

My sabbatical of sorts that summer continued when, leaving Habitat, I accepted a ride to Seattle from one of the many challenging activists I had met. She was a comely and accomplished lawyer representing several Native American tribes that she contended, and convincingly argued, had been exploited by the greedy white man conspiring with federal and state governments for the last century. She was convincing, and I was no one to argue otherwise.

I have forgotten her name, too, but not her advocacy, as she both lectured and entertained me for several engaging and educational days, showing me what she labeled the "other Seattle," where some of her clients persevered: the substandard housing, nagging unemployment, and a skid row. She also proposed introducing me to a sympathetic someone at the *Seattle Times*, which she felt needed and would welcome an informed, experienced writer like me, and gave me a tour of a houseboat on Portage Bay where I could live cheaply and not, coincidentally, near her landside home.

The offer was tempting, but Seattle was a long way from New York City and my children, and ahead of me was a long road of promised experiences and employment to which I looked forward. I declined, though when leaving for my next adventure at the Aspen Design Conference, she gave me a heavy silver Navajo bracelet to wear to remind me of the offer. And it did for several years, until I wrote her that I was moving West, not to Seattle, but to Los Angeles, to be the activist writer she implored me to be. She replied with a curt request to return the bracelet, which I reluctantly did.

There was no such drama, but there were temptations at the Aspen conference; the most popular, I felt, was just kicking back, going to the public hot baths in nearby Glenwood Springs, and dancing and laughing into the early morning hours. The conference was fun, but as I recall not very illuminating and challenging.

Unlike the socially aware, politically savvy, activist-challenging cauldron of causes Habitat had been, the conference seemed to feature morsels of self-important design professionals floating on top of a gazpacho of sycophants, subordinates, and students. There was hardly a whisper of low-cost housing needs, city and suburban planning issues, and environmental concerns, the grist for my writings. Instead, design was not viewed as I did, and still do—a tool to solve societal problems—but as an expression of fads and fashions, users being at best an afterthought.

As a result, the newsletter I edited with then emerging talented graphic designer Milton Glaser, ignored the mostly self-aggrandizing presentations, and featured among chatty items about hot baths and cool exhibits, a full-page cartoon by Milt of individual speakers cutting loose fart balloons of cliches I had culled from their talks. It did pinprick some inflated egos on the speaker panels and conference board, and Milt and I took a perverse pleasure in it. My return to New York City in time to celebrate the nation's bicentennial, unemployed, was left unaffected, however. But not for long.

Beckoning among other prospects was a planning consultancy at the Pennsylvania Avenue Development Corporation (PADC), which had reached out to me with a proposal that was intended to tap my skills learned as the downtown renewal director of New Haven and my critic's concern, generally for a sense of history, but at a more modest scale, to better serve pedestrian life. In discussion with its director, John Woodbridge, I felt the wide avenue favored vehicular traffic and the once every four-year parade, and not the daily users, the office workers, and tourists, who really were its lifeblood. Housing was needed, too. He agreed, and I signed on for a year.

So much for urban planning. After signing on for what turned out to be six months, I spent most of my time writing memorandums recommending that the landmark Willard Hotel, then vacant and awaiting demolition, be saved and restored. It took a lot of memos and meetings, but the building was spared and, a few years after I had left, an open competition I proposed was held to rehabilitate it, albeit as a luxury hotel.

Allowing some relief from part-time bureaucratic battles, I was commuting to New York City for four-day weekends to see friends and the children, from whom I feared I was growing distant. I also continued to write book reviews, however sporadically, for the *Washington Post*. Missing the buzz of a newspaper, I hung out there whenever I could, mostly in its Book World office to schmooze with its always engaging and judgmental editor, Bill McPherson.

I had been doing reviews for Book World for several years and had only met Bill recently through my companion at the time, Jane Howard. The best-selling author of *A Different Woman* (Dutton, 1973), Jane, a close friend of Joan Didion at the then-celebrated *Life* magazine, was a longtime friend of Bill's, and we would visit him in DC, as would other writers, in effect transforming his book-cluttered office into a literary salon. There, opinions flowed freely, like the wine from the bottles he kept in a small refrigerator under his desk.

On a particular day in the spring of 1977, he was chiding me, but not for a book review I had just turned in on *The Abuse of Power: The Permanent Government and the Fall of New York* (Penguin Books, 1977), by Jack Newfield and Paul DuBrul. Bill in fact said he loved the review, in which I wrote that the authors "have combined their outrage and talents as a journalist and planner, respectively, to piece together the sharpest, most unforgiving document about misrule in the city" in recent years, noting that a network of elites milked the city for personal power and private gain. And when their greed triggered a fiscal crisis, "they manipulated the media to blame it on the city's policies of doing 'too much' for its citizens."

What bothered Bill was that I was in DC "playing" planner and paper pusher when I should be in New York, like Newfield and DuBrul, muckraking. He stated that he didn't know anyone in the media more knowledgeable about urban affairs than me, and more forthright and persuasive. That is why he said he happily assigned me books to review, but he really would be happier for me to be a critic or a columnist, even if it meant my writing for the *Post*'s competition, the *New York Times*. He felt that the paper would take me back, just as the *Post* had taken him back to be an editor after he had wandered off to cavort as a book publisher for several years, though he granted that A. M. Rosenthal was not as magnanimous as Ben Bradlee.

Bill's sermon set off applause in the office and a call for a toast. Bill was, as usual, right, reminding me that as an editor he had the last word over what a writer might think and put down on paper, and sometimes felt he knew what the writer was thinking even he or she didn't write it. Meanwhile, I also had been thinking how much I enjoyed the catbird seat of a journalist, and the writing, too, hard as it might be at times. Would it be turning the clock back in my relentless journey forward?

But Bill had scratched an itch. So the next day, I scratched, and instead of proofreading another proposal for the PADC, I updated my resume, though the people I planned to call were friends, and I probably wouldn't need it, but others up the ladder would. What I had to reassure them was I wouldn't be a pain in the ass, go off on self- motivated tangents, write things I shouldn't, and embarrass them and their publication. Whatever, I had felt the little push from Bill on my back. It was time to jump to another rock.

My first call was to Syd Schanberg at the *New York Times*, a recent recipient of a well-earned Pulitzer Prize for his Cambodia coverage, which was to inspire the 1984 film *The Killing Fields*. A friend from my early days at the *Times*, on his return from Southeast Asia I had arranged for him to sublet Jane Howard's Riverside Drive apartment, she off to the Pacific Islands researching another book, this one on Margaret Mead. Syd was the newly anointed city editor at the *Times*, Abe having clawed his way to executive editor.

We met in New York City, in a West Side coffee house, the cups getting cold as we talked. I was excited and so was Syd, who related he was planning to form and launch an investigative team to take a hard look at the city's elite and power brokers. It would be raw meat for the caged tiger in me, and we agreed to a date for me to start work. All that was needed was for Syd to inform Abe that he intended to hire me, and to pick a launch date for the proposed team.

Syd was optimistic Abe would heartily agree to establishing the team, and certainly hiring me too, given that my books had been hailed by the *Times*. Syd related that the *Handbook* was a constant reference in the newsroom, and my having both public and private experiences in urban development, New York's honey pot had to impress Abe. We agreed that the city's rapacious real estate development in particular was ripe for a probe by the paper and should be an initial target. But Abe curtly nixed the plan and told Syd to also hold back on the investigation, pending his review.

Maybe the thick-headed, thin-skinned Abe, who took no prisoners, suspected that I had written the *Village Voice* exposé of the *Times* a dozen years ago; but, in retrospect, it's more likely he just wanted to fire a warning shot across Syd's bow to demonstrate that he, Abe, was sovereign, and warn his underling not to try to outshine his legacy as city editor. Shaken by Abe's paranoid management style, Syd apologized to me. No need, I replied, I wasn't surprised, and I thanked him for the efforts and friendship, warning him to beware of Abe, reminding him of the decade he'd spent observing the convoluted palace politics of Asia.

Syd was to serve as the *Times* city editor just three short, unpleasant years, to be kicked upstairs to write a local column, only to have it cancelled a few years later by Abe. Syd kept moving in a stormy career that I could relate to, writing provocatively for *Newsday* and the *Village Voice*, to pass in 2016, at eighty-two years old.

The hope to return to the *Times* behind me, I sought out another friend I had known there, Robert Lipsyte. Very much a kindred soul, he had left the paper, where he had been a heralded young sportswriter and budding columnist, some years before, to also jump from rock to rock as a correspondent for both CBS and NBC, a late-night host on public television, while all the time writing novels for teenagers and sports-themed books for adults. His latest gig was as a columnist at the venerable *New York Post*, which had been recently bought by Rupert Murdoch, then an upstart Australian publisher with dreams of a world media empire.

Ever the enthusiast, Bob thought correctly that the *Post* needed a New York City-born and ill-bred presence in the newsroom to educate the raw alien Aussie staff Murdoch had brought with him. He introduced me to Murdoch, who I immediately liked for his straightforward style and unabashed eagerness to get to know the New York melting pot, with a focus on the *Post*'s readership and how it could be increased. We did not talk politics, but instead about what would entice me to return to the city and work for him.

The offer of pay was fair, expenses generous, and the expectation of returning to New York City seductive, so I signed on as the night city editor. This would entail overseeing the day's stories wrapped up and the paper ready to be printed in the early morning and delivered in the afternoon to newsstands. It was to be a tabloid in the Murdoch mold, with a snappy headline and sassy photo on page one that screamed out: "Buy me!" He also proffered my writing an occasional column.

You can have fun with this, I thought. It certainly would not be uptight like the self-conscious *Times*, which Murdoch learned quickly how to tease and taunt in print, knowing that it would bedevil Abe. I wasn't above enjoying a little redress either, and would occasionally insert some nasty rumor or two in the gossip on Page Six being fed to me by, it seemed, a daily parade of disgruntled *Times* staff, who traded candor for anonymity. It was probably for the better I was at the more proletarian *Post*, and I reveled in putting the paper out, for at least a few months.

LOS ANGELES BECKONS

The summer of 1977 for most angst-ridden New Yorkers was the meanest of seasons: essential services had been cut as the city tried to balance its budget and claw its way back from the edge of bankruptcy: a serial killer sporting a .44-caliber pistol stalking brown-haired women was on the loose, and then came a power failure for an interminable twenty-five hours, setting off widespread looting causing nearly half a billion dollars in damages, some 3,700 arrests, and untold harm to the municipal ego. Unlike the city's blackout in 1964, this one was nasty; looters were emboldened and residents frightened, with the poorer neighborhoods, of course, suffering the most.

Yet for the city's newspapers, it was a great story, especially for the screaming headlined, photo-filled tabloids, and that included the *Post*, where I was rebooting myself as a journeyman journalist. The blackout, if anything, gave me an impetus to encourage more coverage of the city's now exposed underbelly, including its planning and development policies serving special interests. I like to think I enthused some fledgling reporters, including Roberta Brandes Gratz, who became a sympathetic biographer of Jane Jacobs; Jane had a way with us sympathetic scribes.

Ever cognizant of the city's demographics and politics, I also pressed for a more critical laying bare of its obnoxious celebrity scene, in the news section as well as on Page Six, the daily gossip digest Murdoch Rupert had brought with him from Down Under and given full play in the *Post*. I liked and promoted it. In contrast to the *Times*, the *Post* was a scandal sheet, with a liberal bent, advocating for its vast plebian population, which I tried to convince Rupert would be good for the circulation he craved.

But after only a few months as a fledgling crusading editor, I was moved out of news to the editorial page, to become chief editorial writer. Whether I had been too pushy and liberal in the newsroom, or Murdoch had appreciated my being so opinionated, albeit on behalf of subway riders, or that James Wechsler, the venerable liberal editorial editor, was sadly fading, the new post put me in daily contact with the upstart Aussie, as he was considered at the time. I welcomed the opportunity, having read Rupert, perhaps incorrectly, as a populist, "hands-on" publisher in search of circulation, his coarse conservatism then camouflaged. Or perhaps I didn't want to see it in my enthusiasm for having a bully pulpit.

What I did see was that when it came to headlines, as well as the play of stories, Murdoch shed with ease his Oxford prejudices, intellectual pretensions, and the mannerisms of his wealth to display what I labeled a "crassmanship" uniquely geared to attract the lowest common denominator of reader. Then aged forty-six and just a few years older than me, I wanted to like him. Murdoch, and to turn a phrase, looked British, and may not have thought Yiddish, but there was a shrewdness that hinted at the mindsets of both a savvy East Londoner and a raw Aussie.

As per my initial predilection, Rupert encouraged me to vigorously editorialize on behalf of the mayoral bid of Ed Koch, who I considered a progressive from my past experiences, and

Rupert saw as a law-and-order candidate with the potential for being truculent. If anything, this would generate good copy, at the time his bottom line.

Murdoch also gave me license for my planning theories. And after I had argued that no one read the *Post* when stuck in their car in traffic, but did read it sitting or standing in a subway, he agreed to a tough three-part editorial railing against the proposed elevated highway Westway, which would have scarred the Hudson waterfront from midtown to the tip of Manhattan.

Published August 16,17, and 18, 1977, I declared, "Westway is the wrong way"; to favor it "is to embrace the flawed and failed planning theories of the Fifties," and "if there is any transportation priority in the city, it has to be mass transit." That is "what ultimately makes the city tick. It is its lifeline to jobs and shopping and a key to economic recovery." That the *Post* had punched what would be a fatal hole in the balloon of a pet project of the city's establishment, including the *New York Times*, pleased Murdoch and me.

Still, I walked a narrow path at a skittish, paradoxical *Post*. Bob Lipsyte, a good friend and a good writer, who had been instrumental in my being hired there, abruptly resigned that summer, declaring that his columns had been tampered with and that he'd been denied "the freedom to have opinions in counterpoint to the paper's policy." I was comfortable with Murdoch, but not the associates he had brought on, such as Steve Donleavy, who I thought a cartoon of a journalist.

As Michael Leapman would write in *Arrogant Aussie: The Rupert Murdoch Story* (Lyle Stuart, 1985), "If there were a club for ex-editors of Rupert Murdoch's publications, it would be the least exclusive in the international news business. Editing a Murdoch publication is a high-risk operation." I felt nervous back in 1977, especially with child support and alimony payments due each month, on top of the rising cost of living in New York City.

So when John Heimann took me aside in Washington, DC, after his swearing in by President Carter to be the Comptroller of the Currency, the administrator of the national bank system, and asked if I would consider being his special assistant, I was listening with very much an open mind. John confided that he felt he was going to an alien Washington and needed someone he could kick back with and rely on for straight opinions, as the agency would be involved with some sensitive political situations.

This, not incidentally, turned out to be the investigation of the president's confidant and director of the Office of Management and the Budget, Burt Lance, which eventually led to his much-publicized resignation. I had served John when he was the New York state superintendent of banking heading a controversial task force, appointed by Governor Hugh Carey to investigate the State's Urban Development Corporation. I was also appointed to the committee by the governor, having earned the approbation of a principled, if willful, young mandarin at the ECF. As for John, he was refreshingly forthright, and I trusted him, as he obviously trusted me. Impetuously as ever, jumping yet to another rock, I told him yes: "What the hell, I'll come to Washington."

I saw the job as an opportunity to add the very sharp arrow of financial acumen in my planning and development quiver, frankly, which I had viewed as the most influential weapon in urban decision-making. And having toiled in the capitol however briefly as consultant to the PADC, it would be nice returning to the DC scene in a more influential and prestigious position, and at more pay and better benefits.

Though I did have some reservations. Once again, I would not be as close to my family as I was in New York City, especially to daughter Alison and son Mike as they endured their teen years. There also was Nancy Henningsen, a kindred soul living across the street from me on the West Side, who had become a constant companion during my New York adventures. And I enjoyed being a journalist there, and really did not know how long I would persevere in Washington.

Being uncharacteristically cautious, I told Murdoch, Rupert to me at the time, that it was to be a temporary job to help a friend in a delicate political situation, and that in a year or two I looked forward to returning to the *Post* or whatever his next acquisition would be in his quest to be a media mogul. He nodded his head, not saying anything, and turned back to the newspaper on his desk. I would not see him for a dozen years, and when I did at a Milken conference I was attending in Los Angeles, he did not recognize me. I recognized him. He was Murdoch, not Rupert, and was looking much older. His predatory rise was taking a toll.

As for my stint in DC, I looked forward to renewing my relationship with Bill McPherson, who I thought had taken a dim view of my writing as a Rupert Murdoch minion reviewing books from the Left. But he had continued to give me assignments, albeit slyly and with different themes. This included combining three books in a page one Book World review entitled "Single for Better or Worse" (June 4, 1978), in which I wrote to the amusement of friends:

> For those of us adults who most nights sleep single in a double bed, it is small consolation that we have been identified as a book market. We have enough problems being categorized, if not by pandering publishers, then by concerned parents, solicitous siblings, envious marrieds, fickle friends, whispering co-workers, faddist designers, parasitic psychologists, suspicious landlords, fawning hosts and computer dating services.

And I added: "singlehood may not be the American ideal, but today and in the projected future, it is very much a fact of life, for better or worse, to borrow a once popular phrase."

One day at the *Post* in the early fall of 1978, as I stood in Bill's office looking through a stack of recently published books to select something I would like to review, the topic he casually introduced was the end of his tenure as the editor of Book World. My immediate concern was that a new editor, as is their wont, would select his or her friends as favored reviewers, and my assignments would therefore diminish, if not end. But my thoughts also turned to friend Bill, and the question, "What's happening?"

As Bill told it, Ben Bradlee had casually asked him that morning whether he would rather be a writer or book critic than editor of Book World. This would give him time to work on the novel he was always saying he wanted to write and would be more fun than being an editor. We writers agreed, even though we thought editors were paid more for being less creative while sitting in a comfortable office protected from the elements, with an intern close by to get them a coffee. What did they do, really?

Apparently, Bradlee had already offered the editor's job to Book World's dependable deputy, Brigitte Weeks, who had just received an offer from the then-ascending *Los Angeles Times*. Not, incidentally, under Bradlee, overlooking the *Post*'s "soft" news and Book World at the time was the smarmy, smiling Shelby Coffey the Third, who would later become the unctuous executive editor of the *Los Angeles Times* when I was there. Try as he might, Coffey could never exude the spirit and style of the benevolent Ben, and it would have been easy for Bill to stand his ground.

But it was hard for Bill to argue with the august Bradlee, since it was the *Post* that had hired him in 1958, at the age of twenty-five, as a raw copyboy, despite him having dropped out of college twice. And after becoming a reporter a few years later, Bill had left the *Post* impetuously for a job in book publishing, but Bradlee had lured him back with the book editor position. Not only that, he signed the checks. And if you were nice, he and his glamorous wife, Sally Quinn, might invite you to their storied dinners.

There would be no discussion among friends and associates that day, for Bill declared he had accepted the new assignment. He looked forward to being a journalist again, and, in time, a writer. He added that he already had the beginnings of a book on paper, with the story shaping in his mind, though he would say no more.

It was this jumping from rock to rock in the merging currents of journalism and literature that made Bill a kindred soul, since I too had a fractured career. While I had worked on New York's waterfront as a shtarker and upstate as a seasonal farm laborer, Bill had been a merchant seaman.

But I had eventually graduated from Cornell University, which, after a forgettable stint in the US Army, no doubt helped me score the job as a copyboy with the *Times*, also in 1958. Thus we became friends, in the spirit of strangers sitting next to one another on a long sleepless flight, sharing confidences. Except that Bill and I now were again meeting after I had left the *New York Post* to take a position with the Comptroller of the Currency.

And so, in that momentous day in my life, while Bill was talking about his new job and reassuring me that Brigitte would make a fine editor, and, presumably, be pleased to continue to use me as a reviewer, he stopped and smiled broadly. Then, after a pause for dramatic effect— I remember this distinctly, although nearly a half century ago—he suggested I should immediately apply for the book editor post that Brigitte was, at that very moment, calling *LA Times* editor Jean Sharley Taylor to turn down.

He declared I would be perfect for the rising *Times*, having written reviews for the *New York Times* under the tutelage of its book editor, Eliot Fremont-Smith, and for the edgy *Village Voice* under editor Dan Wolfe and infamous publisher Norman Mailer. And, of course, there were the pieces I had written for him at the *Post*, and on my shelf two successful books, and always the promise of more.

Why not? I thought and nodded, yes. He nodded in reply, and handed me his phone, to call Taylor, cold.

As the call was identified from me at the *Washington Post*, I got through to Taylor, who said that yes, Weeks had just turned down the job, and asked how I knew. But before I could answer, she added the paper had a second choice in the wings, its columnist Art Sidenbaum, and he had accepted just minutes ago.

Then Taylor mentioned that the cover the paperback of *The Dream Deferred*, which she happened to have on a shelf, had prominently quoted a rave *LA Times* review, and asked whether I'd be interested in coming to the coast and discussing Sidenbaum's former job.

My hand over the phone, I relayed the query to Bill. He nodded yes enthusiastically. Bill was, of course, right. My professional job in government was instructive, but mostly bullshit, a divorce was pending, my fickle friend Jane had become just an occasional friend with benefits, as were several others in Washington, while friends in New York City were fading away. Los Angeles certainly would be a new adventure for peripatetic me.

"What the hell!" I exclaimed, and flew out to Los Angeles the next weekend, loved what I saw, and moved there a month later. My thought was that the assignment, in effect, was a generous travel and study grant to Southern California, and I'd probably return to New York in a year or two. That was nearly fifty years ago.

I sadly never saw Bill again. We were going to have drinks, but instead said our goodbyes by phone, promised to keep in touch, and didn't. I did send him a note in 1984, congratulating him on the praise he was getting for his novel *Testing the Current* (Simon and Shuster, 1984), but he never answered; and when his second novel, *To the Sargasso Sea* (1988), came out I didn't send a note, but was happy for him.

Bill left the *Post* a few years later, about when I left the *LA Times*. I heard he had gone to Romania as a freelance writer, which would not have been my choice. I became a creative consultant to Disney Imagineering, while continuing to write.

When I asked the writer John Gregory Dunne, whom I had met through Jane and was interviewing me for a television documentary on LA he was to write and narrate, why he thought Bill had become an expat correspondent, he had no answer. This was soon after the great success of John's *True Confessions* (Dutton, 1977), which I had loved.

Changing topics from Bill to me, John asked, ruefully, why I had stayed in Southern California. "It's comfortable," I said. "Corrupting," he replied, adding that it was "not the best place to be a writer. New York City is better. The weather is worse, and you stay inside at your typewriter more."

But he was living in New York then, and I was in Los Angeles, happily married again, to someone I had met at the *Times*, Margaret Mary Hall, who shared with me my captivation with LA, and with whom in time had two more children, Josef and Kyle. It had certainly turned out to be much more than the travel and study grant I had thought it would be, when in November 1978 I embarked on a drive across the country to Los Angeles, to see for myself whether what was being said about the sprawling upstart of a city was true.

WELCOME TO THE LAND OF SUNSHINE AND SHADOWS

"Where you headed?" asked the gawking gas attendant at a sleazy station outside Sikeston, Missouri, eyeing the clutter in my car and my New York license plate, as I made my way cross country in the Fall of 1978.

"Los Angeles."
"Fantastic place," he grinned.
"Ever been there?" I asked.
"Nope," he said dejectedly, grinned again and added: "But I hope to get there someday."

Whether they had been there or not, gasoline attendants, waitresses, motel managers, park rangers, hitchhikers, relatives, friends, and others I spoke to on my way west all had an opinion of Los Angeles. Comments ranged from rejection to reverence, hate to love, though all paid a compliment to the city by their lack of indifference. I was impressed by the emotions it stirred and wrote about in my first article for the *Times* (Nov. 30,1978).

"You'll love it," beamed cousin Alan Cheuse, an occasional book reviewer for the *Los Angeles Times* and then living in Knoxville, Tenn., where I visited with him for a few days on my way west. "LA is the most exciting city in America today," he declared.

"You'll find it interesting," moderated George Malko, a writer born in Copenhagen, raised in Chicago, living in New York City, and thinking about Los Angeles. "Space, sunshine, and a sense of freedom," he alliterated. We had been writing partners on a play that never went anywhere. But we had become good friends and promised to keep in touch.

Like many persons, I formed my first mage of Los Angeles at the movies. Such films in my youth as *The Big Sleep*, *Double Indemnity*, and *The Postman Always Rings Twice* presented the city as a place of seedy bars, slick nightclubs, strange mansions, and sordid hotels in which tough, honest, timeworn detectives confronted criminals and con men on behalf of conflicted, not-so-innocent women. In the shadows there always seemed to be mysterious and morbid characters. For an area blessed with sunshine, there were a lot of shadows. And tragedy.

This was confirmed by some of the books I consumed in my adolescence, which incidentally was then continuing into my forties. The books included *What Makes Sammy Run?* by Budd Schulberg, *Miss Lonelyhearts* and *Day of the Locust*, by Nathanael West, *The Last Tycoon*, by F. Scott Fitzgerald, and *The Long Goodbye*, by Raymond Chandler.

They projected an image of Los Angeles as a city of disillusionment and destruction. Wrote the existential Chandler in *The Long Goodbye*: "A city no worse than others, a city rich and vigorous and full of pride, a city lost and beaten and full of emptiness."

American immigrants, it appeared, had traversed the country in search of a new Jerusalem and instead had found a new Babylon. Reinforcing this image were the views of many of my fellow planners and urban sociologists. With few exceptions, they condemned Los Angeles as a chaotic collection of suburbs, a sprawling abstraction, alienating its residents and destroying the environment.

But visits to Los Angeles had revealed to me that it was more than an autopolis, an amorphous mass of communities dominated by the automobile and held together by a mesh of crowded freeways, my first impression. The communities upon closer look were distinct, their residents real, the potential for the good life unlimited, or so I hoped.

Off the freeways, down the ramps, along the streets, through the markets, at the offices, in the homes, on the beaches there was a vitality. Los Angeles seemed to be alive and kicking. To be sure, there was trendy, vapid narcissism, not unlike New York. But I liked to think there also was concern, commitment, and, particularly, a strong sense of the present and future.

I had always considered, like others, that Los Angeles and New York City were the magnetic energy poles of the United States. It now appeared that the attraction to Los Angeles was the stronger. Whatever its age, Los Angeles seemed young and infectious.

And so it was time to discard the images of the early movies, the novels, the academic theories, the comments of friends and acquaintances, the prejudices of a New Yorker born and bred and see for myself what Los Angeles was like. It could, indeed, be the new Jerusalem or, for that matter, the new Babylon. Or it could be, as I suspected, unique.

Unique also for me was the apartment I settled into, across from the Ocean Park Beach edging the bayside city of Santa Monica, where on my small balcony I could see and smell the glittering salt water. It had been found for me by a friend of the family living nearby, who when hearing I was coming to Los Angeles, commented that if I was to enjoy my stay I had to live by the beach. She was right. It felt like I was on vacation, and in a sense I was.

Living at the beach had also been the advice of a woman I had met in Denver, where I had taken a break from my driving for a few days to tour the city and its encyclopedic art museum. When in cities I don't really know I usually check out their museums and public markets.

She said that, yes, it's where I should live, by the beach, where the light at times could be marvelously pellucid and the sunsets spectacular. As it so happened, her view was that of an art student, which she was, and she was on some business or other in Denver, she wouldn't share with me, on behalf of her employer, Georgia O'Keefe. This spurred interest, dinner, and an extended cordial conversation late into a night.

Talk about light and colors, subjects and paintings! I ended up going out of my way for a few days to give her a lift to a town outside of Santa Fe, where she lived with O'Keefe, with the hopes of my meeting the artist. I didn't. It was late when we arrived. She was asleep, and I had to move on, though the encounter bode well for my Western sojourn.

If now I could only adjust to the lifestyle of LA, which I had been told was distinctively not like New York's. Certainly, the weather was different, something I'd always considered determinant of a culture. Here it was November, and I was in shirtsleeves and dungarees, a tie never to be worn again—never—and walking barefoot on a beach just steps from my apartment.

Trying to define Los Angeles I decided was to be my personal assignment, a theme underlying my initial story; for the city I anticipated seemed to me to be a distant, strange planet I had happened to land on, having taken an abrupt turn west from my obsessed East Coast domain.

Whether called "LaLa land" or "El Lay", Los Angeles seldom had entered my consciousness before I impetuously chose to spend the next phase of my life living there, while telling myself I would be returning to New York City as often as I could, for my children and my sanity, in effect becoming bicoastal. And to think previously I had thought being bicoastal referred to people having to commute cross-town Manhattan.

Given the prerogative of finding my own stories and setting my own pace by a generous and supportive, if not indulgent, *Los Angeles Times*, I turned at first to distinctive scenes I was familiar and comfortable with and that might appeal to the archetypical reader.

Whom that might be, of course, is the eternal debate among journalists. At the *New York Times*, I remember being told, perhaps sarcastically, that it was a precocious nine-year-old; at the *New York Post*, a Jewish garment worker riding the subway; at the *Washington Post*, a bright special assistant to a calloused congressman; by *Life* magazine writer Jane Howard, a suburban, educated housewife.

I would, no doubt, soon find out who my reader was in an evolving Los Angeles. Though my ego told me it was myself, as explained in the infamous quote from the comic strip *Pogo*: "We have met the enemy, and he is us."

My first self-assigned assignment in Los Angeles was a scene just a block away from the *Times* offices, Grand Central Market, the city's public market. Then seemingly neglected and catering to a mostly Hispanic working class, family-oriented population, I considered it a softball assignment to flaunt my urbanity.

As expected, I found the market slatternly, but colorful and congenial, and wrote an animated, solicitous article (*LAT*, Dec.12, 1978) drawing upon my varied experiences of public markets; in my local East Harlem, at 116th Street beneath the Metro North tracks; the city-wide serving wholesale Washington Market then in the West Village, when I was a fruit and vegetable inspector in two college-year summers; and in Paris, as a tourist, the historic Les Halles before it was demolished to become a shopping center.

The positive feedback I got on the Grand Central Market piece, and being the gourmand that I am, the tacos I enjoyed prompted me to take the advice of a reader, who had written me a letter of praise, to drive to the predominately Hispanic community of Boyle Heights, in East Los Angeles, and check out the market, El Mercado, specifically on a Sunday.

And so I did, and found a welcoming three-story, teeming indoor bazaar there, with not only produce, but several restaurants serving Mexican cuisine accompanied by competing live mariachi bands. It was a blast, and to think I also was clocking a workday while reveling in an ethnic celebration.

The article in turn generated more letters from readers informing me of farmers' markets persevering weekly in scattered neighborhoods, which of course I publicized. This again raised a few eyebrows at the *Times*. Apparently, it was then an anomaly to write feature stories other than breaking news not blessed with a press release or the presence of a public relations person, and to be serendipitously open to the unexpected. To me, that was the fun of feature writing.

Or as further explained to me by a kindred reporter, perhaps it was because the Pasadena market I wrote about was a struggling low- to moderate-income neighborhood, not usually written about in the establishment-conscious *Times*, and that I had added impolitically that the weekly event was where residents shopped for lower-cost produce, as well as gossip and air grievances of poor services and an unresponsive city hall. "In this respect," I wrote, "the market carries forward one of the older traditions of an urban neighborhood, the function of which over the centuries often focused on a central area, call it a square, plaza, piazza or marketplace, where residents could gather to trade and talk."

As for the urban design perspective I was expected to bring to the *Times*, I commented that the engaging public markets thrived by offering lower-cost foodstuffs and work clothes and footwear to a predominately Hispanic clientele, even if they weren't the paper's readers, though hinting they could be. And this despite the establishment planning profession's then clichéd vision of public markets and pushcart vendors being unsavory and unattractive, not your upscale shops and markets in idealized neighborhoods and the suburbs, and so blinded to the social capital and cohesion that public markets can generate.

Then there was also, for me at least, the experiences in my youth in Brooklyn of horse-drawn pushcarts plying our street, where food could be touched, custom cut, or perhaps tasted, not something packaged off a shelf, to be scanned at the checkout counter. Shopping could be fun at a public market, not rushed or anonymous, playing bumper car with your food cart, as in a supermarket. Jane Jacobs would be proud, and

I thought of maybe sending her a tear sheet, as a way of telling her about my move to LA and to counter her vision of a sprawling faceless collection of suburbs.

There was also a seasonal story in which I wrote in my early days in Los Angeles that "Christmas brings out the city in Los Angeles, more than at any other time of year, its shopping streets and malls swarms with pedestrians in search of goods and gifts" (Dec. 12, 1980). The urban critic that I was continued:

> Here at last is a chaotic consumerism replete with people brandishing elbows and packages, a crying or curious child or two in tow, creating a scene long associated with a traditional city in its traditional mode as marketplace.
>
> With the crowds, Los Angeles sheds its image to be viewed through a windshield. Cars are parked, and shoes touch the pavement, as citizens join the throngs to experience the city at less than 55 miles an hour. It becomes a different, more vital city.

I continued:

> Out on the streets, faces are no longer blurs behind glass window, voices no longer drowned by horns... [to create a] pedestrian physics in which a small crowd becomes a critical mass, setting off a chain reaction much like that of a fissionable material, creating a larger and larger crowd. In short, people tend to attract people.

The result, I added, was congestion, which retailers loved, the involved bureaucrats not so much. I continued:

> For the city's planners, traffic engineers and development officials, the congestion presents a conflict. They say they want people to flock into the centers, knowing well that good business means a healthy tax base and needed jobs. But in designing and legislating the city to supposedly give people easier access to the centers, they have often discouraged congestion. . . . In a desire to move traffic, city engineers have a record of widening streets whenever and wherever possible.

Winning no friends at city hall and raising eyebrows at the *Times* with my Christmas-in-the-city article, I noted that the Los Angeles City Planning Department's answer to the congestion was the construction of pedways, pedestrian bridges to connect downtown buildings at the second and third levels, prompting me to write: "What happens here is that pedestrians and retail activity becomes thinned out on all levels, with the street being hurt the most. So much for the planning in the interest of pedestrians."

I went on to attack the city's proposed people mover that had been cheered editorially by the *Times*, as a gimmick, sure to line the pockets of construction and real estate interests, while hurting pedestrian life. On a roll, and with space to write, I also attacked the city's recent ban on sidewalk street vendors: "Few things in a plaza or on a sidewalk attract and stimulate a crowd more than a food vendor," I declared. "They provide a convenience, a focal point and a sense of security to almost every place they pause. And with little competition, the food for the price is usually not bad either."

Though my shtarker father would not necessarily approve, for a truism of his shared with me was that standing up eating was for schleppers, and a true goal in life should be to eat, as well as work, sitting down. But in my business, I replied to him, you couldn't always, and besides, standing up eating could be more social.

Trying to end my widely cited Christmas article on a positive note, I wistfully added:

> but whatever the city in its myopic vision bans, plans or allows to be constructed, people will find a way to create congestion. That is because a city by nature is organic, a shifting, expanding marketplace of services and goods attracting people who in turn attract others. It is a thought to cheer a resident while walking an extra block or two from his or her car through a crowd and into a store to buy that one last gift for Christmas.

If there was a solecism I made in my ebullient views of Los Angeles, no doubt affected by the benign weather of my first Winter in sunny Southern California, was that I wanted LA to be more like New York. That initially meant living in an elevated apartment building, parking in an underground garage, gravitating to the few crowded enclaves recommended to me by other expats, frequenting delis and Chinese restaurants, getting to know the waiters, and as urban affairs writer for the *Los Angeles Times*, welcoming density and extolling urbanism.

It was a mistake that I soon realized, and consciously tried to correct in what turned out to be a decade-long search for LA's soul, its sense of place, and, as an aside, lighting my view of other cities and a perspective as a critic.

But first I still had to define LA, as if any city could be summed up in a sentence that isn't a cliché.

"L.A.'S THE PLACE"

"L.A.'S THE PLACE" proclaimed the bumper stickers in 1981 promoting the city's bicentennial battle cry, to which at the time I added a question mark, having lived in Los Angeles for a year and been anointed the *Times* urban affairs critic. Whatever the *Times* wanted to label me was fine, for the assignment was what I had expected when I had impetuously taken the job which I had, in effect, considered a travel and study grant from a generous foundation for an urban critic, at midlife.

Though perhaps too hastily, for in my last days at the Office of the Comptroller of the Currency, word had gotten out that I was leaving, prompting several job offers. Citing my newly found knowledge of capital markets and toleration of bankers, combined with development experience, at the ECF and my New York *sechel*, smarts, add a dash of journalism, and I was the choice of a few select investment firms for a new venture, labeled REIT, for real estate investment trusts. It would have literally added an estimated zero to what the *Times* offered of about $40,000 a year, plus the other $10,000 I added on from my books and freelancing. In contrast, the however equivocal prospects of earning a half a million dollars a year on Wall Street had been tempting.

But I had already said yes to the *Times* and was very much looking forward to a change of scenery and the vaunted California lifestyle, at least to give it a try for a few years. When I mentioned the choices and my decision to a friend, her reaction, that still echoes in my mind, was "how adolescent" of me.

And in a way it was, for having hustled as a teenager, working full time during my last years at high school, then also employed part time while going to college, I felt I'd never had an adolescence. Going to LA as a single man in the permissive '70s, I would be, in effect, an "arrested adolescent," according to psychological terminology. Wall Street and the big bucks could wait.

So adhering to my mother's adage not to look back, instead of evaluating real estate investments at a downtown desk in a corner office looking out at Manhattan, I was out and about sunny Los Angeles in a two-seater English MG convertible with the top down, onto the freeways, across the shrouded sprawl, down the beckoning ramps, and into the city's disparate communities, on a self-affirming assignment, asking strangers what they thought was LA's place, its image, its identity? As expected, the answers varied.

Sunset Boulevard, suggested a UCLA sociologist. "From Union Station to the Pacific, it cuts through the whole L.A. scene: Chinatown; the Latinos of Echo Park; the gays of Silver Lake; the transients and tourists of Hollywood; the nouveau riche of Beverly Hills; the just plain rich of Bel-Air; the liberals of Brentwood, and the conservatives of the Palisades, in all their manifestations; you know, cars, clothes, houses."

The Farmer's Market, commented a senior citizen sitting near the fast-food and fruit and vegetable stands: "I can sit here all day in the shade when it's hot, and covered when it's raining and, thank God, not have to buy anything. And the people you see coming through here are a regular show, and it's free." This was written Nov. 28, 1980. Today it doesn't rain as much, and the hostile security guards at the privately owned market may not tolerate anyone sitting all day, especially if they appear homeless.

Other answers were the beach and the freeways, teeming Broadway on a midday Saturday, the vistas from Mulholland Drive on a clear night, the sunsets viewed from the Santa Monica promenade, and the sprawl of the city itself seen twinkling on a dark night from a plane descending into LAX.

The list continued, as varied as the contributors. No image dominated; no skyline as in New York City; no boulevards as in Paris; no Boston Commons; no White House; no Big Ben; no cable cars. Like the land it sits on, LA's identity appeared to shift from place to place and from time to time.

So if there was no image, stated a native, then for him it was the weather. But as the volatile fires, winds, droughts, heat waves can attest, the weather changes, affecting the city multitude of sub-climate zones, sitting as it does beside an ocean and edged by mountain ranges. And now there is the erratic, worrisome factor of global warming.

Also noted, as constantly changing were the city's varied lifestyles, but holding fast, commented a few, was a sense of freedom, which though lacking a single image they felt above all else should be valued. I was impressed by the mostly ruminative replies. But this made the writing a challenge but not a worry, thanks to the largesse of my editor, Bob Epstein, who told me to take all the time and space needed. This was unlike any of my previous newspaper assignments; one of many surprises at the tranquil *Times*, obliging to a fault.

What emerged out of the mosaic of images, the profusion of words, gathered on the beaches and bus stop benches, in neighborhood stores, mini and mammoth malls, parks and plazas, as it did in New York City and wherever I happened to find myself, were the presence and diversity of people. That to me was the image of LA; not something specifically conspicuous in the variegated natural and manmade cityscape or pithy statement. Here, for me, the people dominated.

Coming a year after I had moved to Los Angeles, I considered the article published on Nov. 28, 1980 a milestone of sorts; the end of my introduction to Southern California as a transplanted social critic, rather than an urban affairs critic, as I had been labeled, my critical experience founded on design, and how it could be more imaginatively contrived and constructed to make Los Angeles a more livable, aesthetically pleasing city.

After all, as a reform-minded advocate, if I couldn't affect meaningful change to better the lives of the less fortunate, I thought I might as well move back to New York City, accept the still-open offer to direct a REIT, and really improve my life, as well as that of family and possibly friends. That would be tangible.

I felt I had mined enough of the cliche of the indomitable New Yorker warmed by the sun of Southern California and awakening to the pleasures and surprises of Los Angeles, an ever-popular motif that editors never seemed to tire of assigning transplants. If I couldn't become the architecture and design critic for the *Times*, the province of an enervated John Dreyfuss, I saw preservation, public places, and pedestrianism ripe for advocacy and planning for criticism.

But editors beyond the *Times* persisted in suggesting freelance articles from me on the attractions of Los Angeles, and faced with alimony and child support payments, and the happy prospects of a new family, I accepted them with an open mind and an open hand. I still think a few resonate, with some truths relevant to all cities.

For *Oculus*, the magazine of the New York AIA, edited then by the ebullient Kristen Richards, I wrote in a column in retrospect headed "Lessons of L.A." that New York City had been for me "the center of the universe." Therefore it was natural for me when I moved there "temporarily" to want LA to be more like New York:

> But as I settled into L.A. and experienced its eclectic architecture, engaging hidden spaces and places, and its marvelous mix of culture, I began to revel in its uniqueness. L.A. was not New York. I felt its benign climate and collage of contexts demanded a singular architecture that should neither mimic New York's, nor be a self-conscious response to the clichéd prejudices of the eastern design establishment perpetually visiting L.A. We have more than our share of wannabe "star architects" lining up wanting to be validated by counterfeit critics.

I wrote that LA was a city where every style seemed to have its moment in the sun, and a parade of architects their fifteen minutes of fame, and declared that unlike New York, there was a distinct tolerance in LA for follies and fantasies, and an embarrassment of self- and public-conscious conceits. Or maybe, I commented with a twist of a literary knife, all that was just the result of the city's regrettably shallow design standards, adding that there are serious, social minded, environmentally sensitive, user-friendly efforts out here by a cadre of concerned architects from which to draw hope for a livable city. But, unfortunately, an undiscerning starstruck media too often ignores them. That is a problem in L.A., where, unlike New York, a cult of amiability compromises open and informed debate over the shaping of an evolving cityscape.

"And its evolving," I noted:

> [l]andmark office buildings downtown are being converted into lofts, a subway is running, one-story mini malls are being replaced by mid-rise mixed-use developments, parking is going underground while housing is going up and up, and streetscaping for pedestrians is happening. It may not yet be a sun-blissed-out New York, nor will it ever be. But it ain't chopped liver either.

Recognizing that this would be an article read mostly by architects, I concluded that all this was "great grist for the architecture mill, if you look for it. And now when I visit my native New York, I wonder why it can't be more like L.A. Where is the sky, the sun, the serendipity?"

For Academy Award winning producer Brian Grazer of Imagine Entertainment, who was guest editing a special opinion section of the *Times*, I wrote about the city's approval of abstract ideas. But the section was second guessed as too favorable to the industry, and killed, so I had it published in the then-thriving *Downtown News* and the looming social media:

> If anything distinguishes and drives L.A. in the present headlong rush of the moment it is the bloom of ideas. More than one single commodity or cause, ideas have become the true cash crop of an evolving Los Angeles, to be seeded by the determined migration from across the country and beyond of the best and the brightest, as well as the avaricious and ambitious.

"Wall Street may be the marketplace for companies, but Hollywood is definitely the marketplace for ideas, be they for scripts or startups," I quoted a writer who had ventured from New York to Los Angeles to launch his career as a writer/producer. "Most but not all come referred by the usual suspect friends, family or acquaintance, almost always with an idea, for a book or a script," added a "creativity" agent, for writers, and directors: "The knocks at the doors are getting more insistent, the pile of scripts in the hallways higher and higher."

The entreaties were not just reverberating in the city's storied entertainment and music business, I noted, but also in its emerging architecture and design practices, the fashion, furnishings, and food industries, and research and development, from genetics to astrophysics. Wherever ideas dominate, one result being that "intellectual properties" have become "one of the hottest things in law in L.A.," said a venerable local attorney, adding that "We are talking viable and increasingly valuable products of the mind, hi-tech products to yoga modalities."

I observed that those I labeled as creatives drawn to Los Angeles were coming clutching their sketches, screenplays, theories, inventions, improvisations, formulas, concepts and, most of all, dreams, ready to elbow their way into the multitudes already here that included those who had succeeded and those still scratching out an existence, hope triumphing over experience. These were actors, artists, architects, authors, designers, and directors, as well as chefs and composers, and the unspecified inspired others in the creative arts.

> Each hopeful harbors an idea they believe will set them apart and bring them fame and possibly fortune. And if not, well, then there is always the benign weather and its diversions, the night job and maybe graduate school. Meanwhile, with a touch of hubris they have transformed Los Angeles into the disputable creative capitol of the world, a category to be christened and chronicled by urban demographers and those who keep lists

I considered this happening very much in the tradition of LA as a trendsetter, which it was first as a boomtown, then as Tinseltown, where the aerospace industry was spawned later, as well Disneyland, in the present the reality shows and artificial intelligence, and tomorrow the next best thing. Who knows, but if you have any ideas and get lucky, I added, there was probably someone out there equally wanting, maybe sitting in some Starbucks, willing to listen, and perhaps package and pitch it.

Making this more likely to happen, I ventured to say, was the blossoming multiculturalism of Los Angeles, for where there is cultural diversity there is usually creativity. "And there was no city in the world as culturally diverse as L.A.," observed Dr. Fernando Guerra, director of the Center for the Study of Los Angeles at the local Loyola Marymount University. "That it should become the creative capitol of the world follows."

Rhapsodizing, I added that this cloud of ideas was almost perceptible, that "you can see it in the sparkle of eyes and animated gestures of the creatives; hear it in the intensity of their voices and the rhythms of their music; feel it in the touch of the materials in their designs; and taste and smell it in their inventive cuisines." These were "the young and forever young pursuing their muse, infusing L.A. with a distinctive joy of discovery. It is an idea of Los Angeles whose time has come," I concluded, wishfully.

Recently married, embracing an extended family, I had become smitten with Southern California; it obviously was not to be a short, several year sojourn, a travel and study fellowship, as I had thought when I accepted the *Times* offer. I had put down roots and begun reading the literature on Los Angeles.

Also wanting to know more of the city's past, while becoming more specific and relevant, for my weekly self-assignments for the *Times*, I focused on the burgeoning historic preservation movement's push for adaptive reuse. This, I felt, had been all but ignored by the paper's lightweight sections of view and calendar.

Apparently, architectural landmarks were something New Yorkers might get excited about, but not Angelenos. So I pitched it to the real estate editor, Dick Turpin, who to his credit saw that the coverage could enliven his Sunday section and attract new readers. He gave my initial story a major play, replete with photos (*LAT*, Dec. 7. 1980):

> Los Angeles is at last becoming aware of its rich architectural heritage and, more critically, is attempting to adapt it to today's needs," I proclaimed, continuing with some excessiveness: "Public and private efforts within the last few years have saved dozens of distinctive buildings from demolition by demonstrating that the structures can be given new life with new and updated uses

Citing select prominent landmarks in such cities as San Francisco (an abandoned fort), Boston (a decaying wharf), and New York City (a train station façade), I noted that beyond sentiment for their preservation were some hard-nosed economic decisions. I went on at length to list examples in Los Angeles, giving publicity to the developers and praising the efforts of a burgeoning Los Angeles Conservancy; I argued that, offering hope that the city's past could be used to enrich its present, its expanding core of enlightened residents was "changing the image of preservationists from a small group of elitists to a broader amalgamation concerned with the city's sense of history and community renewal."

Pleased, the heretofore shunned conservancy reciprocated in kind, praising the now responsive *Times* in letters and me with a newly created journalism award. And I had an issue I liked and that my conscience could happily flog.

I also struck up a friendship with the *Times's* Art Sidenbaum, whose place as an urban commentator I had taken when he became book editor. He reminded me of quick-witted Bill McPherson, and like Jim at the *Washington Post* and before him Eliot Fremont Smith at the *New York Times*, he assigned me a wide range of books to review, short pieces such as the end papers I had done at the *Times*.

In one month alone, September 1981, I reviewed the first volume of a photographic history of the American Civil War—*Shadows of the Storm*, edited by William C. Davis (Doubleday, 1981), *A Theory of Good City Form* (MIT, 1981), by Kevin Lynch, *Zero Fighter* (Crown, 1981) by Robert Mikesh, *The Journeys of David Toback* (Schocken, 1981), by Carol Malkin, and the *Joys of Jewish Folklore* (Crown, 1981), by David Max Eichhorn.

Like the topics themselves, the reviews were mixed, as I fired away with quick-drawn pistols. For the tasty longer reviews and smorgasbord holidays wrap-ups, I used a surgeon's knife. The book reviewing was diverting, something done at leisure, at home, but it was observing the cityscape, out and about, that was my forte.

PERSEVERING PRESERVATION

The article on the incipient preservation movement in Los Angeles, extolling its social and economic benefits and praising its adherents, prompted a surge of story ideas, as I had hoped.

The interest in preserving the city's rich architectural and cultural history was certainly present, but like so many things in Southern California it was scattered, and as a result was being paid scant attention by the local media. The media instead catered to the constant stream of real estate development flak, principally to the new and secondary single-family residential market, with its generous advertising budgets. It certainly made for a thick *Los Angeles Times* in the heady days before the Internet.

The timing of the article, Dec. 7, 1980, was propitious too, I thought, for the city's bicentennial celebration was upcoming in 1981. One assumed that this would be an opportune time for some recognition of the city's architectural landmarks, though aside from the planned self-congratulations and the publication of several histories, there was no real call for civic preservation advocacy.

Certainly not out of city hall, then occupied by a benign, distracted Mayor Tom Bradley, seemingly more interested in bulldozing buildings rather than protecting their possible historical importance. It therefore really was dependent on the few residents of scattered neighborhoods to somehow rally support to save a building, a place, a landscape, or simply a tree that might be standing in the way of "progress." But now they had an energized Los Angeles Conservancy and its stalwart founder, Ruthanne Lehrer, to appeal to for help, and the *Times* for publicity, me.

Without doubt, I was prejudiced in favor of preservation due to my association with Jane Jacobs, my various planning pursuits, and my understanding of its importance in lending communities and cities a sense of history. My prejudice was also, frankly, visceral, having once owned and rehabilitated a pre-revolutionary war landmark in Port Washington. To be sure, the house at three-hundred-plus years old had needed constant repair in the eight years I lived there. This included a new kitchen and no less than a new foundation, replacing the rotted wood with steel, and taxing my cash flow and stretching my knowledge of construction, which in fact was useful in my critical writing at the *Times* in Los Angeles.

Word among the stalwart Angeleno preservationists in 1981 was soon being circulated that there was a sympathetic ear at the heretofore editorially aloof *Times*, with the result that I was being pitched varying preservation-themed stories, from every angle, by community activists and several enlightened developers.

There were archetypal preservation laments about threatened historic landmarks, such as churches. More often than not, churches embody the more notable architectural designs and stand out amid the usual residential and commercial municipal clutter. That is why, even if their congregations are shrinking, they are prized and protected by most world cities of note. And if not for their history alone, then for the tourists they attract.

But not quickly enough in Los Angeles, where I found that what sentiment there might be, was secondary to cashflow. This was the case downtown, where diminishing congregations and increasing land values were prompting the sale and demolition of several architecturally significant churches. And in some instances, this was with the unfeigned approval of the remaining parishioners who pleaded poverty, while looking forward with their ministers to relocating to a new church in fertile suburbia.

I nevertheless took up the cause of church preservation, and not surprisingly usually lost, despite some of their being declared landmarks and eligible for the National Register of Historic Places. Labeled elitist, preservationists were no match for entrenched parishioners and the city's religious consortiums.

The city's weak architectural and cultural landmark laws didn't help, nor did city hall's lack of commitment to preservation. But the community activists were not daunted, and neither was a chastened me, as we anticipated other more promising battles to raise the city's preservation consciousness.

We had better success with public buildings, such as the Pan Pacific Auditorium, one of the nation's outstanding examples of streamline Streamline Moderne architecture. A fading movie theatre, in need of major repairs, it had been slated for demolition by the county, until I wrote several articles, bolstering the landmark's enthusiasts and rallying support. No doubt, it was given consideration because it was an entertainment venue in a city where entertainment is a religion.

Closer to my heart was the preservation of housing, though not necessarily of historic interest; rather, I felt instrumental to community revival; especially when it aided under-served minority residents in redlined neighborhoods. Though long exposed as flagrantly discriminatory, redlining was previously an issue scrupulously avoided by the *Times*, which had a long history aligned to the real estate interests of Southern California.

Exposing it under the banner of preservation gave me a certain pleasure, if not some notoriety in the tradition-bound quarters of the *Times* and in the city's conservative establishment, which I was told winced when I wrote the following (*LAT*, May 22, 1981): "Though no one in a local bank is known to have taken a red marker to actually draw a line on a map of the area, northwest Pasadena for years was redlined." Getting a mortgage there was considered about as hard as finding a parking space near Colorado Boulevard on New Year's Day morning, for the Tournament of Roses parade.

I also exposed the city's lauded freeway construction program to be a form of minority removal, noting in the same article that "Proposed freeway and redevelopment plans had cast a pall over the area. Not knowing what the future held prompted homeowners who could sell and scurry to suburbia, leaving those who remained to watch house after house sink into disrepair and streets into neglect."

This I described as "a typical vicious cycle of decay, aggravated further by the fact that about half of the neighborhood's estimated 10,000 residents were poor and Spanish-speaking or Black." Investors worried that a ghetto was in the making." And I added that "despite its tree-shaded streets with some of the city's more distinctive historic homes, the area had become, in the jargon of realtors, undesirable."

But the neighborhood was turning around, I continued, thanks to a private agency, preservationists, and the city's community development department. Land clearance was stopped, and an ambitious rehabilitation program to help existing homeowners was launched, while young couples looking for reasonably priced houses with character were solicited. The neighborhood became stable, racially integrated, and desirable, and a paradigm for several similar efforts I publicized, locally in the *Times* and nationally in *Historic Preservation* magazine (Summer 1981).

Trying to make the preservation movement less elitist and more egalitarian was a constant challenge in Los Angeles, as was making the architecture profession more aware of preservation and its importance and benefits.

Indeed, in doing the research I considered imperative to my critical matrix, as well as for simply enjoying my new Southern California home and habitat, I was enthralled with the rich architectural history of Los Angeles. It became my off-hours hobby for five years, eventually to become a book, *L.A. Lost and Found*, which I wrote with the renowned Julius Shulman the principal photographer.

Published in 1987 by Crown, it was immodestly described as a "lavishly illustrated history of the diverse and rich architectural heritage of the city that has been called the earth's first experimental space colony, the new Eden, the new Babylon, Lotus Land, Lala land, Autopia, and simply a mistake." The book blurb continued:

"Los Angeles is a city of constant contradictions, a brash, eccentric, energetic place filled with promises and problems—where a rare sense of freedom and place has created in L.A. an uninhibited, exuberant architecture . . . [;] much of that architecture has been lost, but much remains." The book went through several hard cover printings, to become a local best seller and then a back seller, and eventually a paperback, and still can be found in circulation, years later.

Though the preservation movement has expanded with the respected LA Conservancy very much a presence, preservation continued to be a challenge in Los Angeles, obscured as landmarks and cultural enclaves tend to be, in a fractured political and physically evolving cityscape, constantly compromised by an indifferent governance and privately by rapacious real estate interests.

And I continued to expose these compromises in my writings, be it for social media or the more august publications, principally the *Los Angeles Review of Books*. Stirring up a particular storm was my (July 11, 2021) critque there of *Preserving Los Angeles: How Historic Places Can Transform America's Cities* (Angel City Press, 2021), by Ken Bernstein. Longtime head of the city's Office of Historic Resources and Urban Design Studio, and a survivor of bureaucratic battles, Bernstein, understandably politically sensitive, takes the high road. Presenting a more sanguine state of preservation in Los Angeles, he cited the revival of select neighborhoods and downtown renaissance and celebrated an arbitrary selection of architecturally tangible and culturally transcendent landmarks.

Self-aggrandizing and self-serving as they appeared, I commented that they were excusable. In many ways, I added, they reflected the politicized posture of preservation in an unsettled Los Angeles, and the need for its validation, lest it be ignored in the city's precipitous growth. There was indeed a wealth of landmarks in a relatively young Los Angeles that at its founding in 1781 was a desolate cow town of forty-four persons, and a century later just eleven thousand. With the railroad, it then became a boomtown, a resort, and finally a destination, all of which was spurred on by imported water, the discovery of oil, motion-picture making, an aircraft industry, and continued migration. What it has become, I noted, was a cityscape of distinctive architecture and noteworthy neighborhoods, as well as of the infamous suburban sprawl that still defines swaths of Southern California.

But as I added, and the book documents, landmarks somehow persevere, distinguished by their diversity and random locations. Featured are the obvious office towers and theatres that have been restored and recycled downtown and other commonly identified monuments, that the book dutifully describes with beautiful accompanying photographs.

Nice, though I added that perhaps a more revealing portrait of Los Angeles might be found in the book's expanded appendix. There displayed were everyday residential, commercial, and industrial buildings, to be sure of historic interest. And lending the portrait a perspective was an added survey of the city's many cultures, corroborated by the estimated and impressive 220 and more spoken languages in LA.

Essential to identifying the landmarks was the help of some three hundred professionals and volunteers, myself briefly included, which took over a dozen years in an unprecedented digital survey of structures and locales of potential historic interest—no modest undertaking in a city of 470 square miles. That is about ten times the size of San Francisco.

In addition, and critical to the book's production, was the munificent, local J. Paul Getty Trust, and to a lesser extent a long list of like-minded public agencies and institutions, and private firms. This prompted some concerns, for having such a gaggle of a group, I suggested, would most likely influence the book's research and writing, and also might explain the omission of the more heated local battles over the designation of problematic landmarks, involving a politically sensitive city hall and the capricious fidelity of real estate interests, the entertainment industry, and community groups.

However covertly, this erratic consortium has nonetheless at times, in my opinion, colluded to frustrate worthy preservation efforts, while compromising a leadership sensitive to staffing and funding as the noble endeavor became institutionalized. Specifically, I noted that this could account for the glaring omission of the protracted protests in recent years by concerned preservationists and design community members, and immodestly myself, to block the ravaging of the iconic Los Angeles County Museum of Art and its redesign.

I also took exception to the allocation in the book of several gratuitous personal profiles, written by the subjects themselves, an odd addition that no doubt was in deference to the surreptitious politicizing of the preservation movement as it gained prominence and influence. This subversion should be a concern for preservationists; that despite the increased awareness for the need for a continuum of a sense of place and community, our architectural and cultural landmarks are constantly, furtively threatened.

Consider the fate of my former, much-loved landmark Baxter House, the prerevolutionary structure I lived in for nearly a decade and spent much of my sparse spare time proudly restoring. But after I moved out in 1975, and the house sold by my estranged wife, it was acquired by a rapacious absentee owner in 2003.

To the dismay of neighbors, she illegally converted it into apartments and let it sink into disrepair. Only after it became an eyesore and a story in the local weekly newspaper did the conservative Baxter Estates Village become involved and order an inspection. But the night before the scheduled inspection in 2017, and the prospect of multiple code violations, there was a suspicious fire.

The house was trashed, and subsequently condemned and demolished, despite the protests of an incipient local preservationist group. The house's prominent waterfront site was divided for several dwellings and put up for sale. Having raised two of my older children there and labored to preserve the building, I was crestfallen, especially knowing that it could have been saved, and truly sad for Baxter Estates, Port Washington, and Long Island for the loss of a fragment of their history and pride.

My commitment to preservation in Los Angeles also went beyond writing. I reported on the historic Ennis House, a singular concrete block creation of Frank Lloyd Wright, which was in desperate need of repairs, and was subsequently invited to join its nonprofit board of overseers. They had been directing patchwork repairs from the little funds available from rental fees for movie locations, while trying to get foundations interested.

It was tough going, and eventually—with me on the board, as well as the architect's grandson, Eric Lloyd Wright—the landmark was sold to a preservation-minded supermarket mogul, who conscientiously maintains it for partial public tours. At least it was repaired and has remained open to the public.

PLANNING, FOR BETTER OR WORSE

As the newly anointed urban affairs critic for the *Los Angeles Times*, my purview included, in addition to preservation, planning. In all my varied exploits, as activist, journalist, bureaucrat, educator, in various communities, principally New York City and Los Angeles, planning has been the most incongruous of pursuits, private or public, and to write about it and do it has been the most challenging.

Charged with providing a guide to a more livable, sustainable, and egalitarian city, planning, as practiced by bureaucracies, pandering politicians, and a comfortable claque, had become principally an ambiguous paper-pushing, in-and-out basket exercise, confusing the public and consuming scarce municipal dollars. According to a frustrated gaggle of practitioners and academics, at least.

To be sure, among the abiding professionals and the public, there was an argument that the admitted failures of planning should be treated as a call for the pursuit of more enlightened planning initiatives, in which, of course, the surviving apparatchiks and the powers-that-be would be preserved. I was naturally skeptical, which I considered the proper perspective of a journalist, whatever my personal prejudices.

And prejudices I certainly had, among them experiencing the lack of planning in my native Brooklyn, my awakenings in East Harlem, vain attempts in New Haven, New Jersey, and some successes in New York. I had reflected on these experiences in my writings in the 1970s, and now would draw on them again in the 1980s as a critic, their radical and reasoned postulations sharpening my take on the Los Angeles cityscape.

Among books remembered and relevant was Robert Goodman's *After the Planners* (Simon & Shuster, 1972). An architect, planner, teacher, and community activist, Goodman argued that new programs, priorities, and money were not enough, that a change of attitude of those trying to do good was needed—that empowering target populations should replace patronizing them. It also meant no less than radicalizing the economic system to better serve the oppressed.

Then there were the less shrill and more reasoned planning professionals and polemicists who, while recognizing the fractured cityscapes, and the dearth of informed citizenry, argued that communities pressured by inexorable growth desperately needed a planning vision to ensure their idiosyncratic character and tentative future, however imperfect the process. I was primed for the debate.

Actually, I had been moderately surprised that planning and preservation were not in the purview of the *Times*'s architecture critic, John Dreyfuss, as they had been for the venerable Ada Louise Huxtable at the *New York Times*. Sharing a corner office with John in the soft news department of the *Times*, I found him amiable—though disturbing to me was his allowing select prime sources to approve draft copies of articles citing them.

Our editor, Jean Sharley Taylor, felt the same, apparently. She had other complaints as well, including the paucity of his copy. This was mentioned to me as an aside when I was hired, Jean hinting that she hoped I would be more like the paper's crusty music critic, Martin Bernheimer. Taylor added that she thought a little in-house controversy would be good for the paper and, in fact, it was why she hired New York journalists when she could.

This emboldened me to question John about his reading his drafts to sources over the phone. He replied that it was ostensibly to make sure he had gotten the quotes and facts right. I noted ruefully that, at the *New York Times*, it would be the basis for dismissal, continuing that there seemed to be something I labeled a cult of amiability at the *LA Times* that was compromising its journalism.

After that exchange we seldom talked, but John apparently repeated the gist of my remarks to a few friends in the newsroom. The cult suggestion was the most cutting, I heard, and I soon found myself singled out for derision. True, I was clearly not the amiable type, certainly not when I felt the tenets of journalism were being abused.

So when John picked up the phone, copy at hand, ready to read and, in effect, to be edited by the story's principal subject, I would abruptly leave the office, under the pretense of getting coffee. The *Times* staff, with several exceptions, left me unimpressed, and I tried not to let it bother me and get in the way of a good story, which in journalism is paramount. Furthermore, now in sunny California, I was enjoying myself and didn't want to cause myself problems.

Meanwhile, I was happily consumed by the challenges of the city's haphazard, mostly ineffectual planning practices, which provided me with a constant flow of grist for my writing mill, as well as exclusive news items from an increasing chorus of conscientious, if frustrated, city planners who wanted to be heard off the record. These included almost weekly articles in the early '80s on the varying planning and redevelopment efforts of diverse communities across the Southland. (i.e., Hollywood, Nov. 7, 1982, Pasadena, Nov.13, 1982, etc.) and commentaries on the failings of the practice of planning itself (*LAT*, May 30, 1983).

From the increasing response to the articles, I felt I was influencing at least a few outliers in the bureaucracy and scattered residents and their communities. I considered all co-conspirators in attempting to make the government listen to the public, and the city more livable and equitable.

At home, there were also the joys of my recent marriage to Margaret Mary Hall, and her support. Not incidentally, I had met her soon after she had been hired by the *Times* as a specials writer in 1980. Added to that, she was a winsome and staunch political liberal, and I soon became enamored with her and then fell in love. That she was also a fledgling journalist with a respect for deadlines and the unconventional, if not obsessive, work habits of media types, made for a sympathetic partnership. She was a great help when I began researching a history of local architecture that became my book LA *Lost & Found*.

Over-achieving as ever, it was as if I had never left New York City, still recognized there as a planning advocate, including by my alma mater, the *New York Times*. Identifying me as an *LA Times* critic, but also as the author of *The Dream Deferred*, I reviewed for its Sunday books section (July 28, 1985) *Looking at Cities* (Harvard University Press, 1983), by Allan B. Jacobs. Putting it into context, I wrote that

> following the urban riots of two decades ago, city planners were very much involved in a variety of

> well-intentioned efforts to make cities better places to live, work and play. and pursue the American dream. Planners could be found on the streets, organizing neighborhoods, leading rent strikes, advocating community-oriented designs and immersing themselves in local concerns.

I then lamented that in recent years, however,

> reflecting changing national priorities and prejudices, the profession generally has drifted into dabbling in the rhetoric of sweeping theories and grand designs. While the nation's cities and suburbs are being shaped and misshaped by developers, real-estate lawyers, market researchers and obliging architects and politicians . . . seem content.

With unfeigned approbation, I noted that Jacobs agreed with me, urging planners and others involved with the fate of cities to "leave their desks and computers, step out from behind their lecterns and go for a walk through actual streets." And I added that "the more conscious we are of relationships between what is observed and what actions are taken, the more likely we are to have better, more humane, more livable cities."

I was truly warmed that my review went national. But first and foremost on my plate was my daily journalism as the *Times* urban affairs critic, and typical of that was a column also of July 28, 1985 bemoaning the effect on planning of LA's convoluted political system, which divided the city into fifteen fiefdoms, I declared:

> The city is in desperate need of some planning, what with its varying degrees of frustrating traffic, pollution, haphazard development, bad design, poor and inadequate housing and threatened landmarks and the environment.
>
> However, the planning should not be on a grand, regional scale, replete with thick studies and multicolored maps presented at seemingly endless series of seminars and conferences presided over by pedantic professors and babbling bureaucrats. We have had enough of those efforts for a while.

I contended that what was needed was real planning "on a practical, block-by-block, neighborhood level involving those who will be affected. It is time for fewer reports to be filed away in some cabinet, and for more sensitive plan reviews, perhaps even a suggestion of an amenity or two, such a tree planting and street furniture...," and added that it was time "for city planners to be assertive and involve themselves in the urban design process, to turn off their computers and desk calculators, to rise from their paper encrusted desks and to get out of their cars to walk the streets of the neighborhoods of their concern." And I continued that it wouldn't be a bad idea if all city officials involved in the planning process did the same:

> perhaps they would not be so quick to approve a street widening, a demolition of a landmark or the construction of some out-of-scale, out-of-neighborhood character projects. Perhaps then they would begin to understand how planning can, if carried out

> on a human scale and with those affected in mind, can make a good city great.

I urged planners bluntly to become relevant, "that they should plan like it is where they live, next door or across the street."

What provoked this diatribe was asking some sources the simple question of what, if any, is the future of planning in Los Angeles, specifically then in the wake of the rejection by the courts of the Hollywood Community Plan, a bellwether of sorts of the thirty-five community plans that in accordance with state law constitute the city's required general plan.

After several years involving more than 120 community meetings and much acrimonious debate, the Hollywood Plan was considered a viable compromise by most involved. Blessed by the powers-that-be, it was approved by the LA Planning Commission and adopted by the LA City Council, only to be subsequently challenged by a consortium of local groups that, among many things, argued it was an outdated, flawed document.

I agreed, and so did the courts. The plan was subsequently struck down, but left faintly breathing, at least enough so to put it on a pricey life support system in an intensive care unit of bureaucrats and consultants, where they were kept employed. If packaged with care to a bureaucracy, planning could be the gift that keeps on giving.

The near-death experience of the heralded planning efforts in which so many were invested prompted a flurry of forums and seminar workshops, which offered conflicting explanations but no collective conclusion other than that the quest for community plans must continue, however flawed and questionably useful.

You would think that the city's succession of professed progressive mayors would have taken the initiative and somehow revived the plan, especially the more recent Eric Garcetti, since he had been the council member representing Hollywood during much of its drafting. But when asked, he just smiled and shrugged his shoulders, in keeping with the city's timorous tradition that, despite words and studies to the contrary, considers planning as something to be mollified.

I persisted, for if I couldn't raise the planning consciousness of the city, I thought I could at least shame the bungling bureaucracy and posturing politicians. And I did, which led to some reassignment and early retirements, including that of Calvin Hamilton, the pleasant planning director. I didn't win any friends at city hall for this. So much for polished press releases from politicians and studied position papers by aspiring academics; my perspective as usual was bottom up, the view of those who'd be affected.

Missing from these protracted proceedings and all the political posturing was the reaction of the rank and file. When seeking their opinions, as someone who had been both a longtime witness and participant in the private and public sectors, and promising anonymity, I learned about the frustrations of planning in Southern California. I opened the floodgates, and those in local governance, rarely asked for their thoughts, reacted with a passion I expected and welcomed. And it made for good quotes.

Community plans in LA, and specific plans and their stepchildren, were regarded in the municipal backrooms as a waste of time and resources. "We give them lip service and then put them away on a dusty shelf. Planning is really done on a project-by-project basis," said a planning department veteran. Asked why he continued to do what he considered the unnecessary, he replied, "When you are at the end of a rope, you make a knot." Another added that planning was purely an academic exercise for her. She cited the department's publication of the user-oriented and neighborhood-sensitive "Do Real Planning" guidelines. They were much ballyhooed when produced a decade before she felt they read well, but were unfortunately badly translated into practical paradigms.

Asked for a more positive perspective, it was noted that the court decision had prompted a needed reconstitution of community plans to be more generic to avoid legal action and with additional emphasis on preserving neighborhood character. Still, working on the plans was seen as being in a sort of purgatory. More appealing to those interviewed was the department's focus on local projects, such as streetscaping and small lot design guidelines.

Most agreed, with a touch of envy, that "real planning" was not done at city hall, but in the offices of deep-pocket developers, attended by land use attorneys and planning and public relations consultants. Bonded in a real estate-driven Los Angeles, these people constituted a consortium that might be described as the city's mandarin class. They tended to thrive on the continued confused state of community plans, which necessitated their crafting of amendments, zoning changes, and other costly strategies to ease the approval of select favored big-buck projects.

Their success in Los Angeles depended on the support of local councilpersons, in keeping with the city's twisted political tradition that considered each of the fifteen councilmanic districts fiefdoms. Though each district had at least one planning potentate, "real" planning was, frankly, viewed as secondary to photo opportunities, press releases, political contributions, and what could be discreetly labeled personal considerations. Rarely a year goes by without some council office being exposed shaking down a developer to "pay to play."

Despite being suspect, public planner posts in the city of Los Angeles remain desirable. Pay, perks and pensions are generous, though few stay around to vest, moving to the private sector or public posts beyond California.

Acutely aware of the confused state of community plans were the professional planners toiling at the varied academic constructs, and in the nearly one hundred small cities that compose Los Angeles County. Their perspectives offered off the record also revealed a conflicted profession questioning their relevance, and explaining, in part, why the Southland was a planning calamity.

For me as a planning advocate, it was all grist for my mill, while writing for the *Los Angeles Times* and after for a host of professional publications and websites. These have included Planetizen, the Planning Report, and the California Planning and Development Report, which in general have been good sources, Planetizen's website in particular. But a reader must be discerning, for paying freelance writers little or nothing they suffer the prospect of suspect contributors and veracity. Planning needs public exposure, which I feared it wasn't getting enough of from the new media.

And frankly I didn't think it was getting enough "ink" when it was a prime focus of my journalism, even when I was the urban affairs critic of the *Times* and could choose my assignments. Planning, design, and development were seemingly happening almost everywhere across the Southland in the 1980s, and whatever was to be the subject of an article needed to be seen. You could not trust the press releases of the developer or whomever, nor could you necessarily trust the community. For me, being a critic, was a challenging boots on the ground beat.

But despite its challenge to me, it became problematic early on during my stint with the *Times* when in the summer of 1983 I was asked by Taylor if I would help the paper's respectable Washington bureau for a few months as a correspondent, given my *New York Times* credentials and praiseworthy performance in Los Angeles. The flattery was nice, the promise of a raise and a more liberal expense account nicer, and there was my wont of never saying no.

The assignment was diverting, and facile me dutifully turned in my stories, clean and on time. Since it was known I had served however briefly in the Office of the Comptroller of the Currency, an offshoot of the Treasury Department, I was assigned stories involving the economy, several page one-bound, such as pieces on unemployment reports and interest rate fluctuations. Important, but inherently dull.

Though I did try to punch them up, writing with some latitude, attempting to translate the bureaucratic babble into scenes to which readers could relate, hence this lead sentence: "Like a little boy looking through a store window at a candy display, the public sector savors the emerging economic recovery but knows it probably won't get a very big bite of it." (*LAT* 8.4.83)

Still, I also was able to slip in some stories concerning design and development in DC. These included the on-and-off, long-planned rehabilitation of Washington's Union Station, once grand but then decaying, and the renovation of the lower floors of the landmark Post Office building on Pennsylvania Avenue with specialty shops and trendy eateries. Gentrification was coming to Pennsylvania Avenue—nice for tourists, lobbyists, and the comfortable, but not necessarily for the city's predominately Black, low-income underclass, in an economy where trickle-down Reaganomics ruled.

Though there were stories to be written, Washington was not enticing; not in a single industry city of bureaucrats and Republicans, and especially not in the summer. In addition, I missed being in my new home in Santa Monica with the anticipation of starting a new family there, commuting was a strain, and the thought of possibly moving to Washington was daunting, just when I was getting a handle on living in Los Angeles. I was therefore happy to return to LA, which would give me the opportunity to update my prosects, hustler that I was. It was good to be back in a welcoming LA.

Having ingratiated myself with Taylor, I found I could talk to her in confidence, and the conversation my return soon focused on was design and development in the city. When I told her as an aside that I would prefer not moving back to the office I shared with Dreyfuss, that I found his work habits annoying, Taylor smiled and nodded in agreement. Then after a pause, she raised the question as to whether I was interested in becoming the paper's architecture and design critic, replacing Dreyfuss. I had anticipated the question and had my response at the ready. Yes.

Though agreeing with a sincere thanks, I asked to be labeled urban design critic to let people know that I would continue to cover planning and preservation, which I felt was integral to architecture. I added that I also liked the tag "urban," as it implied that my job encompassed social issues, such as affordable housing, instead of the singular design conceits then being promoted by architects, consequentially pigeonholing the profession. And of course there would be a salary increase. There were no tears for John: congenial as he was, he wasn't a discerning critic. I would take the beat, and like everything else, I would not look back. Instead, I'd look forward.

THE ART AND ANGST OF ARCHITECTURE

Ever open to change and a challenge, in September, 1983, I donned the cloak of the newly anointed urban design critic of the *Los Angeles Times* to principally cover architecture. But also planning, preservation, and redevelopment; in effect, whatever shaped and misshaped the built environment, with a focus on Southern California. In effect, I was given a coveted free hand.

As my mixed-media writings up to then should have clearly indicated to the design community, my perspective was that of a user; my critical matrix was that architecture was a social art, its prime purpose the shaping of the places and spaces for human endeavor, heedful of context and climate. Mistaken if not disappointed were the architects, and others in design, development, politics, and the media, who had assumed back then, in the "Me" generation years, that if the position became open it would probably go to a well-connected pedant pursuing fun, fame, and fortune.

Not me. I consciously saw my role as being a resolute advocate for a more livable and equitable city. I had given up what undoubtedly would have been an uptight, pressured job on Wall Street with the potential of earning an added zero or more to my income, for a holistic lifestyle in a benign LA, married again, a triumph of hope over experience, and was enjoying it. And that included bringing to my new assignment the discerning experiences of the past as a social and cultural critic.

This was in contrast to what I observed as the drift of architecture criticism into debilitating elitism, not incidentally at the same time as a concurrent fracturing of journalism and the promotion of soft news which celebrated celebrities and conspicuous consumerism. The reams of words that I felt did not speak, unfortunately, to the gut issues of how we could make our habitations more livable, rather than trendy follies. As I was to observe and repeat in several reviews, if it didn't work as architecture, the so-called, star architects called it art, their shallow vanities fed by fawning critics wanting to be modish.

Tempting as that was at the time, it was not me. I was not going to prostitute myself to have lunch with a self-aggrandizing architect, be invited to appear for a four-figure fee at a developer-sponsored weekend retreat, or for an equally generous stipend to write a forward to a monograph, as has been the convention of some of our more prominent critics.

So my first article (*LAT*, Sep. 12,1983) intentionally was not on a latest singular conceit of the local gaggle of vain architects, but on in-fill, affordable housing in a pronounced liberal neighborhood in transition, and not a clichéd suburban community typical of Southern California:

> With view of a reservoir, nearby hillsides and distant mountains from its undulating landscape and respect for privacy and tolerance for varying ethnic groups and sexual preference, Silver Lake is one of the most popular residential areas for singles, gays and Asians. Its views and hills also have been the

testing ground for such architect masters as Richard Neutra, Rudolph Schindler and John Lautner

I continued:

However, Silver Lake's popularity heightened by its short commuting distance to downtown, has in the last few years prompted a spate of development that is changing the area's image from an eclectic single family neighborhood to an eclectic collection of small condominiums and rental complexes, interspersed by individual houses. . . . The process is known as in-fill housing, and it's going on not only in Silver Lake, but also in adjacent Echo Park and other areas of the city convenient to growing concentrations of offices and institutions. Slowly, inexorably, two- and three-story residential complexes of mostly anonymous architecture are being squeezed onto vacant lots on side streets to lend a new shape to the cityscape.

I added:

Unfortunately, much of the in-fill housing has been designed out of scale and out of context, with little respect for the character of the street. A few appear as if they have been dropped down on the site from another region, if not planet. One wonders if the architect or developer, before having the buildings designed, bothered to get out of their cars to walk the site and streets to get a sense of the neighborhood, or whether the plans were just pulled out from some bottom drawer.

Probably.

I went on to comment on several new projects, praising a select few for their respectful scale and sensitive landscaping, but sharply criticizing others, describing several as no better than matched indecorous motels, and others as bad neighbors, blocking views with blank walls. I noted why some were selling and others not; and I also identified their designers and developers. My first shots as the paper's new architecture critic were fired—a shotgun blast, hitting several targets.

Then it was onto Pasadena, where I observed that developments had risen in and around its downtown: "[they] have destroyed housing, disrupted neighborhoods, cluttered the skyline, unleashed a flood of frustrating traffic, savaged streetscapes and all but denuded sections of a genteel quality its residents hold so close." While I conceded some development may work as individual buildings, "they simply did not fit well into the urban context that is Pasadena or with those who care about Pasadena's unique qualities want their city to be like," and who were pressing for a more sensitive, restrictive downtown urban design plan (*LAT* Sept. 19, 1983).

Their efforts had splintered the city, and as I wrote had exposed the ravaging by bulldozing urban renewal and freeway construction programs that targeted predominately Black neighborhoods. This was not collateral damage; rather, it had been tacitly approved by many of Pasadena's old guard, in an unholy alliance with real estate interests, and had been supported in past years by a patronizing *Los Angeles Times*. I like to think the article that also called attention to Pasadena's landmark status as the heralded "City Beautiful" beaux arts movement of a half century ago, and explained the planning process, which in the past had been conducted behind closed doors in cigar smoke filled rooms, drinks at elbow.

Alerted, motivated, and now quoted and validated, neighborhood groups asserted themselves. I noted that the resulting plan was "an extension of the City Beautiful movement by recognizing the distinctiveness of all downtown Pasadena's diverse districts and trying through zoning to maintain and reinforce them." Though I added it was not as tough as some local purists would like it: "the plan would be an important tool to stop the drift of downtown Pasadena into a mold undistinguishable from other outcroppings of commercial real estate ventures blurring the San Gabriel Valley." It also critically had the reasoned support of Claire and Bill Bogaard, who had been two persevering preservationists cut from old Pasadena and well respected, with Bill going on to become mayor.

Though community activists such the Bogaards, several outlier bureaucrats, and a few scattered architects promoting affordable housing responded to my "urban design" articles with praise, story ideas, and personal appeals, having been down this path before at the *New York Times*, I was appreciative yet dispassionate.

What I was waiting for were the appeals direct or indirect from a confederacy of architects themselves riding on the wave of new design, principally encouraged by an assertive Frank Gehry. I had suspected but never confirmed he was one of the architects with whom Dreyfuss would confer before turning in his copy, for usually when the story appeared, Gehry would be quoted liberally credited of his trendsetting designs.

Serendipitously, I was living in a comfortable if pricey neighborhood in Santa Monica, in an unadorned Spanish bungalow, just a few blocks away from Gehry, in his distinctly idiosyncratic house. The house also served him as a showcase for his singular talent, and whether it was labeled a "deconstructivist" icon, a punk exercise, or a middle finger to the neighbors, it was attracting national attention. Gehry thrived on it, and though he had yet to design a major building, he'd become an architect to watch, an aging enfant terrible of design. Unquestionably, Gehry was the elephant in the room that was LA architecture, and I looked forward to meeting him.

Researching him in anticipation of a meeting he had suggested in his office in funky Venice, I was predisposed to liking him. We had grown up in modest circumstances, he in Toronto, me in Brooklyn, culturally but not religiously Jewish, and both our mothers were named Sadie, his coming from the possibly distant related Caplanaski clan, in Russia. Also into his second marriage, as I was, he had named a son Sam. In addition, he had been described as a hustler, as I had been, and having worried at times in my youth in the Depression where the next meal was coming from, I considered it an attribute. And we were both overachievers.

It was therefore discouraging that Gehry at the first meeting was obsequious to a fault, as a result of which I could not take most anything that he was saying as sincere. I felt that he was playing me, feeding me a mix of clichés and compliments. Noting my "welcomed" writing about the need for affordable housing, especially in minority neighborhoods, he confessed he had socialistic leanings and wrongfully assumed that, because of my concerns, I was a socialist too. If I was to be labeled anything, I replied, it would be a liberal.

Further to my rising displeasure, he played what I would call the infamous "Jew card"; that "we," as ever-paranoid "landsmen," should bond together against "them." And when I suggested that his name change, from Goldberg to Gehry, was timorous, he said he did it at his first wife's urging. She thought it would be good for business, he claimed. This blaming of others, be it a client or a colleague, I found to be another unappealing trait of Gehry's when confronted with whatever faults or failures might be found in his designs. I came away from the meeting distrusting him, which made me cautious when viewing his projects in the future. And there were many in the decade I was the *Times*'s critic.

There was his own house. He'd taken a modest pink, a plain, two-story Dutch Colonial structure, built in 1922, exposed portions of the framework and wrapped it all in an expanded shell of angled metal, plywood, and chain link. The raw materials made the house appear to be still under construction, or deconstruction—a cluttered expressionistic effect Gehry said he wanted to achieve.

I viscerally liked it. As a cheap-tech construction fashioned with off-the-shelf materials, it demanded attention, and living just two blocks away I would many mornings walk my dog there, stop, and contemplate it. The dog would take that as a signal and use the time to relieve himself. I thought that funny, the urine harmless, and mentioned it off handily to some architecture professor, who broadcast it, in quest of his five minutes of fame. Hearing of it, Gehry did not find it humorous and filed a complaint with the City of Santa Monica, charging me with littering. It was summarily rejected, but it soon became a gossip item in a magazine article about dogs and their owners, and was repeated locally, attracting yet more publicity for Gehry. He was if anything irrepressible in his quest of ink, it being good for business. And it was.

Gehry's commissions increased considerably in the '80s, with my liking some of his work and sometimes praising in my reviews. But I also took exception to others, and for that would be accused of heresy by his followers, who urged that the *Times* replace me with someone more sympathetic to Gehry's artistry, and of course theirs too. Despite the acclaim and awards, fame and fortune, Gehry never reacted well to criticism, however constructive and respectfully couched. Designs aside, I found him conceited to the point of insufferable.

As a New York-based critic who asked me whether Gehry was always ill tempered, having been curtly put down by the architect when she questioned the context of one of his projects, I replied, no. "Urban design is not Frank's forte," I answered in an e-mail, adding that his focus is usually on the buildings as objects rather than their contexts and users. "He might state otherwise, but you have to look at what Gehry the practicing architect does, not what Frank the celebrity architect says," I wrote. "And beware, when praised he can be a warm puppy, when criticized a mad dog. Watch your hand."

In addition to his deconstructed house, the landscaping of which had been preferred by my dog before I stopped walking him past there, I praised his design of Loyola Law School.

Hinting at a raw classicism, the fragmented school formed a much appreciated urban campus, making a singular statement about its downtown context and as a focal point.

More confused was the Aerospace Museum, in LA's Exposition Park, where trying to find the main entrance was an adventure, as was wending through the exhibit halls. I also trashed Gehry's awkwardly sited Cabrillo Museum in San Pedro, with its excessive use of chain-link fence and poor circulation. User-friendly it was not. But both museums were ballyhooed from afar by critics, and I wondered whether they'd ever visited the projects.

Then there was the residential Indiana Avenue complex, a modest exercise in cheap materials, unpainted plywood, and blue stucco, mimicking the tone of its Venice neighbors. What I found distressing was that all the oversized windows that were to provide soft light for the artist occupants at work faced a glaring south instead of a shadowed north. It was a mistake that, when asked about it, Gehry blamed on an associate in the office who'd been confused by a survey, as if no one, including himself, had ever actually walked the site or supervised the construction. I wrote this reluctantly, knowing that it was sure to invite some nasty asides from Gehry and his sycophants. Though more important to me was writing what I had felt and experienced; that was what the public expected of critics, acting as their advocates.

But as I had observed in New York and now Los Angeles, getting ink was the name of the game for architects, and in this Gehry was a superstar. The Santa Monica architect may, or may not, have been the most imaginative designer since Frank Lloyd Wright, but he certainly was the most publicized.

And whatever I thought about him, I was compelled to cover his designs, be it a public library in Hollywood or a trendy restaurant in Venice.

As for the library, I wrote (*LAT*, Aug. 17, 1986) that it was a qualified success, its "cubist massing of the structure is well-scaled to the street and friendly, but not so friendly was the fifteen-foot wall and wrought iron gate fronting the street, constructed for obvious security reasons. But the horizontal, light blue tiles somewhat relieve the impact." I wrote that it was nice to note that Gehry did not use chain-link fence, once one of his trademarks, that there was enough of it already in the neighborhood, and that "one does not always have to mimic context." What I particularly liked was the naturally light interior and an inviting informal children's area, but I continued my praise with a slight damn:

> There are few surprises, which was a surprise in itself, given Gehry's usual penchant for architectural excesses. Rather the Goldwyn library is a fairly simple, straightforward, somewhat austere, well-detailed construction, very much in the modernist idiom. A broad postmodern pastiche or deconstructionist exercise, styles Gehry at times has played with, it is not.

As a result, I commented, it was not something that would prompt the excitement a Gehry design usually generates among those architects, magazine editors, and jury members hungry for something different, "as if different necessarily makes design successful."

If the library could be considered a result of Gehry's ego, Rebecca's, the Venice restaurant he designed at about the same time, in 1986, was a product of his id. Having no sense of entry, no drama, only confusion and poor circulation, I dismissed it as a disaster. But the nouvelle Mexican food was a delight.

Meanwhile, the design columns continued to mount, and in response to reader requests and architecture and planning schools, where there was a dearth of critical commentary, a book was proposed. The columns were culled down to about one hundred and organized under nine headings meant to be provocative. These included "Why L.A. Looks the Way It does," "Whose City Is It Anyway," and "Architecture, for Better or Worse," ending with "Personal Prejudices."

Entitled *L.A. Follies* and subtitled *Design and Other Diversions in a Fractured Metropolis*, ten thousand paperback copies were printed and most sold. Though a book publisher who I had not solicited gratuitously observed more would have been sold if I had praised Gehry. "Never occurred to me," I replied, "but thanks for the advice," adding "maybe for my next book."

MOVING ON

Before ascending to a critic, I had been nurtured as a journalist at the *New York Times* on hard news, first banging out five-minute broadcasts, "every hour on the hour," then as a police reporter, court reporter, and a city hall correspondent, always on constant deadline. In time, the journalistic mantra of who, what, when, where, and why became instinctive, characterized by the cliché of "having a nose for news."

Very much in the news at the turn of 1986 was the National Aeronautics and Space Administration's launch of a space station. This prompted me to think that the innovative design of the station as living quarters might make a good article; that no one else would probably be writing about it, and that it would therefore be an exclusive. The editors agreed, and off I went to Houston to view a model of the station, interview its designers at NASA headquarters, and, being at command center, also witness via monitors its launch from Cape Canaveral.

So there I was on January 28 in command central watching on the two big screens *Challenger* rising to the sky on liftoff to a chorus of cheers, and seconds later, in horror, seeing it explode, the capsule hurtling in flaming pieces into the sea, its seven crew members perishing.

The scene in command center still haunts me, as does the echo of one of the NASA specialists I was standing behind, he sitting starring at the blank screen of the computer in front of him, repeating urgently over and over, "Do we have a downlink?

Do we have a downlink?" Tech talk for communications with the crew.

Then there was, for what seemed several minutes, an eerie silence in the room, before the phones started ringing and I was abruptly escorted out of the center to the press room by one of the NASA public relations liaisons who was in tears, as I was. I dutifully phoned in my story "Cheers to Tears," that made print to be page one in the *Times*, headlined "SPACE CENTER TRIUMPH TURNS TO TRAGEDY" (*LAT*, Jan. 28, 1986).

Emotionally drained by the scenes at NASA, I returned exhausted the next day to Los Angeles, where writing about design did not seem as important as in the past. As for my awkward dance with Gehry, it continued, though I was finding him a bore, as it was distracting me from reviewing the projects of other architects and chronicling more of my concerns and those of the paper's readers: a rising urban design consciousness in a Los Angeles in the middle of growing pains not unlike a gawky adolescent's.

"From San Pedro to Sunland, from Boyle Heights to Venice, across dinner tables and back fences, at supermarkets, shopping centers and gas pumps, on the job and at the beaches, weather is no longer the prime topic," I observed in a feature article in the *Times*'s Sunday magazine (Oct. 26, 1986). "It has been replaced by such issues as traffic, planning and zoning, and whether Lotusland is disappearing in a cloud of exhaust fumes or in the shadow of a high rise."

The article appeared when the *Times*'s management was receiving apparently orchestrated complaints from architects and their publicists, which were echoed in some corners of the newsroom. I should be devoting less space to public concerns, they argued; they were the purview of the news department and reporters, not critics; I should be paying more attention to the design professionals and the real estate industry, then in those halcyon days before the rise of the Internet.

Perhaps at the time I had not been as politic as I should have been, as if I ever was. I could have insincerely agreed with my critics while doing what I wanted anyway. I was not one to respond with a humble smile at choice desks. Rather I answered obliquely, within my regular weekly Sunday column, inside the *Times*, also appearing Oct. 26, 1986:

> There has been an echoing lament from who else but the architects that this column pays an inordinate amount of attention to planning and preservation issues and not enough to architecture. My contention, of course, is planning and preservation issues are architecture issues, and if architects don't address them, they will soon find themselves in a small corner of the design world.

I added that "corner was getting quite crowded, something the A.I.A. should be concerned about."

I contended that too many architects appeared to have designed themselves into that corner, preoccupied as they were with the look and symbolism of their structures, rather than with their functions and social and cultural contexts, and continued:

> No doubt their efforts titillate peers and editors of regressive and indigestible architecture magazines,

> but in the larger scope, particularly important, or worthy of review . . . the perfidious pursuit to become a superstar, these self-appointed serious architects seem to work as hard at promoting or trying to explain their projects as designing them. There is talent out there, but to what end is at question.

I didn't bother addressing the editors at the *Times* who had wagged their fingers at me. If anything, they lived day-to-day in the production of the paper and seldom looked beyond, a failing for which they, the paper, and its readers would suffer soon enough in the wake of the internet.

For all Gehry's self-promotion and off-putting personality, at least from my experience with him and, if it could be believed, hearsay of his put-upon students and underlings, he was indeed a talent, and a homegrown one at that. Thus I supported him during the coveted Walt Disney Concert Hall competition, in which he was one of four finalists. It would be at the time his most ambitious project, consisting of an unsurprising underestimated program calling for separate concert and chamber music halls, boldly sited on top of Bunker Hill downtown, adjacent to the city's nascent cultural center.

I declared Gehry's design most lyrical, featuring a limestone-clad sculpted façade, fronted at the structure's most prominent corner with a foyer in the form of a glistening glass conservatory, to be filled with native California plants. That and the adjacent plaza would in effect create "a living room" for the city, according to Gehry's statement, a place for promenading, sitting, exhibits, and outdoor concerts. In effect, a public place of the kind I was recommending in my urban design articles. It also was clearly the most promising of the four schemes submitted, including those from world-renowned and touted designers. I subsequently praised and championed the Gehry scheme (December 11,1988) for which I was thanked by the local sponsors.

The column was published to much fanfare, shortly after which in early 1989 Gehry was chosen as the architect. His being awarded a Pritzker, the highest honor for architects, would also come in 1989, and the much sought-after design commission for the Guggenheim Museum in Bilbao, Spain, the next year. He was on a roll, with commissions in short time in France, Germany, Spain, and a host of other countries. His hustling was paying big dividends.

Not that I would have eaten crow, for I was pleased for him, and liking to travel, looked forward to the possibility of all-expense paid assignments abroad to write about how an LA-based architect was winning over the world. He had certainly worked hard for the Disney commission, as I assume he did the others, his office a beehive of activity, however reportedly difficult he was to work for and ungenerous. To be fair, these were dubious complaints I also heard from other offices of so-called star architects, where schadenfreude seemed to be the only common pleasure.

Though not wanting to get personal with subjects whose works I was reviewing, I found that Gehry's international acclaim made him even more of a pain. I therefore felt a certain amount of relief that I wouldn't have to attend the inevitable press conferences and write about the piling on of accolades. I left it to others at the *Times*, as a moment of truth for me was fast approaching.

By the end of 1988 I had been at the *Los Angeles Times* for a decade. This was near the point in time in other jobs, at the *New York Times*, the Educational Construction Fund, and the City University of New York, albeit part time, that I would grow restless and look for new challenges. Some friend with an astrological bent suggested it was because I was a Sagittarius, another because I had the mindset of a survivor and never wanted to get too comfortable anywhere so I wouldn't feel bad when I had to abruptly pick up and flee. Few appreciated or accepted the pronounced need I felt to be stretched, to see things anew, and as a result feel alive. Turning fifty-five then, I also didn't know how many more choices I would have.

Disney Imagineering had been at the time interested in my placemaking theories, discreetly inquiring whether I would consider consulting with them as a senior creative analyst, focusing on their existing and planned parks. The hours proposed would be flexible so I could remain at the *Times* as a critic. However accommodating, I felt that this would be a conflict, if not in the actual assignment, but in my dedication to the jobs at both Disney and the *Times*. I said I would think about it and discuss it with my wife and friends.

I pondered this for more than a year, into the spring of 1990, for though not having an affinity for the *Times* or a real kinship with colleagues there, I did like being a critic and immodestly felt my columns were both enjoyed by the public and made a difference in the shaping and misshaping of a young LA. I was also, frankly, apprehensive, having once left the more august *New York Times* and turned down more lucrative development and financial jobs in the private sector, each one of which

I had regretted in moments of disquieting reflection, only to snap back to the echo of mother's axiom of don't look back.

But I was truly growing weary of the *Times*, overbearing architects, and a cloying design community, and I really did think I would enjoy the stimulation of a new job, at least that was what I was telling myself. And if the family or me needed it, I had a good medical plan from the Writer's Guild of America, which I had joined nearly thirty years ago when writing for television during the newspaper strike of 1963. I also was vested in the *Los Angeles Times* pension plan, as well as New York State's for my teaching and public planning there.

So taking a deep breath, I resigned from the *Times* in June 1990 and signed on with Disney, part time, for I also liked the idea of freelancing, writing for print and broadcast, perhaps doing some more teaching, and being open to the occasional odd assignment.

Indeed, all this would happen in time, some unexpected and a few quite odd. It would include becoming an Emmy-winning television news producer and writer, doing special effects, appearing as an actor on the successful television series *90210*, varied teaching associations, a few adventures abroad, and some hopeful planning assignments locally. Though the latter turned out to be disappointing, as I found that the development scene in LA was not as stalwart as New York's. However, it was remunerative, which was a consideration of mine since my later two truly gifted offspring would soon be off to college.

But meanwhile, though no longer the *Times* design critic, and try as I might to move away from the morass of the media enveloping Gehry and the Disney Hall plans, it kept "calling me back," to mimic the lament of a conflicted character being cajoled by the Mafia in the then-popular television series *The Sopranos.*

The fate of the concert hall had become a melodrama following the completion of its plans in 1992, accompanied by a construction cost approaching $300 million, far exceeding the Disney Family gift of $50 million. The cost of the underground garage alone, that was to serve as the hall's sub structure, was $110 million; it would be built and paid for with bonds issued by an increasingly nervous Los Angeles County. The construction was launched, even though at the time the private funding for the hall itself was faltering.

The garage was completed in 1996, but then work was completely stopped, prompting Gehry to threaten to quit. As the project wallowed, I was asked to do an opinion piece on the hall's future prospects for the *Times* editorial page, an assignment I considered not unlike a piece of raw meat thrown into the cage of a hungry tiger.

I dutifully wrote that the hall's scope be dramatically shrunk and the design altered, adding that if a larger venue was needed for the city's aspiring orchestra, a portion of the funds should go to the needed renovation and upgrading of one of the landmark movie theatres on historic Broadway. I argued that it certainly would be less expensive. The prominent site of the Disney Concert Hall could be used for a public park, with a placemaking sculpture as a focal point and city icon. I turned it in and got no response from the *Times*, not even a request for an edit, and the piece remained unpublished for several weeks.

Then came a surprise phone call from the Walt Disney Concert Hall Committee's public relations consultant. The *Times* had given the committee's chairman, Frederick

Nicholas, a copy of my still unpublished commentary, a tacit violation of journalistic ethics, and asked him to write a reply to be printed alongside mine. Agreeing, he had then asked the consultant to ghost the article under his byline; she had a few questions and, being a friend, called me to help her. I reluctantly said I would, but she had to tell me, out of curiosity, how much she was being paid. She replied $1,500, on top of her generous monthly retainer.

I answered her questions, and soon after heard from an editor that my piece would run, for which I would be paid $300,000. As an aside, he mentioned that the same day a piece taking exception to mine, written by the chairman of the Disney committee, would run. Asking him how much they'd been paid, he replied he didn't know, but assumed $300,000. I then told him the person writing it whom I'd helped told me she was to be paid $1,500.

Getting no response, and after a dead silence, I stonily said that next time if the *Times* wanted to print conflicting twin stories, I would happily do both for a negotiable fee. There was more silence and then the click of the phone being hung up, followed by the finality of a dial tone. The pieces ran, mine the last I would do for the *Times*.

As for the project, it was altered, and new funding sought in a revitalized campaign under the direction of local philanthropist Eli Broad, who was not a fan of Frank. Sparks flew, and the cladding became flashy steel, presumably to save money; the glass observatory was scrapped and the plaza changed to a stairway that would be used more often as a location for automobile commercials than by pedestrians; the frontage on the area's major street became a high blank wall, protecting from public eyes a private garden for donors. So much for a living room for the city Gehry had proposed and I had praised.

But however altered, when construction was finally completed, in 2003, fifteen years after the competition and ten years after the groundbreaking, at a cost of $274 million, thanks to Disney upping their gifts, the hall was unquestionably a success.

If it wasn't a fluidly functioning architecture for gathering, circulation and listening, it was certainly a glistening sculptural art piece that dazzled and captivated. And while no longer the design scold for the *Times*, I still had my critic's credentials, and would be covering the hall's protracted grand opening, internationally for the BBC's *Front Row*, nationally for PBS's *News Hour*, and locally for Fox Television News and the *LA Downtown News*—more arrows in my quiver.

Sharpening those arrows was my winning a local Emmy for feature writing in 1997, as well as having several newspaper articles herald my broadcasts. These included a rave review by Howard Rosenberg in the *LA Times* for my "vibrant," "refreshing," TV segments for Fox, which he declared were "distinctively witty and literate for Los Angeles" and "deserving of a wider audience." The welcomed review indeed prompted several new gigs and, judging by my increased mail, a wider audience. There was no looking back at the *LA Times*.

DISNEY HALL AND ITS DISCONTENTS

The rave reviews started several months before its opening. Among the early comments from out-of-town architecture writers: "A stainless steel masterwork," "an exuberant pile of twisting steel encasing public spaces of generosity and wit," and simply "Bilbao Two," a reference to the similarly styled museum that had lent Gehry his star architect status several years before and given new life to the gritty city in northern Spain. I was then an Emmy winning reporter/producer with Fox Television News for its local Los Angeles station Channel 11, not incidentally distinct from Fox's hard-right cable news network.

While essentially a part-time employee and discouraged from freelancing, it was nonetheless excused in my case and looked upon with pride by the station's enlightened news director, Jose Rios. So however premature my review would be, at the behest of several of my freelance editors, I wrangled a tour of the hall, then in the last throes of construction, though I was denied an interview with a very testy Gehry. In addition to monitoring a punch list of the project's defects, always taxing for an architect, he was also curating a major retrospect of his projects at the adjacent Museum of Contemporary Art, to go on display concurrently with the hall's gala opening.

"To date only the privileged, the patrons and select members of the media have been allowed to pad through the downtown structure, and fewer still have listened to the orchestra test the acoustics," I wrote in my premature review for the *Downtown News* (July 21, 2003), and repeated in my weekly City Observed commentaries on public radio station, KCRW. They reportedly were dazzled, at least according to a fawning few who perhaps may have traded acumen for access.

As for the public, they were being held at bay, I commented, their noses pressed against the peekaboo glass facade on Grand Avenue, while those wanting to take photos were directed by officious guards across the street away from the glistening hall to snap photos. I suggested that the unveiling should be thought of more as a slow striptease to a chamber orchestra conducted by a cadre of publicists; that they couldn't be too cautious when lots of reputations were at stake.

To be fair to all involved in Disney Hall, I did feel a proper review of such a conceit critical to the future of the central city as a cultural nexus should await the true test of public use. That included experiencing the crush of crowds attending performances in the new auditorium and looking in on the multiuse theater and art gallery. Also on my critical matrix was to sit down for a meal at the restaurant, have coffee in the café, mingle with the masses in the hall, and meander in the adjoining gardens.

But given the increasing comments of others, and having toured its interior, I felt some first impressions were in order. Labeling the critique an overture, I declared in several of my multimedia platforms:

> From a distance, the concert hall fulfills its promise as a singular icon for Downtown, and L.A. Its billowing shape attracts the eye and holds it. Though

the cladding is stainless steel, and the structure static, the design conveys movement, an exciting concept for any architectural exercise.

Whether meant to be a boat at full sail, a flower in bloom or an unfolding artichoke, the building shimmering in a shifting light is alluring. With its emphasis appearing to be more on form than function, the Hall as a design springing from the idiosyncratic vision of the 74-year-old acclaimed architect must also be viewed as a sculptural exercise.

The resulting computer-aided sculpture appears to be more in the spirit of a kinetic composition of Calder, rather than, say, a raw, rooted imposition by Serra, one of Gehry's artist pals.... An up-close view of the hall from the adjoining streets and sidewalks leaves little doubt that it is a Gehry concoction. It's also a disappointment. His buildings from afar may twirl, but up close they are flat-footed, and not particularly pedestrian friendly. Urban design is not Frank's forte."

I went on to detail my criticisms, noting that "The First Street north frontage consists of a forbidding wall edging the sidewalks and is more appropriate to a minimum-security prison than a public building. It cries for views, places to sit, landscaping and art." I did concede, though, that "the Grand Avenue south frontage is somewhat friendlier, thanks in part to the afterthought of streetscaping now in the throes of construction and hinting at inviting people places. As for the entry, nothing special here, like there is with the steps of the Sydney Opera House."

As for the interior, I declared that another kettle of fish, to use a popular Gehry image. "The reception hall and foyer are bathed in light, attractive transitions to the Hall's centerpiece, a 2,265-seat main auditorium. This is the building's soul, and it's where Gehry's design both embraces and soars. It is intimate yet grand. Declaring the effect was a singular, memorable space, I continued: "The so-called "vineyard" shape of the interior wrapping the orchestra Platform, staggered seating, hardwood walls and ceiling, the backdrop of natural light, the colorful seats, and the varied sight lines, all promise a captivating concert experience. And I love the spiky organ." And I concluded that this deserved praise, but that the more modest spaces and landscapes scattered in and about the Hall had to await the madding crowds, and the music, for a more considered judgement.

Then came the protracted opening over several days in October, where I noted in a subsequent review that the "waves of the privileged and the press, the wandering tourist and jurist (from the nearby courts). And the welcoming staff, all lent life to this long-awaited project. There is nothing like milling crowds and the patter of pedestrians to spark the starkest of spaces.

"It was a memorable several days," I commented in and on my multimedia platforms, "full of pride and promise for the new uptown Downtown. The $274 million cascading complex at Grand Avenue and First Street may be a civic indulgence and architectural anomaly, but there is no denying its sculptural presence and power." And I declared in broadcast (KCRW) and in print (*Downtown News*): "The Disney Concert Hall is a success, if judged only by the heavily promoted grand opening, media raves and money generated. This apparently is just too big an event for the city's civic and cultural communities to entertain any notions that the Hall is anything less than extraordinary." And for perspective I added: "The Concert Hall no doubt will generate renewed interest in downtown, and for a few, serve as a door to other diversions here. I do not envision crowds from the Concert Hall spilling onto the surrounding streets, as they do after performances at Carnegie Hall in New York." This most certainly would not happen, I wrote, until at least Grand Avenue was developed as an engaging and urbane space, vitalized by an edge of eateries, shops, cinemas and clubs, topped by offices and housing.

The Disney Hall boosters and Gehry acolytes trashed the review as a damnation with slight praise, while I considered it praise with slight damn, and reminded them I was a critic, not a publicist. This was a point I drove home with a heavy hammer in my subsequent review of the Gehry architectural retrospect at the Museum of Contemporary Art across the street from the hall and appearing the day before the grand opening.

I found the exhibit a clutter of Gehry's study models and sketches, "that left me unimpressed," continuing:

> What is revealed in the artless squiggles and the varying study models is an almost obsessive focus on form rather than function, a preoccupation of a Gehry inherent in what he has labeled his intuitive approach to design. Missing is any appreciative consideration of context, climate, cost and, most unfortunately, the user, those who will ultimately experience the structures. . . . Function appears to be at best an afterthought.

I went on to label some of Gehry 's collection "plop architecture," and say that in the far future some of his more celebrated, ego-encrusted designs will, I suspect, "be looked upon as anomalies, representing a time in history when a self-indulgent society worshiped celebrities and showcase buildings, to the detriment of humanism and livable places."

I did have a modicum of praise, stating that "The Guggenheim, Disney Hall and their derivatives of Gehry's designs can be, and should be enjoyed as spectacles. There is no denying their sculptural power." But I added that "to call the designs the cutting edge of architecture is to misread the true purpose of the profession as a social art in the public realm, and to distort it as surely as Gehry's computer aided conceits corrupt the siting and purpose of his projects."

With this harsh summation echoing on air and vibrating in print, I went to a preview of the exhibit on assignment for Fox Television News, not to do a commentary but to capture the social scene which promised a smattering of celebrities, this being LA, and when called upon by my news director, I could pose as a so-called red carpet correspondent.

Out of the crowd, catching my eye, was a red-faced Gehry. Breaking away from a cluster of well-wishers, he pushed his way toward me, fuming. I told my cameraman to roll the tape, but Frank was already in my face, screeching: "Sam, you don't know a fucking thing about urban design." I heard this loud and clear, as did several bystanders, who would repeat it for the always voracious gossip columnists.

Nonplussed, I nevertheless answered him, inquiring whether this was a bad hair day for him or what, to which he replied that I could "go fuck off." Newsman that I was, I asked him whether I could quote him, and according to witnesses, he said, "Yes, fuck off," and turned and walked away. One of the many public relations aides who had rushed over to see what the ruckus was about profusely apologized, which I accepted, though annoyed that none of the outburst had been captured on tape, my cameraman frozen, stupefied. No matter, the item made the gossip columns, the "fuck you" and all.

I was amused, having received worse in my days as a critic. Frank at least was not a spitter, as were a few other persons who have verbally attacked me. Not amused reportedly was Ruth Seymour, the then-officious general manager of KCRW, a popular NPR local station where I was delivering a weekly commentary.

It was no coincidence. Frank was a friend of the station and occasionally volunteered his presence in its aggressive fundraising drive, the success of which was the pride of Seymour and the basis of her community prominence. She was also an infamous petty tyrant, who shuffled the station's commentators arbitrarily. Thus, I was duly informed by her apologetic aide, Sarah Spitz, that my show had been canceled. My slot not incidentally to be filled by Ruth's dilettante daughter, with a music commentary, which to no one's surprise subsequently bombed. Ever the hustler, I jumped to a rival public radio station, KPCC in a blink, continuing sporadically with my City Observed commentaries.

I also missed the hall's grand opening concert, which was the scheduled culmination of the week's celebration. I was to cover it for FOX, but instead was reassigned to the San Bernardino mountains as an on-air reporter covering a disastrous wildfire. It raged for a week, killing six people, consuming ninety thousand acres, destroying 940 residences, and causing $1.2 billion in damages.

Though I could not be at the hall to salt the ceremonies and perhaps pepper Gehry that week, over time I still found various opportunities in both print and broadcast venues for my curmudgeonly reviews of the Hall.

One memorable incident came a year later, when attending a concert on my own time and nickel, for I had been purposely avoiding the hall and its sustaining fanfare. The occasion was a family event, as revealed in a most personal review I did for both broadcast and print. It was subsequently widely reprinted and praised on social media, perhaps because it was so personal and pointed.

"Dear listeners, indulge me," I prefaced the KPCC script that I saved as a family memento. "My antithetical feelings for Disney Hall continue, especially after attending a concert there that included my 15 year-old son, Kyle, performing on the bassoon. There is nothing like parental pride to further cloud one's critical faculties," I declared in a commentary that also appeared in the *Downtown News* (Aug. 30, 2004) and on social media. "Ever since the Hall began to take shape a decade ago, I have found it a particularly difficult project to comment on—not only because of its distinctive if arbitrary and indulgent design, but also because of its hype and multiplexity of purposes." I continued:

> The sails and swirls of the stainless steel aside, the Hall on a personal level is an international icon for its arching architect, Frank Gehry, and a laurel for its local boosters galvanized by philanthropist Eli Broad.

> It is hard to think of the three hundred million dollar exercise separate from the many egos involved.
>
> However viewed, its significance cannot be denied. In the flush of its dedication less than a year ago, the Hall has become a symbol of the cultural aspirations of Southern California, another piece of the puzzle of an emerging Downtown, and a critical focal point for the recently launched redevelopment of Grand Avenue.
>
> To be considered also is the perspective of those who experience the building, whether purposefully attending an event there, and thus having to find a seat and possibly a bathroom, or just driving or walking past it, or living and, or working nearby.

I also noted that the people who perform in the building or who service it were to be considered: the musicians, maintenance personnel, ticket takers, and ushers or the persnickety person who tells you to put away your camera even at intermission when your son is on stage gathering up his reeds. All have their differing needs and priorities, which I maintained should be considered when commenting on the architecture.

Reminding listeners was my calling. I wrote that "generally I have welcomed the building, which I've described as an arresting ego encrusted icon." Further contending that I had questioned its excessive cost, contorted urban design, while trying to be fair and balanced, out of respect for the professionals involved in shaping, styling, and serving the hall, as well for the public. Then after a pause, I announced: "That is until last week."

I then professed that all pretense of being a critic faded when my youngest progeny performed with the Festival Wind Ensemble as part of an evening program staged by the Idyllwild Arts Foundation. The program that also featured the Festival Choir and Orchestra filled the hall with friends and family of the several hundred talented youths from Southern California and beyond who had studied at the foundation's internationally renowned summer program in the San Jacinto mountains.

Kyle was excited, I confided, and so was his mother, my wife Peggy, his older sister Alison, who flew in from New York city for the gala event, and one of his two older brothers, Josef, who happened to be the music critic for his college paper. Also attending was Kyle's much revered bassoon teacher, Sara Banta.

It was impressive that Kyle had found time between his schooling, studying for the SATs, surfing, soccer, and ascending social life to take up one of the most demanding musical instruments. I remember being excited, too, and proud. Of course, I had attended concerts in the hall when writing my commentaries, but now having to meet my family in the lobby and then go to hear my son perform heightened my anxiety and also my awareness of the design.

The lobby, I wrote, "does not work particularly well as a welcoming space nor as a place to comfortably meet and mingle. Unlike most other great music halls and opera houses, the entry from Grand Avenue is unexceptional, no hint of ceremony, no perspective for a processional. It is rather sadly more in the mode of a multiplex movie house."

I added that there was no real center point or focus in the main lobby, some spot you can easily mark as a place to gather, and that, as a result, I had spent several long and anxious minutes searching the crowd for the various members of my party.

> Not helping was that the lobby has no real edge, and drifts off and up into fragments of spaces on five levels. Circulation seems to have been an afterthought, the interior spaces squeezed to accommodate the exterior shape.
>
> The focus of the Hall, of course, is the main auditorium, a dramatic curved wood lined space in a vineyard shape with staggered, wrapped seating that promises a more intimate concert experience. And much to my pleasure that's what I had found in my previous visits when I moved around the auditorium to experience different views and listening posts, and a few seats with limited leg room.

As for the concert, I had purchased seats in the third row of the orchestra, which I was expecting would be a good location for me and family to view and hear Kyle play. But me and my wife's seats were off to the far left and had a limited view of the ensemble, and none of our son. The others in my party could glimpse him, if awkwardly.

We were devastated, and I reacted as any parent and New Yorker would most probably do in such circumstances, which was to ignore the ushers and determinedly scramble to command two vacant seats two rows up in the center of the orchestra in clear view of the musicians. With furtive glances to the left and right, my wife and I settled in with the nervous hope that the people the seats were for some reason would not show

Disney Hall and its Discontents | 183

up, not at least during the first two offerings on the program, in which Kyle was performing.

They didn't, and we saw him and he saw us; beaming smiles were exchanged, and we settled into our purloined seats and watched and listened with parental pride as he played.

Incidentally, the acoustics were excellent, at least for us and I presumed for the near-capacity audience, less the two persons whose seats we were in and never showed, to enjoy the balance of a stirring performance that included a memorable Copland's *Appalachian Spring*.

Kyle later said that the acoustics prompted some adjustments by him and the ensemble for, unlike other orchestral experiences in other halls in which he had played, in Disney he could not hear the other musicians but oddly could clearly hear the audience. All this was in my commentary.

Also included was Kyle's dismissal of my perhaps over-exacting observations; that they were irrelevant to the thrill of performing in a clearly singular space before an obviously appreciative audience that included his family and teacher. And while to me it was an illustration of the importance design makes in shaping experiences, I was thrilled to tears for him, myself, and the family.

CRITIC AT BAY

Having been unceremoniously dropped by Santa Monica's KCRW (89.9 FM), I was hired a few days later quite ceremoniously by another and more popular Southern California public radio station, KPCC (89.3 FM), but still bruised by being the brunt of Frank Gehry's anger over what I thought was fair criticism, praising his Disney Hall design for its sculptural qualities while questioning its urban design. There was no appeasing Frank, apparently.

Be that as it may, it was nice to be lauded by KPCC in its announcement of my hiring for being a singular "unapologetic populist," championing "an architecture that serves people, not artistic pretensions." Occasionally, belabored critics need to be reminded of their merit in an increasingly shameless, blameless world.

So said the station's John Rabe, the host of the show *Off-Ramp* I was to join, who added that my "reluctance to pull punches" was as much appreciated as my "critical bona fides." Cited were my television Emmy, writing for the *New York Times* and *Los Angeles Times* newspapers, and my books. Also cited was KPCC's numerous awards, but not its intense competition with KCRW for public radio dominance in Southern California.

Working with Rabe was a delight; he was a sympathetic soul who cared greatly for Los Angeles and enjoyed its fragmented urbanity. Unlike the remoteness I had experienced at both the *LA Times* and KCRW, John took an interest in my segments, as did Jose Rios, the news director at Fox News. This was very much appreciated, for the wordsmith that I confidently felt I was, based on my extensive print background, I considered myself a broadcast neophyte, my Emmy and other awards notwithstanding. For me, being live on air was anxiety-inducing, as was having to look into an unblinking eye, try to smile, and talk coherently into a microphone.

Still, I truly enjoyed being a multimedia journalist, especially away from a desk and on location, for, as I had advised on air and in print, "to look at LA for curiosity, or love, one must go off-ramp, down the main meandering or mean streets, and experience the spaces and places in their context, climate and culture." Understanding this, and encouraging me to follow my media instincts, was Rios. Seemingly content to be persevering at his executive post at Fox, a mild-mannered and plain-spoken Rios, frankly, was the most instinctive and personable newsman I ever worked under.

So unfettered, wearing yet another hat, I was out and about in Los Angeles, looking beyond the megaprojects I had mostly focused on as an architectural critic; instead, I was examining some feature or facet that I felt lent the city character and that revealed more the closer you looked.

Many of my broadcasts were simply about walking here and there on select stretches of downtown, or a neighborhood, about finding a bench on which to sit, a park for my growing children, garage sales for my curiosity, or a friendly eatery, where they would pour you an extra cup of coffee without being asked and smile without always expecting a bigger tip. I wrote ecstatically about these places.

But I continued to be as someone labeled me, the city scold, as in this *Off Ramp* script that also saw print with the title "The Right to Walk" attests. In it I castigated the bureaucratic mindset of LA's overbearing traffic engineers, writing that, "the prime mission of the Los Angeles Department of Transportation is, simply put, to move traffic, be it surreptitiously in and out of residential neighborhoods in the far reaches of the Valley or lumbering fitfully through Downtown Los Angeles." Let's face it, I exclaimed,

> the presence of pedestrians tends to be a pain, at least to most traffic engineers and impatient drivers. Put-upon pedestrian advocates always seem to be complaining about something or other: not enough crosswalks and traffic lights, too narrow sidewalks, poor street lighting, boring storefronts, excessive curb cuts and overflowing trash receptacles.

So when there was yet another traffic circulation study for downtown, and a call for a pedestrian perspective, I cautioned we should be wary, and be excused if we found ourselves whining. "Yes, we are whiners," I wrote, "but then again there is so much to whine about in our fragmented, auto-obsessed Downtown where, I'm afraid, walking is still looked upon through the windshields of cars as déclassé." I added that one didn't need to be an architecture critic to observe that downtown LA just did not have the street life of a world-class city.

As for the proposed study, I obviously did not hold out much hope for it, given that it apparently would be conducted by the usual suspects: traffic managers and academics. I observed that beyond the shuffling of papers on the desks of bureaucrats and their preferred consultants, such studies have mostly resulted in the knee-jerk widening of roadways, the designation of one-way streets, and the timing of lights primarily to speed traffic. And concluded: "In L.A. the car is king and queen, and parking is a major determinant of the design of residential and commercial projects. Automobile movement in and out of the Central City drives the planning of roadways. Pedestrians are truly the pawns on the Downtown chessboard."

Thinking specific and small, I continued to write about downtown, rewriting and expanding my *Off-Ramp* scripts into print for the *Downtown News*, where I was being read by my former *Los Angeles Times* followers. I had been read as a critic there by Nicolai Ouroussoff, a fan of Gehry's and several other self-proclaimed deconstructionist designers, while all but ignoring social architecture causes which I had championed. If anything, this motivated me to pay particular attention to projects I knew the *Times* and Ouroussoff would not be writing about, though should.

Included were several decidedly modest developments that in their less regaled ways held an equally important promise of a more urbane downtown. This I observed was happening incrementally, one block at a time, on a neighborhood scale, which is the way most cities traditionally transform themselves over time:

> These are not the promised idiosyncratic icons of spiraling steel and glistening glass that grace the pages of glossy magazine and gossip sheets, and

transform architects into celebrities, and some architecture critics into fawning publicists. They're something you might call backdrop buildings, designed first and foremost to maximize developable square footage and minimize construction costs, and somehow make the packages more marketable by underscoring their context. Fads and fashions are fun. But trumping all is location, location, location!

While continuing as the city's scold, disparaging several new residential projects downtown, I also praised others, especially when I could add a personal perspective. I noted that one project had balconied units with direct access to the sidewalks, in effect creating "something akin to people-friendly front porches and stoops that just might encourage tenants to perch there and turn a friendly face and a watchful eye to the street."

Waxing nostalgic, I exclaimed: "Indeed stoops, such as where I grew up in Brooklyn New York a half century ago and which served as grandstands where we could view the daily soap opera of our street that was much more entertaining than what was then on television." Their finding a foothold in Los Angeles, I added, was "vital to the success of the city's emerging urban developments."

Among the learned sources I was using to gain a perspective on downtown at the time was Fernando J. Guerra, the director of the Center for the Study of Los Angeles, at Loyola Marymount University. A professor of political science and Chicano studies, he seemed to be everywhere, serving on blue ribbon committees, and ad hoc task forces for the City of Los Angeles, the State of California, and regional bodies in Southern California.

For me, he was a great source who I got to like and respect, and when sharing with him some of my hands-on experiences in New Haven and New York City, suggested I really should get involved again; and as he was so well connected and was serving as a political consultant, he had, of course, something in mind.

That is how I embarked in 2005 on a brief association with Meruelo Maddux Properties as its planning consultant. It was a rollicking if not lucrative time, the company in a few years building an impressive portfolio of more than one hundred acres and fifty properties downtown. Its mercurial president, Richard Meruelo, had me working full time repurposing and reimagining many of them. Something had to give, either my journalism or my planning.

Still true to my precepts of try to keep moving forward, and when in doubt, do it, with some regret I decided to leave Fox. I had been there more than a decade, the usual length of my past major employments, and though having truly enjoyed the freedom afforded me, as well as the fun, it was at times too hectic.

And those times were increasing as I approached seventy years of age, and recently having suffered a heart attack that required being rushed to the hospital for an emergency operation to receive two arterial stents and the medical advice to slow down. The message was clear. If not smelling the roses, it was time to at least spend more time in my garden, at least tending them. It seems I was indeed mortal.

In answer to inquiries from faithful followers who noted my absence on television, I detailed my departure with some license in a column in the *Downtown News* (April 4, 2005) that was picked up on social media and circulated widely:

> It wasn't the fanatical right harassing me for being a member of the liberal media elite that prompted me to recently say goodbye to FOX11 News.
>
> Conversely, perversely, it also wasn't the hostile left insulting me for working for FOX, unable as they are to differentiate between the puerile reactionary talk shows on cable and the reportage of local station KTTV, where I had been a member of the weekend news team since 1994.
>
> I frankly have been long inured to insults from ideologues, idiots, architects and others in a maverick career spanning nearly a half century in print and broadcast, with sporadic forays into the public and private sectors.

I continued:

> More influencing my decision was one morning several months ago when about to deliver the snow report from Big Bear I was introduced on air by show host Steve Edwards as one of L.A.'s leading urban authorities, a kind reference to my writings and abiding passion for planning and design. And there I was a virtual snowman on the ski slopes being buffeted by a blizzard.
>
> While defrosting in the news van on the long trip back to L.A. I decided it was a good time to start

thinking about moving on and pursuing my avocation of urban design and development. Fox was agreeable and generous.

My work also at Meruelo Maddux had become difficult, in part by the Cuban contingent's habit of coming to the office at the crack of noon, having their signature strong, thick coffee, then going out for lunch, and actually not starting work until the late afternoon. And the projects I was involved with were getting increasingly frustrating, as I related in an article that appeared in the January, 2006 issue of the *Planning Report* and on select websites, with the preface: "There is a planning adage that postulates cities are shaped parcel by parcel, project by project, the sum determining whether a city became memorable, mediocre, or marginal."

I then went on to relate the sad history of one parcel I had been involved with which I had high hopes; if imaginatively planned, it could have become a paradigm for the development along the forlorn LA River. Known as parcel F, its twenty-three acres off San Fernando Road in Glassell Park north of downtown Los Angeles had been widely advertised for sale as "industrial land" when it first caught the eye of developer Richard Meruelo in early 2004. He purchased it a year later, envisioning it as a vibrant, high-density mixed-use and mixed-income, new town, in-town, development.

The immodest vision consistent with Meruelo's pursuit of low-end properties with high potential in and around the central city was very much in the spirit of what I had been advocating in my commentaries promoting the unappreciated and under-developed river in the *Downtown News* and on select websites.

So when he and partner John Maddux challenged me to put on my old, battered hat as an urban designer and direct a planning and architectural team to shape the site that had been part of the Taylor Yards railroad maintenance yards into a distinctive riverside community, I, said yes, of course.

How could I not, seeing as I did the potential of the LA River as an engaging spine of natural habitats, active parks, and mixed-use housing developments, offering a viable inner city alternative to the continued noxious suburban sprawl consuming and compromising the region. I also agreed with the Meruelo Maddux firm's refreshing stated commitment to "socially responsible" development that would serve an evolving, burgeoning Latin population, while having a sharp eye for fringe properties.

But there were problems, needless to say. The parcel also had been identified by the LA Unified School District as one of several possible sites for a proposed high school. Though when Meruelo entered the picture, the district staff had reportedly recommended against the site and the board was wavering and not pursuing the purchase. This prompted the anxious owner to turn to Meruelo.

It also was obvious to those familiar with the area that the adjoining Fed Ex site immediately to the south was a far better location for the school, being directly adjacent to a newly designated forty-acre state park and its potential for joint use, as well as ease of access.

Subsequently, I recommended that the Fed Ex property be included in the site, and the proposed 2,295-seat school sited there to take advantage of the park. Also included were the unsightly adjoining strips of commercial and industrial, creating a projected $1 billion multi-use development, to be called Riveredge. Ever optimistic, the proposal fed the hopes of a dramatic planning paradigm for my adopted Los Angeles, not unlike what I'd achieved nearly a half century before with the ECF in New York City.

Various options were developed, calling for the school as centerpiece, along with a mix of housing types in a variety of architectural styles totaling from 950 to 1,290 units, including up to 20 percent affordable. There also was a range of neighborhood and river-related stores, shops, and eateries, and local serving offices, totaling up to eighty thousand square feet, gracing a network of pedestrian-friendly streets and spaces to form a flavorful village.

Woven throughout the proposed various ideas were lushly landscaped pathways, so-called "green fingers," that would link a local park to the anticipated inviting LA River. Also proposed were assorted traffic calming devices, encouraging pedestrian, bike, and bus use. Further reviews with the local community prompted the addition of an aquatics center featuring a twenty-five-meter pool, and a family health care clinic. I loved it.

The planning effort that involved the firms of RTKL and the Quatro Design Group had been relatively easy. Turning out much more difficult, to my abject disappointment, was the processing of the plan, due to the pernicious politics and petty parochialism that tended to plague such undertakings in a fractious Los Angeles.

Not helping was an article in the *Los Angeles Times* speculating that the plans were just a deception; that the firm's true intent was to flip the property, presumably at a substantial profit. And there were whispers in the catty, if not prejudiced, real estate industry about the involvement of the fictious but nonetheless feared Latino mafia, Meruelo being Cuban and a deep-pocket supporter of local Latin political candidates. The effect of this negative publicity haunted Riveredge. While local representatives and their staffs privately praised the joint-use design, they were reluctant to publicly promote it out of fear of being identified with the fog of politics and payoffs.

Meanwhile, and complicating matters further, was the school district, which reportedly under political pressure was reconsidering pursuing parcel F as the site for the high school, to be sure separate from any joint use development it felt would compromise the project and most certainly delay it.

Much to my consternation, this prompted the LA River revitalization advocates that had praised the ambitious Riveredge plan to back off, not wanting to take a position on the school site which would alienate the now divided local community. Some wanted the school as planned; some a smaller school; some saw the benefits of the joint school, housing, and park development, while others were simply concerned it would aggravate traffic.

Slowly, painfully for me, the support for Riveredge faded. "Too ambitious," "too complicated," I was told; this was a recalcitrant Los Angeles, not the New York City where I had championed joint use projects involving public schools and housing with success. It was soon ignominiously scrapped. The school would be built. The Meruelo firm would take a financial hit, and so did my pride. Trying to "do good" is hard, but I already knew that.

This was followed by another rejection of an innovative project I had been working on: an off-site constructed modular apartment house of small apartments, to be located a block from SCIARC in the arts district that would serve as student and artist housing. The city planning department had been enthusiastic and supportive, too. It had radically waived its parking requirements, which would have been costly, and approved the four-story structure as a walkup, with the hope, as I and affordable housing advocates had nurtured, that the project would become a paradigm for desperately needed lower-cost housing downtown.

But the project did not pencil out enough profit for the now skittish Meruelo Maddux firm and was rejected internally. I protested, and with the architecture firm Killefer Flammang proposed buying the site and developing it ourselves. This also was rejected, for the firm was then suffering much more serious financial problems, wheeling and dealing its large portfolio of properties at a time of tightening credit. The firm subsequently went bankrupt. I was left with some stock that went for pennies on the dollar. More hurt was my pride.

Having problems at that time in 2009, too, was the *Downtown News*, where my column was cut back from once a week to every other week. I noted this in my popular social media blog, adding that the paper was ailing, and where I could be read elsewhere. This didn't fare well with the owner, who was trying to sell the paper at the time, and so I was also soon out of that job.

Undaunted, at seventy-four years of age, I still had several outlets, among them the respected *Planning Report* and various design publications and websites. There was also a consultancy pending with the region's burgeoning mass transit agency, METRO, and teaching, the latter most rewarding.

TOUGH LOVE URBAN

It was during several flush years as a consultant in the late aughts that we bought a co-op apartment in New York City. Principally at first it was for our son, Josef, who had graduated college and taken a job in the city, and his companion at the time, Sayo, who had lived near us in Malibu and had gone to high school with Joe. They were fine as friends. But living together as New York City neophytes was something else, and they soon each went their own way, Josef to Williamsburg, Brooklyn. So we got the full run of the apartment, to use as a pied-à-terre every month or so, and also spent extended vacations there. In effect, we became bicoastal, albeit for about four years, until I was stricken with cancer, which limited my travels and my work. We rented out the apartment for a few more years, before selling it in 2014.

In retrospect, the time there was well spent. It allowed me to see my large and loving family more often: two of my four children were then living in New York City, a third, the youngest, was at McGill University in Montreal; my brother was ensconced in the borough of Queens, my sister in nearby Upper Nyack, and until she passed at age106, my mother, alert to the end, was in a co-op in Rockaway. Scattered in Manhattan, there also were several persevering friends from my teaching days at City College and before; they and my visits there provided me with a renewed perspective of the evolving urban design of the city.

Though I had been back visiting New York City regularly since I had left it in 1978, on various media assignments and to see and celebrate my family, nothing was as palpable as living in an apartment there, even sporadically, when we were bicoastal from 2008 through 2012. Certainly it was patently different than in the intervening years when visiting we had been nomads of sorts, staying with family or friends in a guestroom, makeshift bedroom, on a couch, or in a convenient hotel. Always a visitor, be it on assignment or for pleasure.

Now, however intermittently, we were residents, part of the milling crowd seen on sidewalks and subways that distinguish New York City as an urban conglomeration, for better or worse. My years in California notwithstanding, being back in "the city" brought out the New Yorker in me, deep rooted to be sure having been born in a once mocked, outcast, though proud Brooklyn. Yeah, "Brruklin," that evolving bourgeoise motherland where craft beer in my long absence had replaced the egg creams I had craved in my youth.

I might not have sounded like a New Yorker, my diction having improved, due in large part to the necessities of my radio and television experiences of a thousand voice overs, the countless corrections by friends, and a brief stage presence. But apparently not my attitude, as I believe my years of being a critic and commentator bore out. Though California-based and tan, when asked I always identified New York City as my hometown. I was, and would always be, a New Yorker—opinionated, contentious, and quick on the offensive, and ever ready on the defensive.

And as an occasional city dweller of common expectations, to be sure, one had to contend with the rudiments of eating in, as opposed to dining out, furnishing, and maintaining the apartment, and the daily concerns of making do and getting by. Then there was the building, the neighborhood, and the commuting, the noise and the nudnicks, all influenced by the real estate determinant of "location, location, location."

I had at first looked to score an apartment in the familiar Upper West Side. But there and elsewhere convenient to midtown Manhattan had become prohibitively expensive. The parochial city where l had come of age and had written about in *The New York City Handbook* and the *New York Times* was long gone, along with the housing costs that I achingly recalled.

These included my first apartment, a large studio on the southwest corner of Lexington Avenue and East 71 St. that I rented in 1958 for seventy-five dollars a month, including utilities, or the three-bedroom co-op in then gritty East Harlem that cost me $2,500 to purchase in 1961 with a monthly maintenance of $113, or the four bedroom on the more desirable Upper West Side I bought for $4,500 in 1965, that with some regret I never moved into. In the late '70s when I moved from Port Washington back to the city, single again, the rent for my large studio apartment on West Ninetieth was $310, and though I found it very comfortable, felt I was overpaying. As a New Yorker, past or present, you remember the rents.

We eventually purchased a co-op what was considered by my New York friends a good deal, paying $460,000 with monthly maintenance charges of about $800, for an attractively appointed, sunlit two-bedroom, one bath, top floor apartment in a classic, six-story modern 1920s-styled building on 186th Street in Washington Heights. It is an area I once labeled as "upstate Manhattan," and mostly knew as the site of the

Cloisters, the Metropolitan Museum of Art's inviting replica of a medieval monastery, and for its idiosyncratic population of principally Orthodox Jews and immigrant Dominicans.

Being just twenty minutes by the A train express to Times Square from the 181st St. station, and for us a more convenient 184th Street entrance, it also was the affordable neighborhood of choice for Broadway musicians, striving actors, and people like ourselves who enjoyed the theater midtown and downtown.

I liked the neighborhood, for it reminded me in many ways of the Upper West Side I had known thirty years prior and Flatbush fifty-plus years before, with small owner-occupied stores and walkable streets. In 2008, these included a Jewish bakery that baked its own challah and pastries, pieces of which were always at the ready to be nibbled with a fifty-cent cup of coffee, free refills, if you sat on the raised stools facing the window on 187th Street. There was also a pizza parlor that in addition to its fresh-baked specials, sold its own homemade ices; a shoe repair shop, attended by a crusty shoemaker with an Eastern European accent; an authentic Hungarian beauty parlor and facial clinic that my wife loved, and a drug store with a druggist who got to call me by my first name, albeit in Yiddish, Shmuel.

That our co-op's board of directors were dominated by the portentous rabbi of an adjacent Orthodox synagogue and his resident minion was a mixed blessing, but that they kept the elevators running on Shabbos was appreciated, and the lobby full of black-hatted *kindeler*, children, their sidelocks, *payots*, flailing. And on the nearby sidewalks, a friendly, resident Dominican contingent, the venerable of which seemingly always sitting and playing dominoes. All this was in sharp contrast to the Malibu that was our main residence, making us occasionally, idly, think about someday perhaps moving back to New York City.

Meanwhile, from my new catbird seat I began writing more about the new New York City I was seeing, for periodicals that included *Oculus*, a monthly published by the New York AIA, the LA-based *Planning Report*, and the urban design and planning websites Planetizen and ArchNewsNow.com.

New York indeed was changing, its housing market that I had been so familiar with years ago now seemed alien and adrift in a turbulent ocean of pirate ships manned by voracious real estate and financial crews. I frankly didn't like the drift I saw in the development of high-rise luxury residences punctuating the skyline, particularly in the face of the increasingly pressing need for affordable housing and the homeless problem. The focus seemed to be all on money, money, money, now the bottom line of public planning and private design and development. I feared that me and a smattering of others expounding social concerns had become relics.

I hinted at this in a commentary for Planetizen (April 11, 2012) on a controversy in my old haunt of Greenwich Village, my memories of which I wove into the narrative:

> If not an architectural landmark for New York City, maybe it can be a planning landmark, or, simply, a dash of nostalgia. There is a certain irony in community stalwarts in testy Greenwich Village wanting to have the stale housing slabs hovering over a bland park composing Washington Square Village

declared an architectural landmark that will somehow thwart New York University from overdeveloping further the neighborhood's singular super blocks.

"Fugataboutit," I declared in the jargon of a hard-boiled New Yorker; the plea seen as a ruse to lure the retro redevelopment realists involved into a backroom negotiation. There the project undoubtedly would be sliced and diced so it can be swallowed by all without choking to a political death.

That process already had started, with NYU agreeing to cut back the project by "almost a fifth," according to the puffs of smoke then coming out of the Manhattan borough president's office. This prompted me to add that we could expect more whittling of the proposal known as NYU 2031, which called for a mix of two million-plus square feet of dorms, classrooms, and commercial space, a total equal to the Empire State building, being crammed into its super blocks already dominated by the two apartment slabs of nearly 1,300 units and edged by a strip of stores and eateries.

"Keep in mind whatever NYU gets will be a windfall, having paid a mere $25 million for the ailing project in 1962 and then watch its value exponentially increase," I wrote, and continued:

> The city's powers-that-be and potentate Mayor Bloomberg see the project as yet another critical element in the city's intellectual and institutional ascendancy, and point to the recent approvals of the ambitious expansions of Columbia and Cornell

universities. NYU's apologizing academic overachievers are somewhat more bias, knowing well who butters their bread.

I was back in New York with a bludgeon, commenting that smart street initiatives hyped by the city's transportation chief Sadik-Kahn might snare the headlines, pleasing planning advocates as myself and stirring the profession's rank and file and students, but that, in New York, the payoff of planning I observed was not finessing public spaces. Rather, it was all about wangling zoning and being able to squeeze the last buildable square foot of out of a site's last square inch, concluding that this was "the city's blood sport and the basis of much of its historic wealth."

I noted that NYU 2031 being typical, the reason for these schemes, the students, of course, would get the short end of the stick, with 770,000 square feet of classroom space to be buried underground. If any user should be interned, I wrote, it was the tenured professors who were rarely in their offices and the administrators who programmed these outrages. I was only sorry I was writing this for an industry website, where I feared it might get lost, and not the *New York Times*.

Then there was the different view I took of the heralded High Line at the time it was being christened and celebrated. Having worked on the line when it was an operating railroad and Chelsea was a gritty, waterfront neighborhood, I was able to lend a unique historical perspective, again for Planetizen (June 21, 2012): "The High Line curving through the west Chelsea section of Manhattan bordering the Hudson River has to be one of the most successful planning and design stories in

New York City in recent years, touted as a crowning achievement of the reign of Mayor Bloomberg, to be emulated in cities across the country."

Then came my zinger. "Testimonials and awards notwithstanding," I wrote,

> I am wary of the cloying elitism of a crowing Bloomberg. Having followed the project's promotions for the last decade and the community's evolution for the last half century, I am skeptical of its heralded success, given the embrace of the High Line by its high stepping sponsors and a middling media making it hard to criticize. There can be no denying the feel good publicity it has generated. Whether labeled a park or a promenade, the finical design of the former freight train spur sensitively landscaped with sustainable plantings and mod furnishings has become a major tourist attraction and an even more considerable real estate asset.

I added:

> The elevated tracks certainly have been transformed from when I worked there as a fresh fruit and vegetable inspector for the Perishable Foods Inspection Agency on the night shift on the original B&O line and in the nearby NY Central RR Yards.... To know Chelsea during those days was to walk its mean streets and work on the waterfront and in the rail yards, a bailing hook at the ready.

Given the neighborhood's rough trade and its predators, I would not use "affection" to describe how I felt about the area then, flavored as it was by a bar scene catering to an S&M leather crowd that did not include the MBA types as it does now. "Wary" would be my more apt descriptor, which prepared me well for my future work as a journalist and planner. It also made me appreciate the nuances of neighborhood change. The passive open space of today's High Line design—with its ban on bikes and dogs and discouragement of the slatternly, I continued, "is a not so subtle disinvite to the long-time residents shoe boxed into the low rent housing projects and tenements that once lent Chelsea its gritty reputation. They were considered second-class citizens then, as they are now.

I added:

The High Line obviously was not designed for these persevering dwellers, or the neighborhood. If so, from my public planning perspective, the generous funds received from its deep pocketed patrons and the city should have been first used at the street level, to improve pedestrian safety and connectivity, contain the noxious traffic, and purchase a few of the area's unsightly parking lots for active playgrounds, pocket parks and common gardens that have long been on the community's wish list.

The pleasant seating and the arresting views aside, the High Line, l felt, serves principally as the meandering manicured front lawn and garden for the neighborhood's new residential and commercials developments, encouraged by a host of zoning changes and other concessions enacted by a real estate and building trade-friendly Bloomberg administration. To be sure, the project has provided needed construction jobs for the many, investment opportunities for the few, and lucrative contracts for the design teams. The success of the design was coincidental.

Muted had been the criticism that the motivating greed with its over scaled development is destroying the neighborhood. Some feel it already has, and in its place a new Chelsea has arisen, heralded by the High Line and fashioned more in the spirit of a tony Upper East Side in an ever-changing New York. And not changing necessarily for the better, if judged on its livability for most of the city's residents and not on real estate rolls and the lifestyles of the rich and famous. My concerns came more pronounced as our bicoastal sojourn ended and we had to sell the apartment.

To be sure, if anything distinguishes a city as a living, breathing construct of civilization, it is change. Anyone who experiences a city of any major size, be it as a place where they live, work, play, or just occasionally visit, has to notice the constant changes: from afar, the evolving skyline; closer up, the new buildings; on the streets, the increasing traffic; on sidewalks, the diversity of people.

There is no stopping or even slowing change. Certainly not in a world of 7.5 billion, where hundreds of millions of people are moving to cities every year, and in the United States, where the urban population at present is about 80 percent (250 million) and continues to pace the nation's growth. But what is the nature of the changes we are now witnessing, and how are they already affecting the hapless city dweller?

According to Jeremiah Moss, the author of *Vanishing New York: How a Great City Lost Its Soul* (HarperCollins, 2017), the change in his beloved city over the last several decades has been depressingly convulsive, destroying in his view what had made New York the world's urban paragon, engaging and exciting, but also exasperating, making life in it a daily challenge for most.

In his book, that I reviewed (Sept. 30, 2017) for the *Los Angeles Review of Books*,

> Moss is more than exasperated. He feels under siege; his words a dispatch from the front lines of a war zone, where the resident population is losing badly and the cityscape is being ravaged. Most of New York's residents, in Moss's account, are collateral damage in a market-driven economy. For all its liberal pretense, Moss sees the city a capitalistic coven, where if you can't meet the rent, you're "outta here."

Labeling Moss's tome a lament would be too kind. More accurate would be a polemic, unrelenting in exposing the raw greed that has compromised the once-proud city, strip mining its architectural and cultural landmarks, and sapping its historic promise of community and congeniality for aspiring diverse populations. In short, the city's transformation is no less than an apocalyptic tragedy, which Moss condemns with a New Yorker's in-your-face, unbridled passion. Watch out for spittle. "Page after page," I wrote, "Moss documents the rending of the city's historic fabric: landmarks crumble, mom-and-pop stores close, rents soar, while two-faced legislators talk about 'more jobs' and other benefits to an undiscerning media. All this as hordes of tourists from the suburbs and distant shores clog the sidewalks in search of a New York that is no longer."

"However acerbic, there is no denying his outrage," I continued. "And if you, like me, were born in New York and have lived there most of your life, you have to be concerned. You are witnessing the compromise of a singular civilization, cultivated over centuries by immigrants and others in pursuit of the American dream." And I added:

> If New York is fucked, as an unrepentant New Yorker might say, can Los Angeles be far behind? A gaggle of citizens may have rallied to protect the rich architectural and cultural history of the aging adolescent city from the ever-avaricious real estate industry. And there is a righteous rising tide of concern over the lack of affordable housing and the homelessness epidemic. Nonetheless, the city is vulnerable to the twin social diseases of greed and social inequality, as New York is suffering.

Moss concludes his reviling with a wish list, offered somewhat like a printed prayer slipped to someone on the gallows. He warns, among other things, against squandering subsidies on tourist attractions and catering to corporations instead of spending them on needed housing and public services. But I ended with the question whether anybody is listening?

His glimpses of New York can be personal and eloquent, such as his yearning for the storied Greenwich Village, once the cultural hub and heart of the city, home to artists and so-called bohemians. I can relate, for this was where a teenage me hung out with the "M and A" crowd, from the sui generis Music & Art High School. It was our sanctuary, and only a fifteen-cent subway ride from school and parents.

That was in the early 1950s, some forty years before Moss arrived in New York as an aspiring poet and free spirit. He naturally sought out the Village, but because the rents there were already expensive, had to settle elsewhere. Nevertheless, he frequented the Village, posting himself, among other places, in the White Horse Tavern on Hudson Street. That's where I, as a neophyte reporter for the *New York Times* in the 1960s, wiled away many an evening, and where I wrote articles under a pseudonym for the then-prickly *Village Voice*. By the time Moss stumbled into the tavern, I was long gone.

Over the next several decades I witnessed the city's gentrification from a comfortable distance in Los Angeles, and, when bicoastal, from a placid Washington Heights. Meanwhile, Moss and millions of workaday New Yorkers were suffering daily, being priced out of their apartments, and enduring the demise of their neighborhoods, shop by shop.

Finding a few flavorful places in the Village, such as the White Horse of my youth, was, for Moss, "a dangerous and painful affair." Every time he fell for what he considered an authentic bar, or a twenty-four-hour diner, "it was snatched away, given over to a successful restaurateur to be gutted and glamorized." He likened the transformation to the film *The Invasion of the Body Snatchers*, in which "the old places look like themselves, sort of, but there is no soul inside."

For someone born and ill-bred in New York, having written indeed of its problems but also its premiums, *Vanishing New York* was a depressing read, from the introduction to the implacable final chapter, which offers Moss's faint encouragement to keep seeking "the unexpected spectacle and the chance encounter." Yet the memories persist, like the smell of cooked cabbage in a tenement hallway, or the delectable aromas from the ovens of the corner bakery, where as a neighborhood waif you were given a free roll and a gruff slap on the head.

As for the compelling cityscape, it was revealed to me in fleeting views from an elevated subway car hurtling through Brooklyn into Manhattan, as if on a magical flying carpet to Baghdad-on-the Hudson. And to climb aboard, all you had to do was follow my father's instructions to duck under the turnstile, to save a nickel. Which was to be rubbed against another nickel, to buy a hot dog off the cart that was always there on Orchard Street. For two cents more you could get sauerkraut.

Above all, I remember, once upon a long, long time ago, a clamorous New York, shining bright and beckoning, with constant wonders and possibilities for those who ventured down its spirited streets. As a child of the Depression, born to a Jewish immigrant family that had fled a scary Europe, the city presented the promise of the future, or at least the prospects of reasonable rents and free seltzer.

The latter, I recall, was to be had out of a dispenser at the accommodating Automat on West 57th in midtown Manhattan, where we waited for our paramours to finish their classes at the Art Students League across the street. As the popular folk song of the '60s has it, "Those were the days, my friend, I thought they'd never end."

But they did end, and we are sadder for it. However, I still love New York, its energy, drive, diversity, tolerance and, yes, toughness. These are traits I feel Los Angeles, and every community, could use more of, including my liberal, libertarian, misanthropic Malibu.

TEACHING AS A DELIGHT

There is in the harsh reality of the grind of journalism the humbling prospect that what you might write as a critic, be it to provoke or lend perspective, will probably have little immediate effect on the life of a reader, and only a vain hope that it will improve where they live, work, or play in their future. The best I could really hope for was to make the reader more alert to his or her environment; to put a few new sharp arrows in their quiver as they ventured forth to wherever for whatever.

Teaching was different. I felt that I could prompt students to simply think and give them the skills to serve themselves and others. And for me, it was also to somehow make education enjoyable, for all of us. I didn't want to teach, exactly, to stand before a class and in essence entertain and instruct. Rather, I wanted to learn, ideally staying a step or two ahead of students, conscious that my knowledge of planning and design was self-taught, experiential, and bookish, my postgraduate degree virtual, my books my thesis.

Particularly instructive and intense was my eight years as an adjunct full professor at the CUNY School of Architecture, acting in effect as the client of the projects the fifth-year graduating students were working on. I was comfortable in the role, for I was then the director of development of the NYC Educational Construction Fund (ECF), shepherding from design to construction public schools in complex mixed-use projects, and for which I had been lauded, and no doubt got me invited to teach at the college.

The ECF had been struggling, its pipeline of projects empty, when it hired me in 1968; so the fund gave me free rein to kickstart the program. And according to author Suzanne Schindler in "The Private Lives of Public Schools" (PhD thesis, Princeton, 2018), I certainly got the ball rolling.

She noted that I had gotten the job, thanks to my "street smarts" and "local knowledge," honed as a *New York Times* reporter and community activist in East Harlem. Though I never met her, she did correctly comment that I had reveled in the job, and by 1972, the ECF had significant progress to show. She noted:

> Its pilot project in the Bronx, funded initially by short-term notes, was occupied, and in April of that year, the ECF issued a first round of long-term serial bonds, which ultimately financed seven schools. It had 23 projects in planning, which would together create 25,000 school seats along with 8,250 units of housing and 1,250,000 square feet of commercial development.

For me, the job was a challenge, and an education, and it immeasurably aided my teaching. Also helping was that I was paired each semester with a professor who was an experienced architect, and thanks to Dean Spring's vetting, compatible. Some, such as Lee Harris Pomeroy, became life-long friends. Having a few motivated students further drove my hope of learning while teaching.

The time I spent at City College, twice a week, eight months a year for eight years were invaluable to my directing development for the ECF and later as an urban design critic. And that was beyond the knowledge acquired to review design and architecture books for the *New York Times*, *Washington Post*, and other outlets.

My educational experience was further augmented when in Los Angeles at the Southern California Institute for Architecture (SCI-Arc). There, once again I team taught a senior thesis class, in 2005, with Ray Kappe, an honored architect, who was a founder of the school and had given up teaching jobs elsewhere to become its first director. Happily for me he occasionally taught, and knowing of my City College experience, he thought it would be educational for both of us. It definitely was for me, and I like to think for the students too.

Knowing students were prone to be computer obsessed, using them for research, designing, and drawing, we intentionally picked a site, a railway yard, across the street from SCI-Arc. We then directed them to put aside their laptops, and step-by-step walk the site, see how it changed day to day, hour by hour, and consider how it might affect what they would propose there. What we tried to do, in a word, was to humanize the research, to reinforce the concept that architecture was a social art, in the real world, creating spaces and places for people, not a computer-based design exercise pursued at a desk.

The process prompted some exciting student projects, which we thought the then-director of the school, Eric Owens Moss, would want to see; we hoped he would even serve on a class jury, as directors are wont to do. Invitations were sent, but Moss never showed up, though we knew he was in his office, just yards from the class studio. We never learned why he didn't respond to the invitation. Perhaps he was resentful of Ray's popularity or didn't like me, for I had once deservedly trashed one of his award-winning designs.

Moss was one of those architects of which there seemed to be a coterie in Los Angeles—self-proclaimed avant-gardists who thought being different meant being good. Believing with the faith of a zealot they were the architectural interpreters of "El Lay," they demanded attention each time they did a project for a style-conscious client.

Sometimes I had to pay attention to them, especially if they won a major award, such as an honor from the national AIA, which an office conversion by Moss did. I found the building overwrought and costly, and I was promptly accused by the owner of trespassing. He didn't like that I had failed to interview him or Moss; I'd spoken instead of the contractor and a prospective tenant, both of whom I met on the site when I visited it unannounced, a door being open and a receptionist welcoming. An editor suggested I revisit the site, and at least interview them, and write a second piece. I declined.

I did teach a graduate course in planning for a semester at USC, but I found getting to the campus at night was a pain. Additionally, I had to pay for parking, so I did not pick up the option of another semester. I considered this a disturbing indication of the prerogatives of an Angeleno I as a neophyte was beginning to sense.

I duly solved the parking problem by fashioning a course at the Art Center College of Design in Pasadena where I had to drive to campus only once a semester, arranging to meet my students weekly at different venues I defined as cultural, spread across the Southland. It could be an art exhibit I wanted to see, a dance or music rehearsal I got us into, or to tour with an architect or client something I might consider reviewing.

The course, entitled "Creative and Critical Thinking," turned out to be engaging for both me and the students. More descriptively, I orchestrated it rather than teaching it, for eight gratifying years, limiting the number of students to about a dozen and turning away dozens more; and I linked it to varied consultant assignments I took on after leaving the *Times* whenever I felt there were no conflicts. Several of these courses became legendary among students while raising eyebrows among the staff and administration.

Having left the *Times* in 1990, I had become for a year senior creative consultant to Disney Imagineering, and was still teaching at the Art Center, when I arranged free entry for a day for my class to Disneyland. On a busy weekend we would view the lines of guests to several of the more popular rides, and then brainstorm how the wait could be made more enjoyable by perhaps designing some sort of low-tech, interactive diversions.

A few of the ideas the students came up with were brilliant, such as designing a thin glass case for an ant farm, to be used as an aisle divider instead of the usual rope on the line to, naturally, the *Honey I Shrunk the Kids* attraction. Talk about teaching scale. And it could be maintained inexpensively enough with a few sugar cubes, greens, and a water drip.

Disney, the students, and me were more than pleased, the Art Center though less so, concerned about parental permissions, a long day and evening for the students away from the campus, and the possible need of insurance. Administrators always seemed to find a reason why you couldn't do something.

But according to what became a school legend, the best class my students ever attended was when I arranged for them to be hired as extras for an episode of *90210*, which was being filmed on the Santa Monica beach, and for which I was a special effects (FX) consultant.

Under my direction, they were to build several sand sculptures I had designed for the beach episode. (I should add that I had a speaking role as the sandcastle judge.) The students would also be on camera, as beachgoers, mingling with the show's infamous cast. And for this they would not only get class credit, eat with the actors and crew, but also paid at the Screen Actors Guild union scale. I of course was paid too, and quite well. I still receive modest residuals from the reruns some thirty years after the shoot. It was a long day, but a day to remember.

The assignment was never repeated, the sandcastle episode was a one-off in the long run of *90210*, though students who subsequently signed up for the course constantly inquired if I planned a similar curriculum experience. Eventually, there was a change of administration in the school, followed by the usual budget cuts in which liberal arts courses were trimmed, including mine, and I moved on to the Otis College of Art and Design, in the Westchester community of Los Angeles. There I would teach a course called "Critical Thinking" for just a year, before looking for a new academic challenge at the more convenient UCLA, in Westwood.

And challenged I was, by Stephanie Landregan, the enlightened director of the UCLA Extension Graduate Department of Landscape Architecture, to develop a course that would explore how forlorn spaces might be designed and developed as community resources that would lend a sense of place, however fleeting. And the more unappealing the subject site in an underserved community, the more the challenge. It was an exercise that peripatetic students, bureaucrats, and community activists termed "guerilla planning."

It was to be a subversive exercise, and it prompted Landregan to team me up with a veteran, like-minded landscape architect, Rhett Beavers, who became a most valued, resourceful, and convivial colleague. We did not need to convince each other that the real challenge in planning and design was placemaking; that big and brutal was no longer winning the hearts and minds of a discerning public. Needed was to think small and green—and local.

Our quest also was in response to the stifling Beaux Arts tradition of instruction still being championed by self-promoting academics and their sycophants mimicking the indulgences of the current crop of suspect star architects. We noted over lunches that often selected in our stale design schools were prepackaged sites lifted from the cavalcade of competitions culled from the internet.

Though these constructs might dazzle students, most were born in a questionable reality promising publicity for their institutions and their promoters and, possibly, an actual project for the usual swarming stakeholders. A cursory review of the internet indicated that, despite good intentions, many of the publicized competitions appeared to end in disappointment and the further dissipation of public good will.

As I commented on social media, these competitions had become a stage for a self-aggrandizing world of star architects, celebrity sponsors, perfidious developers, bootlicking bureaucrats and, not incidentally, a slothful media. I declared it a shame that well-intentioned public servants and community activists were continually subverted by these conceits.

Nevertheless, ever hopeful as teachers tend to be, Rhett and I believed that perhaps our teaching could in some ways enlighten as well as educate; that landscaping is a healing craft. So with the encouragement of a sympathetic Landregan, we combed the fractured Los Angeles cityscape for a test site. To be sure, it wasn't for the miserly adjunct salaries UCLA was paying us or for the pleasure of the IRS denying us tax deductions for our travel costs.

We, nevertheless, pursued the course, and thought we had found a viable site, an abandoned rail line that had become a weed encrusted, beaten dirt path slicing through the back lots of a narrow one-block stretch in Highland Park. One of LA's inner suburbs, its pleasant tree-shaded streets were edged by a mix of modest dated housing, then only lightly touched by gentrification, due in part to a continuous gang presence.

The task was for each student to lend the path a presence, by selecting a defined site and gracing it with a design made with local materials that in time would self-destruct; the hope was that the community would be left a memory of an experience of the landscape. And to celebrate these spaces, the students were further directed to partner with a local artist and devise a ceremony, which we labeled "Ephemeral Performances in Ephemeral Places."

The first presentation featuring a student explaining their design, while a violinist performed and a costumed dancer swirled, was like no other design thesis I've ever reviewed. Drawing an appreciative crowd of friends and relatives, as well as neighborhood residents, the curious, and the site's itinerant homeless, it also generated much comment in the community and social media. This promised an even larger crowd the next week when additional performances were scheduled. It also unfortunately drew the attention of the owner of the property, who revealed his intentions to someday develop it, declared that the class was trespassing, and banned the next week's performances. We were crestfallen.

The artist Margaret Garcia came to the rescue. A longtime resident of the area, who had teamed up with one of the students for a presentation, she rallied the involved residents, led by a neighbor, Tricia Ward, to invite the class to present at a vest pocket park a block away, known for its Mexican roots as "La Tierra de la Culebra." As for having to be flexible, and adapt to the switch in venue, we just made it part of the course and liberally graded the student efforts accordingly.

Ironically it had been Ward who among others had originally lobbied the city to acquire what had been a derelict parcel to make it a park. The community subsequently designed it, and built it, very much in the spirit of the class. This I felt was how communities become more livable, one parcel at a time. No more sprawling sites and pricey plans by alien professionals. That was for a past era of well-positioned and -promoted design and development firms, lobbyists, and government lackeys.

One sensed, at least when out in communities like Highland Park and among dedicated students, that times were changing. Beavers and me felt encouraged to continue our guerilla planning course. And for our students, it was a valuable chance for them to get real and get down, walk the streets, wallow in the sites; to see, hear, smell, taste, and touch design.

For several years we challenged a parade of young and mid-career professionals in quest of landscape architecture licenses to develop plans for a variety of derelict, fringe, and generally forlorn spaces. This included gritty sidewalks, unfriendly streets, forbidding and trashed vacant lots, and alleys.

For bloodied academic veterans such as Beavers and me, this was an invigorating alternative to the capricious and abstract curriculums many of our architecture and design schools were peddling under the sway of self-aggrandizing faculty and administrators, and their favored star architects, patting and scratching each other's back while creaming the top off the schools' coffers.

Occasionally in our less pretentious realm, a project was presented to us that went beyond the usual parameters and expectations. That is what happened one day in class while discussing precedents. A student, Linda Whitney, revealed that she had recently worked on a vest pocket water conservation venture in a planned unit development east of San Diego where she lived. We immediately embraced the project.

Though not the designated class assignment, Whitney's project certainly was in the spirit of the curriculum. What made it particularly engaging was that the student-inspired minimal maintenance project was real: a 1.4-acre site owned by the community's homeowners association that had been an unsightly miscellany of thirsty plants in need of maintenance, serving no purpose. For years it had sat in sight but out of mind on a hillside adjoining a community clubhouse in the sprawling 3,100 single-family unit development on the edge of the city of Chula Vista.

In addition to attempting to be sustainable, the praiseworthy project featured a native wildlife habitat intended to support the strained flyover Western Bluebird population. Created, in effect would be a bird sanctuary at a time they had been shrinking due to the dogged spread of residential development and wildfires. You could not get more real those days in California than contending with the continuing encroachment of urban sprawl on the natural environment. And this was not just another theoretical study; the involvement of a supportive community made it a compelling construct.

We strongly encouraged the project, which in time garnered a host of awards and increased local support by the homeowners association, the local water district, and the University of California Extension's garden program. Linda Whitney was duly honored, and Rhett and I were ecstatic and proud.

The project, of course, departed from the particulars of the class. But as a guerilla planner, in concert with Brett, I tended to bend the curriculum and contexts whenever I could to make such projects relevant. How else as a teacher was I going to keep on learning, if not extended by committed students?

It made teaching one of the pleasures of my unrestrained years after the sinecure of the *Times*, and I was truly sad when I had to end my association with UCLA in 2014, a year after I'd been diagnosed with advanced stage three colon cancer. An emergency operation revealed it had spread dangerously to my lymph nodes. Fortunately at the time there was an experimental treatment program in progress, to which I was a late add.

That and a dedicated, caring team of oncologists headed by Dr. J. Randolph Hecht literally saved my life, monitoring my daily intake of chemo, weekly modifying the dosage, monthly probing me to see its effects, and reviewing the regimen, ever optimistic that a formula would be found to send the cancer into remission. And of course, given no choice, I also had to be optimistic.

But the treatment was debilitating, and it slowed me down. In addition to not being able to teach, I no longer pursued the occasional lucrative consulting contract, though I continued to pick up assignments as an architectural and design critic from a variety of professional venues. These however were from the shrinking market of print publications being hammered by the internet, with a few persevering by cutting freelance assignments and fees.

I also at the time began reviewing, gratis, arts and entertainment for a modest local public radio station. But it did get me invited to a host of engaging cultural events and theatrical openings, selecting one a week for broadcast.

I found I could handle the light, flexible schedule, and appreciated the diversion from the cancer treatments. It was good to get out and about too, and to be constantly challenged to have to think critically in considering the diversity of cultural enterprises, albeit summed up in a three-minute time slot, about three hundred words, and a report with a beginning, a middle, and an end. It was the type of challenge I loved and enjoyed.

And then there were the architecture and design assignments I couldn't turn down.

EVER THE ICONOCLAST

The New York City apartment rented, eventually to be sold, I was back in Los Angeles full time in 2013, though slowed by the experimental chemo treatments I was enduring in my battle with cancer. But I was not going to miss the Getty Center's gala unveiling of its heavily promoted Pacific Standard Time initiative culminating an extended study promising "new interpretations of the city's history and establishes Los Angeles as a developed center deserving of recognition as a model for the future."

I initially was to review it for the opinion section of the *Los Angeles Times*, but the editors there backed off when, on second thought, given my reputation as a stalwart scold, it was felt I might write something that would be embarrassingly counter to a review by its then-temperate architecture critic, Christopher Hawthorne. And there was also the timorous editors' deference to the august Getty.

Disappointed but not surprised, I reviewed the multifaceted initiative for the independent, nationally circulated *Architect's Newspaper*. In contrast to the generally cloying other reviews, my iconoclastic critique generated much comment, and subsequently was excerpted and reprinted elsewhere, including an edited version in the *Planning Report* (Aug. 9, 2013):

> There is nothing middling in the Getty Center's celebration of a half century of modish architecture in Los Angeles, 1940 to 1990. Labeled *Overdrive*, the

evolving city is prodigiously described as "a vibrant laboratory for architectural innovation," at a time when "experimental concepts were tested, and visionary designs realized."

Indeed, I exclaimed, the region does have a rich modernistic architectural history dating back to the early 1900s and including the notable designs of Irving Gill, Frank Lloyd Wright, R. M. Schindler, and Richard Neutra. The tradition carried forward by the Case Study Houses and populist practitioners such as Cliff May and Ray Kappe persevered through the 1970s.

However, I added that my view "from my front row, center seat as the *Los Angeles Times* architecture and design critic for much of the decade, the 1980s was marked by the sad shift in architecture from its social imperative to create places and spaces for human endeavor to idiosyncratic designs, with how things look taking precedence over how things work. It was if architecture and its implications of permanence had become a photo opportunity."

The result was what I labeled "plop architecture," designs ignoring context, climate, and culture that seemed to have been dropped from above to land haphazardly on various city sites. "If their conceits didn't always work as architecture, they hailed it as art," I exclaimed.

The renowned photographer Julius Shulman, whom the Getty embraced and who I had previously collaborated with on a history of Los Angeles architecture, often had dismissed the forced constructs as "junk piles." But he would surreptitiously comment that this did not deter him from taking an assignment. On the contrary, being an immodest commercial photographer he felt he could make almost any building look good. And he did. Many of his photographs were included in the Getty survey:

> As noted by the Getty, the designs and declarations of the 1980s did garner much national and international attention, and many awards, though from my perspective they were prompted by the east coast design arbiters looking for good copy to fulfill the cliché of Southern California as a new age art and architecture spectacle, and anxious to score junkets.

Also, I added, that was at the time the desire to be different, even at the cost of crafting buildings that didn't work very well, was being mimicked by a host of local architects desperate to be in the slipstream of fads and fashions so they could snare their own headlines and hopefully new commissions. Glitz and glamour were the way to go.

I noted that hyped designs, as well as most of those by the so-called LA Ten, failed to become paradigms: they were either too expensive or were simply just too quirky. Interesting sculpturally as they may have been, user friendly they were not. I added that a post-occupancy evaluation of the designs by the Getty would have been revealing.

Not surprisingly, my suggestion drew the wrath of the architects the Getty cited; they were concerned that any negative evaluations would detract from the well-publicized efforts of the Getty they hoped would increase the value of their projects.

Such evaluations I feel still would have been interesting. Certainly they would have lent the gala Getty initiative some much needed scholarly credibility, and at a fraction of the cost of the several million dollars it had spent on affiliated programs and publications promoting the exhibitions and celebrating itself. And I went on to note that numerous distinguished designs indeed were generated in Los Angeles in the 1980s, but they were not the conceits Getty identified. Yet it was these projects in my estimation that persevered as paradigms, a notion in diametric opposition to the Getty's thesis that LA was "one of the most dynamic and influential cities in the world."

Included in my list were the playful open-air shopping centers and a kit of parts for the 1984 Olympics by Jerde Associates, the various residential projects by the firms of Killefer Flammang and Jan Van Tilburg, and the sensitive restorations of Brenda Levin. The Getty aside, it was, I feel, the work of these architects that spurred the resurgence of downtown and the city's incipient historic preservation movement.

"Overdrive" may have been an apt headline for the postwar years, but by the time the 1980s were upon us cars and Los Angeles just were not mixing well. Also not doing well was the hyped avant-garde architecture. If anything put an end to this modern period extolled by the Getty, it was the recession in the late '80s, a time I suggested for development "to down gear from overdrive, slow down, and for people to go beyond the freeways, try to find a parking space, and experience the evolving city on a bike or walking"—to pursue a sustainable, user-friendly city.

The review resonated with the publisher of the *Planning Report*, David Abel, who was the husband of Brenda Levin, an accomplished architect. She and several other talented local architects unfortunately and unfairly were not included in the Getty bonanza.

An avid Abel wanted more, and in an addendum to my review related when turning in my copy that I had been more succinct in my remarks to him, describing the Getty initiative a mixed bag of mostly "poorly presented discursive indulgences, served up with cheeses and whines." And with that in mind, expressing "some trepidation" the *Planning Report* would prevail upon me to expand my review in the next month's issue. I was happy to agree. It was another piece of meat for the caged tiger in me.

The review also continued to prompt comment from other quarters of Los Angeles, where the Getty was seen by the city's bristling alternative cultural community as being a staid, status quo institution, out of step and out of touch with the local artistic scene. They also wanted more critical comments from me, to be circulated with the hope that they might embarrass the Getty into becoming more supportive of local endeavors.

Abel picked up on this, and in a precede to my sequel (Sept. 11, 2013) noted that the previous review of mine in the *PR* had been a reprint, and though welcomed, he as publisher wanted more. "So apparently did others," he added, "prompting us to ask Sam as the former uncompromising architecture and design critic of the *LA Times* to also offer his views on the Getty's broader initiative, Pacific Standard Time, of which *Overdrive* was one of eleven exhibitions and scores of events.

In extending my assignment, Abel challenged me to be my incisive self. I happily complied, twisting my knife a little deeper into the self-satisfied Getty, declaring that the museum's overly ambitious attempt to explain the shaping of the local built environment "perversely reflects the arbitrary practices and personalities of the history and hype of the Los Angeles architectural scene. The result is a muddle of successes and embarrassments." I continued:

> Nevertheless, given Southern California's gnawing nescience, frankly anything that tries to raise the public's design and planning consciousness should be applauded. Albeit for the august Getty, I do so with one hand. Considering the institution's resources, I just had hoped for something more discerning than a capriciously fractured shallow scholarly view.

I did magnanimously declare that the centerpiece *Overdrive* exhibition, featured at the Getty Center and supplemented by a collection of essays, was engaging, well illustrated, and well organized. But added that "unfortunately polished as it was, the effort was not particularly balanced or appropriately critical, presenting what I felt was a strained attempt to promote the city as a 'vibrant laboratory for cutting edge design' and a bevy of professionals as design divas in the years 1940 to 1990."

If anything, I wrote, the late '70s and '80s I was particularly familiar with and had previously noted, was a time for self-aggrandizement for select professionals, and that it no doubt had dazzled the Getty potentates. This was evidenced by the center's largesse to a collection of fawning institutions and applauding historians and design sycophants to the tune of $3.6 million in grants and other goodies for collaborating under the banner of Pacific Standard Times (PST).

For an "egregious" example of this self-promotion, I cited the makeshift gallery of 1979 in Venice showcasing a gaggle of self-anointed avant-garde architects, reproduced for the Getty initiative at SCIARC. The exhibition pretentiously labeled *A Confederacy of Heretics*, the quality of drawings, models, and their presentation were embarrassing. Personally, I would have given them a failing grade when I taught there, adverse to grading as I was.

This event, as most of the others under the PST banner, was cordial and collegial, prompting my oft mentioned observation that there was "a cult of amiability in LA that tends to discourage criticism and lends the local art and architecture scene a certain puerile mindset befitting a high school sorority. Being on a benefactor's payroll helps."

Not so much a muddle, but more questionable, was the exhibit entitled *The Presence of the Past: Peter Zumthor Reconsiders LACMA*, displayed in the county museum itself. Here the history of the museum on Wilshire Boulevard was respectfully reviewed by the prestigious Pritzker award winning Swiss architect Zumthor as a prelude to his pricey, presumptuous proposal to raze most of the present galleries.

Incidentally, they had originally been designed in part by William Pereira, an architect extolled in the *Overdrive* exhibit. I noted that this call for the wanton demolition of a fractured but functional and cherished landmark was clearly a deviation from the PST's heralded celebration of Southern California's architectural heritage.

I added that the exhibit also exposed to public scrutiny director Michael Govan's grand vision for LACMA. It was not enough, apparently, that Govan's design ambitions already had cluttered up a prime entry to the museum with a forest of dated streetlamps and scarred the limited open space with a trench topped by a giant rock, both of which have outlived their novelty. Talk about an edifice complex.

As for the Getty, one had to wonder while viewing this self-promotion, where was the needed perspective, political acumen, and fiscal oversight a tax-free grant-giving foundation was expected to exercise?

Among the exhibits subsidized by the Getty that did shine was a survey of the modernist architect A. Quincy Jones, which was in keeping with PST's purported and well-packaged intent to also explore the region's history at the always perspicacious Hammer Museum. As an architect who practiced in Los Angeles from 1937 to his death in 1979, Jones is credited with five thousand built projects, lending an accomplished style to the region's landscape.

Many of Getty sponsored events were concentrated during a heralded *Architecture Month* in the late spring. While the scheduling gave focus to the miscellany of venues, for those of us not on an academic or some other teat, or had family obligations, it was a challenge to attend all the events.

I did make a special effort to attend "Runway," a part of the "Extreme IDEAS: Architecture at the Intersection" series organized under the guise of UCLA. It also was publicized as the concluding event of the PST initiative, a look beyond architecture's traditional boundaries "to delve into topics arising from unexpected quarters in film, automotive, aerospace and tech industries," exploring their possibilities in concert with architects in an evolving Los Angeles; in short, a promise of a glimpse of the future.

Among the more popular truism heard in LA's dominant entertainment industry is: "drama is easy, comedy is hard." I feel that this could also be applied to Getty's curatorial efforts: "antiquities are easy, architecture is hard." I concluded that "If anything, the Getty initiative could have used less hyped "overdrive" and more erudite oversight."

The review got me bumped off Getty's PR preferred list, its invites to exclusive exhibit previews when the museum is closed and luncheons are hosted and free, which I had enjoyed along with the free parking. I also stopped getting press releases from the museum, for a while at least, until a few years later when I began reviewing the arts and entertainment for public radio and social media. However modest my audience, it was apparently nonetheless a review that could be clipped and an addendum to the Getty's periodic in-house department reports, no doubt justifying someone's job. I was glad to help.

While the Getty was publicizing *Overdrive* and its accompanying print tome, a different, less ponderous take on the architectural history of Los Angeles was published: *Never Built Los Angeles* (Metropolis, 2013), by Greg Goldin and Sam Lubell. Reviewing it for the *Planning Report*, the *Architect's Newspaper*, and Archnewsnow.com (Sept. 14, 2013), I found the thesis tantalizing. It exposed the particularly disparate perspective of unrealized hopes, dreams, and fantasies "[t]he contradictions and challenges of Los Angeles as a metropolitan conceit of perpetual promise continue." I declared:

> Whether it is the city's benign weather, casual character, or the aura of an unfettered society on the move and make, Los Angeles for the last century has attracted

a cavalcade of self-styled and inspired creative personas. The manifest obvious is of course the enthroned entertainment industry with its glimmer of fame and fortune dangling before the panting public.

On a slightly loftier plain, the authors noted Los Angeles has long been a particular attraction to architects. who over the years, in good times and bad, have set up practice there in search of patrons and patronage. So why, they ask, does the cityscape so disappoint as a livable metropolis, especially given its steady if sporadic growth and its engaging if sprawling setting?

Among the noted potentially transformative designs that never made it off the drawing board, according to the authors, were a stunning master plan by Olmsted Brothers and Bartholomew to green the city, a bold and muscular civic center by Lloyd Wright, a futuristic international airport by Pereira and Luckman, and a mixed-use residential and cultural complex for downtown LA fashioned by a panoply of notable architects.

Concerning the latter, I injected in the review an incident I bore witness to during the impressive unveiling of the downtown plan and its eventual ignoble death; that according to the developer and confirmed by a city official, the proposal was rejected because of the failure of the developer to gift an apartment to a paramour of a local politician, then in downtown LA not an uncommon tradition.

It was this and other hints of malfeasance that unfortunately were not pursued by a naïve media wary of the machinations of design and development beyond its comprehension or investigative capabilities.

According to a more politically astute if circumspect Lubell and Goldin, most of the other inspired schemes failed because of a gap "between Los Angeles's genius for design and its public output," specifically aggravated by the city's institutions, citizens, politics, sprawl, and infrastructure. As a student of LA histrionics and history, the book made one wonder what might have been, and weep.

I concluded my review with the adage that people tend to get the city they deserve, adding that some actually don't necessarily want a city of iconic design, fashioned principally after Continental-centric paradigms, by elitist architects. "Rather they are content in Southern California's sprawl, if only the freeways were traffic free."

COMMUNITY PLANNING
CHALLENGED

While my commentaries and book reviews on architecture were acknowledged and generally appreciated by an abiding audience I had unabashedly retained from my years writing at the *Los Angeles Times* and for a host of architecture publications, persisting was my aspiration as a critic to comment on the urgent and what I considered more challenging discipline of urban design.

My concern with the scale of buildings, infrastructure, streets, public space, neighborhoods, districts, and even cities made urban design critical to livability, and was truly the measure of our built environment. That is why when assuming the mantle of critic for the *Times* I spurned the suggested designation of "architecture," for the heretofore unused "urban design."

Though my byline identified me as "Urban Design Critic," I was generally referred to as the *Times*'s architecture critic by the paper itself and the public. Whatever the daily assignments were, I considered architecture, along with landscape design, planning, and public administration all to be in my purview. As the glib adage suggests, "call me anything, but don't call me late for lunch."

Privately, among family and friends, I eschewed the label, for I felt the design of individual buildings had become for many architects an egotistical exercise, follies out of context and with little regard for users. And that sadly was being encouraged by undiscerning critics wanting to be au courant; the result I felt was a debilitating elitism that served neither readers nor the broader public.

It was no surprise my feelings did not get me invites to speak at the profession's many self-congratulating conventions and symposiums, or to write forwards to architectural monographs or for high-end publications, such as *Architectural Digest*. That I once referred to it as the *Architectural Indigest*, perhaps is the reason I never wrote for it—that and my proletariat proclivities.

Publications and websites concerned with the built environment, such as the *Planning Report* and Planetizen, certainly did not pay as well, if at all, and had a limited audience, and at times I took issue with their editing. However, and more importantly, they had a professional integrity that I respected; and I like to think that my work was read by people in the public and private planning and development sectors who cared about good design. Perhaps they were enjoined by something I wrote and urban policy was duly affected.

At times, though, I agreed with my critics and think I may have been too harsh in my critiques and not as constructive as I should have been. I was haunted by my mother's motto: "Be good, do good."

Two articles I wrote for the monthly *Planning Report* come to mind; one on the process of community planning and the other on the people needed to make planning work. Both stirred strong reactions from both planners and the pubic, and I feel are relevant today as they were written several year ago: "Of all the services the City of LA purports to deliver, however packaged and promoted by the self-serving private and public sectors and their apparatchik academics, planning has to be the most incongruous", I declared on July 2014:

> Charged with providing a guide to a more livable, sustainable, and egalitarian city, planning as practiced by plump bureaucracies pandering politicians, and a comfortable claque—has become an ambiguous paper-pushing, in-and-out basket exercise, confusing the public and consuming scarce municipal dollars. At least, according to a frustrated gaggle of practitioners trading candor for anonymity.
>
> But then there are the other less shrill and more reasoned planning professionals who, while recognizing a fractured Southland and dearth of informed citizenry and leadership, argue that a sprawling Los Angeles pressured by inexorable growth desperately needs a planning vision to ensure its idiosyncratic character and tentative future—however imperfect the process.

What provoked this chorus of concern and complaints was my asking some select scattered sources the simple question of what, if any, is the future of planning in Los Angeles in the wake of the rejection by the courts of the Hollywood Community Plan, a bellwether of sorts of the thirty community plans that in accordance with state law constitute the city's required general plan.

After several arduous years involving more than 120 community meetings and much acrimonious debate, the Hollywood Plan was considered a viable compromise by most involved.

Blessed by the powers-that-be, it was approved by the LA Planning Commission and adopted by the LA City Council, only to be subsequently challenged by a consortium of local groups that, among many things, argued that it was an outdated, flawed document.

The courts agreed, and the plan was buried. I feel nevertheless that its history is instructive for those of us who have a faith, however frail, in the future of planning as a critical tool to a more livable environment.

As for the demise of the Hollywood Plan, numerous conflicted explanations offered, among them at a gathering of LA's respected Westside Urban Forum. Typical of such panels, there was no collective conclusion other than that the quest for community plans must continue, however flawed and questionably useful. To be sure, there were the studied smiles, in keeping with the city's timorous tradition that, despite words and studies to the contrary, considered planning something to be mollified with the minimum effort and cost.

Missing in this and other airings had been the reaction of the rank and file. It was when seeking this perspective as someone who has been both a long-time witness and participant in the private and public sectors, and promising anonymity, that the inherent frustrations of planning in Southern California were unveiled. A nerve was touched among those rarely asked their opinion.

Community plans in the city of LA and their stepchildren, specific plans, were viewed in the municipal backrooms as a waste of time and resources. "We give them lip service and then put them away on a dusty shelf. Planning is really done on a project-by-project basis," said a planning department veteran.

Asked why he continued to do what he considered unnecessary, he replied: "When you are at the end of a rope, you make a knot." Another added that for her, planning was purely an academic exercise. She cited the department's publication of the user-oriented and neighborhood-sensitive "Do Real Planning" guidelines. Much ballyhooed when produced years prior, she felt they read well, but unfortunately translated badly into practical paradigms.

Most agreed that "real planning" was not done at city hall, but in the offices of deep-pocketed developers, attended by land use attorneys and planning and public relations consultants. Bonded in a real estate-driven LA, it was a consortium of what might be described as the city's mandarin class. They tended to thrive on the continued confused state of community plans, which necessitated their crafting of plan amendments, zoning changes, and other costly strategies to ease the approval of select big-buck projects.

Their success, I wrote, depended on the support of local councilpersons, in keeping with the city's twisted political tradition that considers each of the fifteen councilmanic districts fiefdoms. Though each district has at least one planning potentate, "real" planning is viewed as secondary to photo opportunities, press releases, political contributions, and what could be discreetly labeled personal considerations. However allegedly demeaning to the few who consider themselves professionals, the position has its perks in pay and praise among peers, however ingratiating. Pensions also are not bad, though few persevere to vest.

I added that less affected but acutely aware of the confused state of community plans were the professional planners toiling at varied academic constructs, and in the nearly one hundred small cities that compose Los Angeles County. Their perspectives offered off the record from the backbenches and veiled cubicles also revealed a conflicted profession questioning its relevancy and explaining, in part, why the Southland is a planning and development calamity.

The commentary raised the issue of the need for a stronger, more committed planning department, or simply someone with cojones. It also drew upon my public administration experiences that countered the comments of some of my city hall critics, as well as revealing my personal history when I had met with Robert Moses, the epitome of an autocratic administrator.

I teased my commentary for The *Planning Report* "with a provocative sentence from the forward by Raymond Moley, a member of FDR's depression-era brain trust, to Moses's tome *Public Works: A Dangerous Trade* (McGraw-Hill, 1970): "All great works have been associated with autocratic power. For pure democracy has neither the imagination, nor the energy, nor the disciplined mentality to create major improvements," declared the once liberal and now autocratic Moley.

Not surprisingly, I had trashed the book in a review in New York City's *Village Voice* (April 16, 1970), writing that it offered "little perspective and much pomposity, served up with bile of an obviously dedicated and sincere public servant, touched by megalomania and the fanatical conviction that he acted in the public interest." In actuality, it was less a book than a scrapbook of letters, memorandums, dedication speeches, and articles by Moses intermingled with run-on paragraphs of hindsight covering his years of dubious public service. The book bombed.

Nearly a half century later I was again reflecting on the controversial, autocratical Moses, this time in Los Angeles's the *Planning Report* (August 2014):

> In the restive world of planning and development especially among the local make-it-happen financial and construction mandarins in New York there seems to be a resurgence and respect in the public works efforts of Robert Moses.
>
> Liberal remonstrations aside, at several recent symposiums and exhibitions on the East Coast, advanced has been a nuanced understanding that Moses had to break a lot of eggs to make his prodigious public omelets. These include New York's vast park systems, sprawling parkways, iconic bridges, power stations and grids, and a diversity of housing projects and a sprawling Lincoln Center—all developed expeditiously under the guise of slum clearance and benevolent good works.

Whether a coincidence or not, the maneuverings and machinations of Moses to garner funds and override parochial political and community interests and objections and the arbitrary achievements of landscape architect Frederick Law Olmsted were, I felt, very relevant to the emanating melodrama of the revitalization of the Los Angeles River.

Among Moses's prodigious projects in New York City was the linear Riverside Park on Manhattan's Westside, built in the air right above active railroad tracks, astride the Hudson River to the west and a parade of apartments in the east, not unlike something proposed for select stretches of the LA River.

To build such projects, as well as his bridges and tunnels and clear paths for his expressways, I observed, Moses strong-armed New York State to create sovereign authorities with him at the helm to override parochial jurisdictions. At one point in his public reign he wore seventeen different crowns, from commissioner of the NYC Department of Parks and Recreation and the head of the mayor's slum clearance committee to chairman of the Triborough Bridge and Tunnel and New York State Power authorities.

A Yalie and a Republican speaking the streetwise tongue of a coarse Democratic-dominated New York City, Moses was a bully and bulldog who in a dominating fifty-year career got things done.

Olmsted, another cynosure of public development, also was a Yale graduate and a Republican, in addition to being known in his day as an imperious personality for developing a host of landmark parks across the United States, often evicting residents from sites and denigrating local politicians. Yet at the time he was depicted in symposiums much more sympathetically than Moses, who remains the ogre of public works.

But Moses could be charming and friendly; at least he was kind to me in at a city-wide Boy Scout ceremony in 1952 when he offered his congratulations as he pinned on me the Eagle Scout badge I'd earned. Talk about serendipity. As a public personality Moses thrived on such events. And when I became a reporter for the *Times* a decade later, he sent a leatherbound copy of his book I still keep.

Still, it did not stop me from trashing the book in a review (noted in Chapter 5) and sympathetically reporting Jane Jacobs' protests of some of Moses's more questionable projects. These included the slicing and dicing of Washington Square Park and Lower Manhattan, and the redevelopment of the West Village. Nor did it stop me from enjoying his achievements that included Jones Beach, where I occasionally played softball on its well-maintained and well-lit ballfields.

With bombastic glee Moses arbitrarily imposed priorities, bent budgets, denigrated opponents, and expedited contracts. The banks and labor unions loved him; politicians feared him; and communities hated him. Though he never learned to drive, preferring to be chauffeured, if he had a favored vehicle it was the bulldozer, as if anyone standing in his way can attest. Public accountability and transparency were not common pursuits in the Depression and the years that followed when Moses transformed the New York cityscape.

Looking at the renderings of the proposed restoration of the LA River and the promise of promenades, walkways, bike paths, and sites for much needed housing was exciting for me. Touring most of the fifty-one-mile scar of the waterway was a lesser experience that put the promised one-billion-dollar-plus project in a tenuous perspective, and in need of a reality check. I wrote in *the Planning Report*:

> Unquestionably, the restoration of the L.A. River at long last has become a magnanimous mien among the city's political and non-profit coterie, generating self-congratulations, and the earnest hope that the warped waterway can become the region's focal point it once was when it attracted the first settlers to the Southland some 250 years ago.

Following the Army Corps of Engineers (USACE) announcement that it would recommend the 1.08 billion dollars alternative, everyone it seems had climbed aboard the fragile kayak I christened "Good Intentions" that has been stuck in the river on a sandbar of studies and recommendations for decades.

The plan as promoted was intended to be a twenty-five- to fifty-year blueprint for implementing a variety of comprehensive improvements that would make the river "one of the City's most treasured landmarks and a catalyst for a sustainable environment," declared the mayor's office in an effusive press release.

It further stated that the plan acknowledges that great and transformative change may not be accomplished in one lifetime; it must remain in the minds of the people who will carry it forward. This Plan includes bold, long-term visions in addition to a series of practical and nearer-term steps that would make the River a much better place for today's Angelenos. To that, I wrote bluntly: "Show me the money."

No one seemed to know exactly where, when, and how the funds presumably promised for the project would be forthcoming. It depended on whom you talked to—the feds, the state or the City of Los Angeles. Persisting was the critical question of how anything approaching the attractive renderings accompanying the volumes of studies would ever be built, with so many public and private interests wadding in the fifty-one-mile course of the river and in particular an eleven-mile stretch bordering downtown targeted by the Corp of Engineers. As those with institutional memories have witnessed, Los Angeles was a city long on promises and short on delivery.

"We need to take baby steps, on a smaller scale," suggested Omar Brownson of the LA River Revitalization Committee, who noted several streets that dead-end at the river were being planned to be landscaped. And for all the talk, one actually was, a three-plus acre park, deftly designed by architect Elaine Rene-Weisman to serve both the immediate neighborhood and the strolling river visitors.

The architect also served on the board of the Northeast Los Angeles Riverfront Collaborative, which with other groups had been studying so called opportunity sites for private development edging the river. It was these designated sites the plan and its authors hoped could spur "an improved natural environment, while also attracting investments that lead to new jobs, increased property values, more livable streets and sustained growth." I was impressed.

But I added in the *Planning Report* that the pursuit of each of these many "opportunities" no doubt would be a very real challenge, given a factious and fractured Los Angeles. Even before there was a plan, interest had been expressed in select riverfront sites, remembering too well a community hearing nearly a decade before for the ambitious mixed-use school, park, and housing project, Riveredge, designed with flair by the firm of RTKL, and for which I had been a development consultant.

The hearing I attended, chaired by the local councilman, dragged on; it was obvious that the proposal would be rejected by a coalition of parks and school people who each wanted to protect their turf. No one spoke out for the proposed housing, jobs, or river promenade, prompting an observer when leaving to confront the presumably pro-river councilman and loudly comment: "Less consensus and more 'cojones' would have been welcome." It was a phrase that would have pleased a Robert Moses and his champions.

As predicted, the phrase was echoed several times over the protracted years as the varied plans for the river were being advanced and promises made by assorted bumptious bureaucrats and political leaders at self-congratulatory press conferences, specifically whether a Moses or Olmsted personality was needed. And they always shrugged and asked: What could he or she do?

The question having been asked, there was no surprise that answering it would be the indominable Frank Gehry, busy as he was with the innumerable worldwide requests his office had been getting in response to his self-promotions. But given that the challenge was from his vaunted hometown obviously could not be ignored, nor the thought it going to some other local firm, along with a promise of a one-million-dollar-plus fee and accompanying publicity.

That Gehry lacked the landscape architecture and urban design prerequisites for drafting a feasible plan the daunting fifty-one miles of river demanded did not seem bother the beaming Mayor Garcetti; he would get his five minutes aside the Pritzker Prize winner who it was noted could always hire the expertise needed.

This Gehry promised to do, though it did not blunt the objections to his appointment by those who had long worked for the environmental restoration of the river. "To us, it's the epitome of wrong-ended planning. It's not coming from the bottom up. It's coming from the top down," stated a chagrined Lewis MacAdams, of the persevering Friends of the River, which he founded and headed for nearly forty dogged years. (He sadly passed in April, 2020.)

Among other things, the Friends objected to the secrecy surrounding Gehry's involvement and the lack of public input, arguing it would create confusion among the public and political leadership and that the star architect would in effect become the elephant in a room crowded with present river advocates, sucking up scarce funds and undermining ongoing planning efforts.

Nevertheless, the appointment was blessed in a city hall ceremony with promises echoing in my red ears that Gehry's involvement and international clout would bring momentum and a bold artistic touch to the river project. That was in 2015.

Six years later and only diffident teases were being issued out of Gehry's office of an elevated park system and a $150 million cultural center, prompting a lawsuit by a consortium of environmental groups wanting oversight. To the city's embarrassment and no comment from Gehry, it argued the groups had been shut out of the planning process and that the river, rather than covered by costly engineered green space as hinted out, should be reverted to actual nature as originally proposed.

A year later, in 2022, Gehry disclosed a draft plan as had been hinted at, of a river covered by a series of parks featuring an array of more than one hundred cultural and community facilities. His office and the city declined to estimate the cost, though, saying only that it would be constructed over many years. Independent sources calculated it at a current $20 billion. It made one worry what Frank was smoking.

The cost-be-damned Gehry plan for the forlorn river was criticized by a few whispering local critics, who compared it unfavorably, if not unfairly, to the High Line and declared it the ignominious project of a virtuoso architect in his later years. I could only shake my head and say I had warned the project's advocates what might happen, as did MacAdams, if Gehry stuck his thumb into the planning process; that architecture would prevail, and the river's revitalization would wallow.

But instead of being contrite, the still alert then ninety-four-years-old Gehry instead turned his attention and that of a sycophantic media to his nearly completed luxury tower complex across the street from his hallowed Disney Hall in downtown LA. If anything, he was indefatigable. You may take exception to some of his designs, as I did as a critic, but you had to admire his chutzpah.

CRITIC UNBOUND

Many years ago in my rollicking media life rooted in New York and flowering in LA, I was offered a choice gig on commercial radio to host a talk show broadcasting out of Sacramento. I was to be the reasoned liberal counterbalancing a then on-air upstart neoconservative Rush Limbaugh.

After giving it a try for a weekend out of a studio in Los Angeles, subbing for a vacationing host, I declined. I did not like the idea of moving from Los Angeles to Sacramento, which I was assured I would not necessarily have to do, but it was clear would be encouraged to do anyway.

I knew my family, then ensconced in Santa Monica, would strongly object, no matter how attractive the expectation was for the promised but not guaranteed lucrative syndication. And I was wary of the notoriety that I had previously felt in my stints on television. They were titillating, but soon after the five minutes of fame became tiresome. And what of my mantra of being good and doing good?

These considerations aside, I really did not like the prospect of having to field the phone calls from what I considered, however prejudicially, the mostly rabid right-wing and ill-informed audience that I had suffered over the tryout weekend. Hosting three hours a day five days a week wasn't appealing; it would not be illuminating. I do not suffer fools gladly.

But what I did like and found stimulating about broadcasting was writing the punchy, declarative, flowing copy attuned for a listening audience. I had been nurtured on that at WQXR, the radio station of the *New York Times*. Helping was my dog-eared copy of *The Elements of Style*, whether I wrote for print or broadcast, both of which were on the wane for me in 2015, and soon for many others.

Approaching eighty years of age, my editorial contacts were passed or retired, while the media was transforming, with print and broadcast withering in the face of a robust internet and an irresolute public. Journalism as I had known it had become fossilized and was fading. So when I was approached by a Malibu-based public radio station to do culture reviews on whatever, be it architecture, art, dance, music, theater, or even travel, I happily signed on.

It wasn't the NBC, CBS or the NET I had known in New York, or the KCET, KCRW, or KPCC in Los Angeles. Its studio was a converted bedroom, its editorial bent was questionable, and, of course, it didn't pay.

But I really did not care. I would be a critic challenged by myself to critique cultural constructs and conceits beyond my previous forte of architecture and design. And, additionally, I'd once again enjoy the perks of complimentary admissions, good seats, preferred parking, and open tables. I knew this could lead to other gigs—and it did.

Having survived a heart attack and cancer and dealing with cataracts and partial loss of hearing, I was content to be very much in the moment, and, if possible, on the cutting edge, especially in the effervescent art and entertainment scene of Los Angeles.

So, unbounded, I soon was happily at large writing pointed and personal scripts, to be delivered on air with the proper mix of chatty enthusiasm and solemnity, which I would later circulate widely in print on various social media websites hungry for intelligible copy.

In nearly three years I turned out over a hundred commentaries, lending a personal perspective on the cultural scene in Los Angeles and beyond. I like to think they resonated with both listeners and readers. No matter, I certainly enjoyed writing and narrating them, and especially liked the diversity.

The visual arts these days can be almost anything, I commented in a review of an exhibition entitled "The Allure of Matter: Material Art from China, at the Los Angeles County Museum of Art" (May 30, 2019). Featured were printmaking, ceramics, drawing, design, crafts, photography, video, filmmaking, and my past prime interest of architecture, as well as art from the everyday world and more. Some results were engaging and stunning, I wrote, adding that when viewing the mix one had to be prepared to be provoked, if not encouraged to look at everyday elements as grist for an artist.

That's what I discovered when looking at in an untitled piece by Gu Dexin, which consisted of an entire room decorated with an abstract composition of brightly colored plastic scraps taken from a factory where he had worked for years, no doubt at a dreary job. Dexin had apparently taken the scraps home and meticulously melted them into a variety of striking art forms, celebrating space and place.

Then there was a particularly striking art piece by Xu Bing, consisting of a large tiger skin carpet made entirely of cigarettes. It was ironically labeled a Tobacco Project, and, more ironically, crafted by him as an artist-in-residence at Duke University, which was established on the tobacco fortune of the Duke family, and Bing being a native of China, where smoking is a major health, social, and economic concern.

I embraced the exhibit as a political statement, as I did the historic implications of silkworm hanging from the ceiling of a gallery—spinning silk, naturally. For more than twenty-five years the artist Liang Shaoji had been orchestrating this fascinating insect on a host of objects, here on hollow metal chains.

Rooted in the Chinese psyche linking the discovery of silk making with the creation of no less than Chinese civilization, the exhibit was described by its curators as a "primary vehicle of philosophical, political, sociological, emotional and aesthetic expression." This was art and provocatively much more, fascinating the cerebral me, ever the student posing as a critic.

What I particularly appreciated about admittedly being a neophyte cultural critic, was that I could better identify with my audience, as in my review of a Jasper Johns exhibit entitled *Something Resembling Truth*, at the Broad Museum (Dec. 11, 2018). If post-modern and conceptual art left you to wonder exactly what the artist might have been thinking when he or she conceived a particular piece, I suggested the exhibit might just provide some answers. And I added there had to be questions, especially if you were as dazed as me by the constantly shifting and ever-challenging modes and methodology of the art world. Johns arguably had influenced nearly every artistic movement from the 1950s to the present day, beginning with no less a rejection of the modernist isms of Dada and Abstract Expressionism that isolated one's aesthetic experience from any cultural context. He, conversely, explored what we actually saw, making the familiar unfamiliar, inviting viewers to look more closely at things the mind already knew.

Illustrating this was perhaps Johns's most widely recognized image, the American flag, here in a parade of subtle permutations. Also displayed were targets, numbers, maps, light bulbs, and several collages that feature broken school rulers. All of this may be commonplace, but it also was cryptic, Johns having been quoted suggesting that "the meanings may just be that the painting exists."

I liked the Broad, despite it being downtown and difficult to get to during the work week. And except for special exhibits, like the Johns, it was free, as I have urged all museums to be.

So too was the Hammer, and being in Westwood and UCLA, much nearer to Malibu, it became a favorite haunt for me, a convenient place to drop in for lunch and an exhibit. And this I did often, for the museum under the inspired leadership of Ann Philbin consistently exhibited artists and movements neglected in the establishment art world, and which I feel played to LA's strengths of diversity, individualism, and support for creativity.

"The Hammer is hip," as I wrote in a review (Mar. 4, 2016) of its comprehensive examination of the avant-garde liberal arts Black Mountain College, situated in the rural Blue Ridge Mountains of North Carolina. From 1933 to 1957, the college hosted a notable roster of influential artists as students and faculty, in art, music, dance and architecture, and also the applied arts and crafts, weaving, pottery, and jewelry making. It was very experimental, adhering to the progressive educational philosophy of John Dewey, which championed free inquiry and learning by doing.

I suggested that teachers and school administrators note there were no required courses at Black Mountain; that students were encouraged to listen to their muse and pursue independent studies. In addition, the students, faculty, and staff also were responsible for the school's operation, including maintenance, meals, and farm work. Among the faculty were the renown Josef and Anni Albers, whose art was featured in the exhibit, and who commented in its catalogue that the college did "not always create 'works of art,' but rather experiments; it is not our intention to fill museums: we are gathering experience."

The emphasis on experience was very much aligned with the Hammer's oeuvre, and I loved attending it and writing about it. Frankly more so than I had about architecture, which by the very fact of its permanence and investment was more formidable. Being a cultural critic was fun, and hopefully this was reflected in my reviews.

And the more off-beat the exhibits, the more engaging, such as the one I attended as the Skirball Cultural Center, a singular, more intimate museum, known for its humanistic Jewish roots and its empathetic exhibits. Entitled Pop for the People (Oct. 7, 2016), it celebrated the idiosyncratic art of Roy Lichtenstein, and included his bold, unprecedented, renderings of comic book images with the distinctive use of lines, dots, and color, all serving his print making well. It also made one more conscious of art as a daily experience in everyday life, which I enthusiastically applauded.

Then there were the quirky "cultural" happenings, like the one I observed entitled Doggie Hamlet, which was staged under a sunny Southern California sky at the Will Roger State

Historic Park, near UCLA's Center for the Art of Performance. I commented (Feb. 5, 2017) that I didn't exactly know how to describe the event conceived, choreographed, and directed by Ann Carlson, or whether it was a dance concert, a dog show, or a happening.

Or even something more. I quoted from the program that the production "dares the preposterous, the absurd, the simple, even silly," asking us, literally, "to sit together at the edge of the mystery and sameness that joins all living things."

However explained, the event was diverting and delightful; it featured a flock of milling sheep trying to snap up a few blades of green grass, several humans cavorting in and out of floppy sheep skins, and a very focused and beautiful herding Border Collie doing his thing.

I concluded the review with the confession that I was partial to the principal dog, named Monk, being a dedicated dog person, and the master of a Corgi, known for good reason as Bobby the Bad. And he was very much a working dog who instead of corralling cattle for which he was bred, had to be content herding other dogs and humans. That said, seated on a hay bale overlooking the park's polo fields, I was predisposed for the event, which I had come to expect from the center.

Promoting this and similar cutting-edge efforts as a cultural critic pleased me, and the word was getting out to press agents that I was a willing scribe for some of their more alternative offerings. Expecting the unexpected, I endured some taxing evenings, but also some rapturous ones that I happily praised—a joy for a critic.

This included the US premiere of the English production of *The Flying Lovers of Vitebsk*, an arresting portrait of the relationship between the Russian-born, shtetl-haunted artist Marc Chagal and his wife of his early years, Bella. The marvelously acted two-character play was stimulating, with bursts of dialogue, dancing, and songs exploding on an open stage that shifted with lighting and props to hint at a synagogue, an artist's studio, wherever. I was transported.

Then there was an awesome evening when I felt blessed being a critic and being able to attend a memorable performance of a *Long Day's Journey Into Night* at the Wallis Annenberg Center in Beverly Hills (June 8, 2018). But I went with apprehension, having seen Eugene O'Neill's masterpiece some fifty years ago on Broadway and still vividly remembering the experience. It had been raw and riveting.

I wondered whether it would still have the same dramatic effect on me; I was now so much older and living at a time when we'd sadly become so unfortunately hardened to shock—school shootings, pervasive homelessness, cruelty to children, the mindless fringe of the Republican party, and so on. My conclusion in my review as a critic was: "Yes!"

Being a critic also heightened my appreciation of modern dance. I saw that it melds music and movement, celebrates the sensuality of sound and the human body, and embodies passion and expresses a range of emotions.

For me, dance was alive as no other art—a feast for the ears and eyes—and being an aging mesomorph, I am always amazed seeing what the body can do. And in Los Angeles there was a plethora of innovative performances to choose from, for dance was very much in the limelight. These included noteworthy premieres and distinct performance pieces, including a memorable Martha Graham duet drawn from her magnificent *Diversion of Angels* and *Canticle for Innocent Comedians* that, in part, garnered her the title of "dancer of the century" and sainthood from her many legions of followers.

I also had a lot of latitude in my broadcasts, and that included travel commentaries, such as when I returned to Berlin to celebrate a New Year's and the music scene there. Berlin also stirred memories like no other trip, as it was the nexus of the last century, arguably, cursed by two disastrous world wars and the crippling Cold War.

It was that war that divided the city with the hateful wall I remembered from some forty years ago when, on a dubious assignment for the US government in 1976, crossing into East Berlin was like walking on eggshells. I took each step carefully through the security mazes at Checkpoint Charlie and the U-Bahn's Fredrichstrasse Station, trying not to look over my shoulder. Returning to West Berlin I was equally cautious, and nervous.

I ventured into Berlin several years later, in 1982, on an urban affairs junket as design critic for the *LA Times*. Though circumstances were more congenial, the city was still divided and edgy. Journalists never seem to be welcomed by paranoid regimes.

Then the wall came down with a crash and cheers in 1989. Germany was united, and a decade later I was back in Berlin, this time for FOX TV News doing a documentary series on a city reborn. The redevelopment and design were impressive, and made for good visuals, and for me another TV Emmy nomination.

The radio broadcasting, however, was not to last. The cultural commentaries were fine and applauded, but there had been exceptions to my weekly, prickly, commentaries on the discordant local political scene over which I found myself at odds with the station manager and his discomfited board of directors.

Recognizing that I had brought some renown to the station, he asked me to discontinue the political but not the cultural commentaries. I ruefully declined and ceased all my submissions, though I continued to successfully circulate them as blogs and began reaching out for new venues.

But we already were in the earlier days of the Covid-19 pandemic, with the visual and performance arts being hit hard. Museums and theaters were being closed, exhibits and productions put on hold, indefinitely, and public life depressingly curtailed.

In addition, my age and medical history put me at heightened risk, and so I had to self-quarantine, albeit in comfortable Malibu. My métier as a visual critic was ending, essentially. And so it was back to book reviewing for intellectual exercise, as well as good company.

READING ARCHITECTURE

Quarantined at home by the pandemic and absorbed in my landscaping projects, I achingly missed meandering through museums, hearing a concert live, seeing a play in a theatre, losing myself in a dance recital, or just being a flaneur in some beguiling city—leisurely enjoying a street, place, or space and architecture, classical, modern, or current. I missed having something to write about and simply going out and about.

But there was the diversion of surprisingly engaging serial dramas on television, and as a voting member of the Writer's Guild since 1962, I watched numerous DVDs of films vying for the seasonal awards. And there were, of course, books, borrowed or bought, though certainly not as many to choose from as in my past.

Among the few that did, however, come my way during the pandemic were several from the *Los Angeles Review of Books*: the long-anticipated opus by my contemporary Joseph Giovannini, who was the architecture critic for the late *Los Angeles Herald Examiner* when I was at the *LA Times*, and who had gone on to the *News York Times*. We had crossed paths and swords on more than one occasion, and now I would be reviewing Joe as a critic, to be sure as a kindred scribe, respectfully.

His disposition on design being, frankly, counter to mine, I approached his book with conscious discretion. So did apparently the *LARB*, for whom he also occasionally wrote. His book entitled *Architecture Unbound: A Century of the Disruptive*

Avant-Garde was noteworthy, and for my review (Mar. 14, 2022) formidable, taxing my conceit as a critic:

"If the contemporary architecture of curving and clashing geometries, convex and concave structures, tumbling cubes and angled walls, eruptions of glass and steel, shimmering in scattered world cities, appears too complex to be simply described," I declared in my lead sentence, "consider trying to chronicle it in a compelling treatise," which, I added, Giovannini had done in his monumental, well-illustrated 876-page tome.

For the last several decades, I'd observed that architecture—considered as a social art creating spaces and places for human life and endeavor—had been experiencing a discernible, if diffuse, revolution, which Giovannini calls "deconstructivism" in his book. I proposed that donning the cloak of a lay historian, as well as being a practicing architect, Giovannini provocatively defines deconstructivism as the confluence of many transformative and oblique architectural interpretations operating under the banner of the avant-garde.

I continued that he then proceeds to offer a history of avant-garde architecture over the last one hundred years through a panoply of predominant styles and a meandering parade of theorists, artists, teachers, students, and schools.

Whatever its origins, whomever its instigators, however labeled, the singular, chaotic architecture that evolved both challenged and fascinated the design community, arguably becoming the most disruptive and controversial of styles, shadowing its precursors that include rational, right-angled modernism and pretentious, fussy postmodernism.

Noting that its ascendancy was no less than a revolution in design and development, I opined that like most revolutions, whether in politics or the arts, it was fraught with intellectual distinctions, both coarse and fine. These distinctions are assiduously documented by Giovannini, who describes the researching and writing of his epic as a "bildungsroman," an undertaking that, he states, came to form "an education that changed the way I see architecture, and at the same time, transformed my own work."

I argued that this also made him something of an advocate for the loosely defined movement the book chronicles, suggesting that this compromises him as a ferocious critic and polemicist. Noted was Giovannini's chronicling of the Guggenheim Museum in Bilbao, designed by Gehry, which followed his then-stalled Disney design experience.

Thanks in part to advances in the digital rendering of curvilinear designs, Gehry created a wavy facade of glittering titanium that lent new life to an abandoned waterfront. According to Giovannini, the "deconstructivst" design is "a masterpiece" that "catapulted this second tier, rust belt Spanish city onto the world's cultural map." Also impressive is that the design and construction of the 260,000-square-foot, four-story structure reportedly took just three years, coming in on budget and on time, an accomplishment aggressively publicized by the architect. Giovannini claims that this helped to silence doubts that structurally complex avant-garde designs, while eye-catching and headline-grabbing, were notoriously pricey to build and maintain.

As for the Guggenheim, its exhibit space was said by artists and curators not to serve the art particularly well, but the criticism was swiftly muted in the wake of the museum's international eminence and the city's burgeoning tourist trade: the so-called "Bilbao effect."

Criticisms of the Bilbao museum and several other deconstructivist designs, as well as what in the architecture profession are known as post-occupancy evaluations—surveys of user experiences—are conspicuously absent from Giovannini's otherwise encyclopedic study.

In short, beyond how a building looks, the nagging question remains about how it works. And when such issues are raised by critics who are considered user advocates, as I was when reviewing for the *Los Angeles Times* in the 1980s, they are dismissed by the self-aggrandizing architects, their sycophantic sponsors, and their academic acolytes.

Nevertheless, Giovannini writes that the Bilbao museum's opening in 1997 was a transformative event that ushered in a host of similarly ambitious projects worldwide, many larger and even more imaginative. If these projects didn't necessarily work as user-friendly architecture, their being labeled avant-garde ensured that they would at least be hailed as art. And they were. Meanwhile, cutthroat competition turned many architects into entrepreneurial pirates, and contemporary cityscapes, with their promise of treasure, the turbulent seas on which they sailed.

Exposing my prejudices, I added that modernism—which is more stable, if static—may be more popular among and prudent for most architects. It's pursued and practiced more often that other styles because architects are trying meet an increasingly desperate and disparate population's need for affordable shelter:

> Yet the singular avant-garde designs surveyed in this
> book continue to mesmerize the profession and the

public, demanding attention, engendering awe, and giving rise to a smattering of schadenfreude. They continue to challenge architecture's long-standing conventional practices, hinting at a more interesting, if not more livable, urban future. That, of course, is what being avant-garde is wont to do. And Giovannini's tome, which respectfully explores and celebrates this tradition, is a distinctive achievement, deserving of both patience and praise.

Despite its length, the review was picked up by several websites, including the Planning Report, drawing respectful comments. I also received a nice note from Joe, which I appreciated, for it indeed was a critical review that I fretted over more than most.

Much easier was my review (*Los Angeles Review of Books*, Jan. 17, 2019) of *An Architectural Guidebook to Los Angeles*—the fully revised sixth edition—by David Gebhard and Robert Winter (with Robert Inman). Here I could indulge my remembrances of a city I had initially thought would be a fleeting experience for a few years in my arrested adolescence, and certainly as a born and bred New Yorker would never call home.

However short the stay, I was determined to enjoy Los Angeles, and happily set about exploring its varied communities for both the *Times* and myself. Having an apartment in Santa Monica, one of the first places I checked out was that seaside city's sleepy downtown. There I found a bookstore, Hennessey + Ingalls, which to my delight was a wellspring of art and architecture books, new and used, and among them a second edition of the guidebook, priced at $13.95.

Knowing that it would be invaluable for my orientation to, and appreciation of, Los Angeles, I snapped it up. That was nearly a half century ago. It still sits on my ready reference bookshelf, along with several later editions, all dog-eared. I have looked for, but could never find, a first edition, which had started as a modest booklet surveying the sprawling Southern California, as well as the fractured cityscape of Los Angeles.

It had been patched together in 1964 for distribution at a national gathering in Los Angeles of architectural historians. Expanded to include modern architecture, the effort dragged on past the conference deadline and was published in 1965. It proved a coveted guide for locals in addition to visitors, and was expanded in a 1977 edition, which I had snared.

My copy quickly became battered, squeezed as it was into the glove compartment of my convertible, a car that was de rigueur transportation for Manhattan migrants like me. You had to love the benign, sunny weather and then relatively light traffic that made touring around with the top down so pleasant and finding a convenient parking space a given. As for the touring, I found the guide invaluable.

So when the next edition was published in 1982, and then the next, in 1985, I quick bought them. In addition to being essential to my toiling as the design critic, they also were requisite for the subsequent research and writing of my architectural history *LA Lost & Found* (Crown, 1986).

Over the following years, that sadly included the untimely death of Gebhard in a bicycle accident in 1996, several more editions by Winter appeared; these contained modest tweaks and kept the same blue cover displaying iconic towering palm trees.

Nearly a score of years later, there was an ambitious sixth edition, by the now ailing Winter aided by Inman, a former student, reorganized and containing several hundred new additions and fresh photographs, priced at a lofty forty-five dollars, by Angel City Press.

I noted in my review that the cover of the revised edition was now accented by a background colored in a smog brown, a tone evoking the dystonic mood of the classic sci-fi film *Blade Runner* and an unappealing futuristic LA which looked more like a down-and-out Hong Kong.

There were no palm trees on the new murky cover, but rather the classical temple-topped historic landmark city hall, framed with a foreground by a distinctly high-tech modern government edifice, the Caltrans District 7 Headquarters building. This was designed by Pritzker Prize winner Thom Mayne of the edgy firm of Morphosis. There was also a plaza with shadowy figures in a descending darkness. Gloomy.

In the preface, the authors write that Los Angeles "seems a different place in many regards." Indeed, though single-family houses do dominate, as in the past guidebooks, there are more multiple-family, mixed-use, and star architect constructions.

There's also an encouraging social consciousness in the book. The foreword states that "the aesthetics and originality of form are often secondary considerations of how a building addresses or fails to address some social goals, such as the need for sustainability and housing many people." Noted are the protests and political muscle of status quo-conscious homeowner groups and the pressure of changing neighborhoods—not only the more affluent communities, but also those of poverty and color.

Particularly prescient is citing the pressing problem, and challenge, of homelessness. "The centerpiece for any discussion about the future of Los Angeles County is the long-term homelessness," which in 2023 was estimated at fifty thousand, their encampments very much in view in an otherwise gentrifying central city.

As much I had enjoyed being an at-large culture critic, attending at whim music, dance, and theatrical performances and art and design exhibits, I principally saw myself as an architecture book critic during the pandemic and after, having survived a bout with Covid-19. Books were and always had been an escape for me; I voraciously read them and sporadically authored them. As I wrote in a radio script in the spring of 2021 that also circulated in the social media:

> E books to be sure are attractive; they don't take up much room, and audio books I feel can ease the pain of long commutes. But I frankly love books, the printed kind, on sheets of paper, in typeface of varied styles, bound together within covers, of evocative designs hinting at the works of fiction or nonfiction within, and the worlds of ideas, emotion and history.

Books for me have been a constant companion, comfort, and stimulation, from the day I got my library card in Brooklyn. Back then, libraries were something akin to an ecumenical house of worship, a hushed community center—and, for a large family like mine, our living room.

As a student, reader, and especially as a critic, over the years I have accumulated thousands of books, literally a ton of them, conscientiously trucking them with me as I've moved from place to place, city to city. I might have left a piece of furniture behind, but never a box of books. Occasionally prodded by largess or lack of space, I have parted with a few, donating them to schools and libraries or giving them to those I know would appreciate them. For me, books are the gift of choice; and there's always been room on my nightstand for another, especially in a pandemic.

But pandemic or not, now coming to the fore of my concerns was parochial Malibu. While I had been tuned to Malibu's myriad of local issues since writing about them beginning in 1979, visiting often, and moving there in 1997, to become a resident, my concerns were heightened during the pandemic, mostly confined as I were to my house and neighborhood.

Meanwhile, my commentaries on local planning and politics that previously had been pointed became more so, as well as provocative, urgent, and widely circulated on social media, misanthropic Malibu now having my full attention as a social critic.

MISANTHROPIC MALIBU

Arriving in Los Angeles in late 1978, I found it as geographically and demographically fractured as I had expected, a sprawling, multiethnic muddle—but engaging, however enigmatic. Having had friends describe it to me and read extensively about it, I was now poised to experience Los Angeles, my appointment by the *LA Times* as a special writer in effect a generous travel and study grant that gave me free reign to pursue articles.

My hope was that the city would reveal its soul—its "genius loci"—to me as I wandered. Everything would be grist for my mill, beginning with my drive across the country, from Washington, DC to Southern California, which was my initial article for the paper.

In contrast was my second article on the Grand Central Market, just a block from the *Times*, and catering mostly to Hispanic working-class families from the city's underserved East Side, and a few adventurous white-collar office workers. The latter now included me.

The article celebrated the market, while raising eyebrows at it being a déclassé subject among a few of the editors I had been introduced to in the paper's congenial executive dining room in its Spring Street building, which had been described as journalism's "velvet coffin."

I therefore made a point not to lunch at the paper's cafeteria, instead following my instincts for ethnic eateries, going further and further out of the center city. This soon led me to the more bustling Hollywood's Thai restaurants, the bourgeois West Side's nouveau health food, East LA's authentic Mexican dishes, the rambling suburban San Fernando Valley's great hamburgers, and for glimpses of the fabled Southern California lifestyle, the outré vestigial spaces beyond, and finally Malibu.

There I found an inviting singular exurban coastal community, blessed with a benign climate. Accustomed as I was to pursuing stories in gritty neighborhoods, going to Malibu for the *Times* was like going on an all-expense-paid vacation.

Only knowing the community by its clichés, the *Times* in its munificence suggested I enjoy myself, spend a few days there, walk on the beach, barefoot, seek out and talk with locals, kick back, and get a feel for what makes Malibu special—and pricey. What I found was something very different from the edgy New York City I had known since birth.

And I liked it. Certainly the weather and ocean front setting, but also the lifestyle. However smitten, I really didn't expect that Malibu would eventually be where I would live, raise a family, and write this in my study overlooking the very beach, Little Dume, where I first dug my toes into wet sand softened by the gentle surf rolling into the sheltered cove.

It was while strolling on the beach and talking with several community activists that my journalistic countenance was won over by their impassioned efforts to preserve Malibu, threatened then by both man-made and natural disasters. So I wrote "Malibu Faces Threats to Life-Style" (Feb. 2, 1979), in which I detailed and dramatized the multiple problems residents faced: the recurring disastrous wildfires, the unchecked development being encouraged by a distant county government, the increasing hordes of tourists and beachgoers, and escalating real estate prices undermining a then-surprisingly economically and demographically diverse population.

It also introduced me to a host of locals who, recognizing me as a sympathetic and potential ally and hearing that I was looking for a place to live, suggested Malibu. Though I considered it then too far from downtown and as a single person too remote for a social life, the thought was enticing. I loved the beach and the weather, the exurban setting, and could imagine someday moving there, to retire.

As it turned out, a few years later I was no longer single. In May 1981, I'd married the winsome, whip-smart Margaret Mary Hall—Peggy—who was a special writer at the *Times* and who'd moved into the modest, stucco hillside house in Mt. Washington a few miles north of downtown LA that I'd bought earlier so I could be near the *Times* offices.

However, now married, the beach city of Santa Monica with its better air and better public schools beckoned; and the move was made in part possible by the emerging internet that allowed me to work from home and only occasionally go to the office. This was good for the family we were anticipating, though not so much for having a presence in the office politics that were heating up as the *Times* changed ownership in a newspaper market being undercut by the internet.

But I blithely continued my writing, including several books, while fathering in succession two boys; and Peggy and I became community activists, me as head of the neighborhood association and her as a president of the parent association at our children's school, Franklin Elementary. Both had their challenges. I had to prod the city to be more pedestrian-friendly and public space conscious, and Peg had to demand that schools become more student- and teacher-friendly. If our efforts accomplished one tangible thing, it was to landscape the local public school with drought-tolerant native plants. Some thirty years later the landscape was thriving.

Santa Monica was comfortable. We had a two-bedroom, one-bath, 1920s Spanish bungalow which we soon upgraded with a second floor and two more bedrooms, another bath, a study, and a darkroom. Adjoining in the rear were three one-bedroom apartments, and above a four-car garage, making the property financially viable.

But Peg had grown up in a rambling ranch house in Salem, Oregon, and wanted more space, and more rigorous schools for our two gifted sons. I had changed jobs too, doing the weekend news for Fox television and select consulting during the week, and could live most anywhere in Southern California.

Being less enthusiastic about moving than Peg, I challenged her to go house hunting and find something she really liked, and that no doubt I also would. Malibu was beckoning—we both had friends there and I had been following the place since I had written about it over the years for the *Times* and done several broadcasts on Fox 11 News.

They were not only reports on the recurring wildfires, but also on Malibu's protracted struggle to become a city. It finally did in 1991, having weaved its way through a governmental maze for more than a dozen years, sustained by enlightened residents with a vision that became the preface of its adopted municipal code:

> Malibu is a unique land and marine environment and residential community whose citizens have historically

evidenced a commitment to sacrifice urban and suburban conveniences in order to protect that environment and lifestyle, and to preserve unaltered natural resources and rural characteristics. The people of Malibu are a responsible custodian of the area's natural resources for present and future generations.

Malibu is committed to ensure the physical and biological integrity of its environment through the development of land use programs and decisions, to protect the public and private health, safety and general welfare. Malibu will plan to preserve its natural and cultural resources, which include the ocean, marine life, tide pools, beaches, creeks, canyons, hills, mountains, ridges, views, wildlife and plant life, open spaces, archaeological, paleontological, and historic sites, as well as other resources that contribute to Malibu's special natural and rural setting.

This indeed was a noble mission to which I could ascribe. The problem was that given its sparkling coastline, benign weather, proximity to Los Angeles, and its history of being a favored haunt for the rich and famous, real estate prices were exorbitant.

But our timing was good, as the periodic wildfires and subsequent flooding depressed real estate prices for a few years. In addition, there is the Irish aphorism that everyone should be allowed at least one good decision in life. And that is what we liked to say when anyone remarked how lucky we had been purchasing our Malibu home in 1997.

Though to be sure the mid-century ranch-styled house and the separate two-car garage and laundry room with a large rental apartment above had its problems. For all its amenities, the house was poorly decorated and the landscape unkempt, and the required inspection revealed the need for many repairs. It was obvious that it would take a costly restoration to upgrade the property from livable to comfortable, and from garish to modish. And that even with both of us being design adept, construction savvy, and financially resourceful, it would take years to do. And it did.

But the property also had, in real estate parlance, location, location, location, being on one of Malibu's more desirable streets, Cliffside Drive, and on a raised lot of nearly an acre that after some deft landscaping would reveal a sweeping view of the ocean. As for access to the coveted Little Dume beach, it was in easy walking distance through a nature preserve on the literal point of Point Dume and down a steep cliff path to the sand. And no coveted key to the beach was needed.

Nevertheless, the house did not show well, and going on the market in a Malibu singed recently by a wildfire followed by floods, it languished on the market for a year and through several price reductions. These all were factors in us making an opportune offer and it being accepted.

We moved in on July 1, 1997, and soon became involved in the community. Peg worked as a part-time writer and editor for the weekly *Malibu Surfside News*, and then later as a grant writer for nonprofit arts organizations, while I worked out of the house just three days a week for Fox. This enabled us to be very present and hands-on parents.

Meanwhile, I served at first on a host of volunteer environmental initiatives, to be appointed to the city's parks and recreation commission, and later to various toothless city task forces, wrote an occasional local article, and settled into the neighborhood. Life was good. By the time our Josef and Kyle graduated and were off to college, I had begun to receive several pensions from my writing, teaching, and television, and was doing less consulting and more gardening, while continuing to write, my search for a sense of place shifting to the extreme opposites of Malibu and New York City.

Slowed however by my illness, we had to sell the apartment in New York, and spent more time in Malibu; a Malibu that I sadly saw was becoming more misanthropic, aggravated by increasingly avaricious real estate interests and an inept local governance.

And so began my social commentaries—initially for broadcast weekly for the modest local public radio station, to be reproduced on the internet—which gradually generated a wide and varying audience in Malibu and beyond.

For my first commentary, May 2, 2015, I thought I'd review some planning issues, which would offer an introduction to my professional perspective and personal prejudices: "Locally in Malibu," I declared, "there is a constant parade of proposals before the Planning Commission and City Council that deserve attention, for I am convinced that cities are shaped and misshaped not by the sweeping plans heralded by political pronouncements, but by small projects, weighed one at a time."

"For an illustration," I continued,

> we have the city of Malibu spending a half a million dollars plus on a study of urban design guidelines for the Civic Center, now not much more than a scattered collection of suburban mini malls and an

> isolated library, city hall and empty park. The over-the top retail stores and restaurants were popular among tourists, but not among residents. . . . An attractive folksy village, which most residents say they want, it is not.

However conscientious the consultants, I concluded, "the study nonetheless seemed destined for a diffused debate, and then to the shelves of city hall to collect dust, alongside the other Malibu studies."

The soft planning hat I'd figuratively put on soon turned into a combatant's helmet, as I became more alert to the drift of Malibu's governance and the pockets of its recalcitrant residents. Seemingly less important, but more personal, items got my attention, such as the application by the new owners of two oceanside houses on Cliffside Drive to remodel them into questionable structures.

I observed that the over-designed remodels would compromise the valued blue-water views of several homes on the land side of the street, and that they were therefore being protested by their owners, including myself. We prevailed, and the heights of the proposed structures were lowered, a rare victory of residents blocking the proposals of wealthy investors—encouraged by local realtors and builders—for larger and more pricey houses.

Other controversies smoldered, small and big, locally and beyond, to be commented on in my broadcasts and social media. Issues included whether Malibu required or wanted another supermarket; the need for affordable and senior housing, as well as for welcoming public places, such as a community garden, to engender a sense of belonging. Meanwhile, I didn't have to remind my listeners and readers that the traffic on the PCH, was getting worse or that if they were at all concerned about Malibu's future they should "stay tuned."

As time went on I became increasingly tuned to the dissonant voices in the community. I turned up the levels of my commentaries and became more explicably critical, such as this heralding in of a new year (Jan. 22, 2016): "Let's face it, Malibu as the manifestation of a city, a town, a village, or however described, is a mess. Of course, there is the ocean. But water quality has become an issue, as well as access and views," I broadcast, summing up my rising and repeated concerns:

> The PCH continues to be a perplexing problem and will be forever, as long as people drive. The Civic Center is definitely not civic or centered, rather several disconnected shopping malls, and an isolated library and what poses as a city hall. And in the marrow of this mess is a raw vacant lot labeled Legacy Park, which an anxious Cultural Arts Commission and entangled City Council are waiting for a team of consultants to come back with a detailed plan for lending the expanse some purpose.

I continued that the so-called park was

> in fact the earthen roof of a city-blessed water treatment plant serving the adjacent high-end stores and pricey residences, packaged by avaricious real estate interests and sold to an undiscerning City Council.

Some have labeled it perhaps more accurately as the leech field, and with derision, Lunacy Park because of the thinking by the city that hyped its approval.

Mine and other protests prompted the city to direct its consultants to again go back to their drawing board. This also gave me some time to walk the forlorn site, keeping in mind its constraints of no structures or ball fields, which had been negotiated away by a past city council and city call.

Meandering along its pathways, I recalled the sage advice of a landscape architect I once worked with in New Haven, Dan Kiley, who'd said that a site will tell you what it wants to be. Just pick up some soil, rub it with your hands, close your eyes, and envision its use.

I did, and subsequently wrote: "The vision that appeared was a community garden, a collection of small plots tended by locals, producing an abundance of vegetables, fruits and flowers, for themselves and for sharing, connecting to the environment, and each other in a singular commonalty, sustaining the park with people and purpose."

But predictably the study quietly died, ending up on some dusty shelf in city hall, no doubt next to the many other studies by consultants who over the years had been hired to placate resident concerns. It was becoming more and more evident to me that Malibu City Hall was all about the status quo. It's bureaucratic arteries had hardened and its budget was a honey pot for civil serpents.

Still, I had not forgotten my comments to the city's Civic Center Urban Design Task Force recommending including in whatever plan was adopted affordable housing for teachers, first responders, municipal employees, and others who serve Malibu and can't afford to live there, as well as resident seniors who need to downsize and want to stay in the community. A few heads nodded, and there were some snide personal remarks by the resident NIMBYs.

Nevertheless, affordable housing for Malibu would be a recurring theme of mine, which I would raise whenever there was a news story to hang it on, as there was in 2017, prompting a broadcast (Oct. 7, 2017) and subsequent circulation on local social media and beyond. "It was no surprise reading an L.A. Times business story recently that major commercial real estate developers are increasingly considering adding housing to their mix of mall brews," I said, noting that more and more shoppers were shunning the malls in favor of online shopping, where in the comfort of their homes they could view a wealth of products, weigh bargains. Free home delivery and easy returns helped. As a result, I reported, some 25 percent of America's malls were expected to close in the next five years, while others would struggle to become more appealing. This included recycling malls in the mode of walkable villages, featuring shops, boutiques, and a range of intimate eateries and entertainment.

Now the latest ingredient was housing, I added, and not coincidentally was needed more than ever, as California already was suffering an acute shortage—of affordable housing, in particular—that was expected to get worse. It did indeed; and in the years since has gotten more than worse. It's a tragedy aggravated by the pandemic and intractable local governments, prominent among them Malibu.

As pointed out then, planning in Malibu was already behind the times, and in some cases unfortunately behind and under the counter, prompting me to declare it was time for the city to recycle its so-called civic center. To this I added that in actuality it was less a center than a scattered collection of suburban mini malls, a planning embarrassment.

Again, I urged the city consider proposing workforce and senior housing in the civic center, specifically for teachers and first responders, and even include a few units for city employees. I suggested that the housing would make the civic center civil, and if designed well could create the livable, viable seacoast village residents had always yearned for.

I added that it also could satisfy the city's affordable housing element then required by the state, suggesting that by taking the initiative no doubt would please the resolute agencies that seemed to have a hate on for Malibu. In conclusion, I declared, "most of all it is the right thing to do. We owe it to those who serve us."

And this was before the disastrous Woolsey Fire in 2018 that destroyed an estimated quarter of Malibu's housing stock, and also before the pandemic, in which people avoided the malls and commercial centers, and increasingly turned to the internet for their shopping,

But in 2017 in self-satisfied Malibu, even the suggestion that housing serve locals in need did not stir a hidebound city council or the neophyte city manager, preoccupied as they were with accommodating friends and special interests, and balancing the city's budgets. Content with keeping a low profile, they ignored a survey of municipal workers that had found that of the nearly one hundred employed, only one lived in Malibu, and she with her parents.

Not ignored was that Malibu's prime workforce consisted of realtors. They were estimated at fifteen hundred out of the city's then population of thirteen thousand; and most of them considered Malibu a monopoly board on which blue chip properties dominated. Any talk of affordable housing was greeted with scornful laughter.

What planning battles there were in Malibu centered on building bigger and overdesigned housing, McMansions, that promised elevated prices and larger commissions. As a matter of fact, I had used the word "McMansions" in a 1990 *LA Times* book review of *Out of Place: Restoring Identity to the Regional Landscape* (Yale UP, 1990), by Michael Hough, and was subsequently cited by Wikipedia as one of its originators.

I was repulsed by McMansions, but recognized that you couldn't really codify against them. In search of a true measure rather than an arbitrary square footage that could be hidden by good landscaping, I suggested as a critic the colloquial expression, "I know it when I see it." That subjective phrase parenthetically was used in 1964 by United States Supreme Court Justice Potter Stewart in attempting to define what exactly constitutes hard-core pornography.

Much of what I was seeing in Malibu could be described as municipal pornography: capricious planning and arbitrary development, an overpaid, underachieving bureaucracy, an increasingly stratified population, petty politics, and the neighborhood public schools being held hostage by a distant board of education in Santa Monica. I felt that the council should be providing some needed oversight and lighting a fire under a sluggish city hall and its bloated bureaucracy and cadre of consultants.

But these and other problems I had been writing about all became moot in the wildfire that ravaged Malibu in November 2018.

Sparked in distant Woolsey Canyon above Simi Valley, thirty miles from Malibu, and so named the Woolsey Fire, it sped south to the coast, pushed by seasonal Santa Ana winds and feeding on the dry chapparal of the rugged landscape.

Confusion reigned in the threatened community. Worse, first responders were "ordered" to save lives, not homes, and shied away from the firestorm. Homeowners had to watch their houses burn as firemen stood by ignoring their pleas to do something.

When finally contained, the Woolsey Fire had burned nearly one hundred thousand acres, killed three people, destroyed sixteen hundred structures, and damaged nearly four hundred more, in Malibu and nearby communities. Within the city itself, five hundred homes were turned to ash and another one hundred damaged, making a total of about six hundred households.

Our house was only slightly damaged by smoke and ash, thanks to a wet wind coming off the ocean dampening and protecting the roof. The wind had been sucked into the vacuum caused by the rising heat from the burning houses just a few blocks inland, and at a crucial moment in time had the blessed effect of turning the blaze away.

However, the city had grievously suffered, the fire having roared through the older, more modest family-oriented neighborhoods with its larger households, the sort that sent their children through the public schools, coached Little League, hosted Halloween hauntings, and were community volunteers.

Many of the more isolated trophy houses and retreats in the canyons above Malibu had been destroyed, further sending shocks through the community. In all, the destroyed and damaged homes accounted for nearly a quarter of Malibu's permanent population.

Malibu was turning from a livable community into a tourist town. The corresponding increase in housing values thrilled local real estate interests and a mercenary city hall, which was only too happy to rake in the resulting taxes and fees. But a core of residents, including me, weren't pleased about it. My computer was ready and the internet awaited.

THE FIRE AND THE AFTERMATH

Like the residue of toxic ash from the Woolsey Fire that is embedded in the soil of my Malibu, the disaster would plague the singular seacoast village for the foreseeable future. And so I declared in a commentary shortly after returning to our ash and cinder-splattered house, where the electricity having been finally restored after ten long days, I could at last turn on my computer to vent anew as the local critic.

"The thought of the fire still haunts me," I wrote for public radio and the internet (Feb. 23, 2019), "as I am sure it haunts many in Malibu, especially the burnouts but also persevering residents who are acutely concerned how it will affect the future city, other than at the present being a cash cow for select public serpents."

Granted, it was a gratuitous term to describe the bean counters in city hall and their detested city manager. But it was an apt reflection of residents' emotions at the time, for "the serpents" had abandoned the city before everyone else while mismanaging the evacuation, then blocked the residents' return, and would still govern remotely for the next several months from temporary offices in Santa Monica where their attendance was sporadic and suspect. "It was like a paid vacation," whispered someone to me trading candor for anonymity.

"Meanwhile," I wrote several months after the fire,

> I can still see from a sandy perch on free Zuma beach that monster cloud, dark with toxic ash,

slowly drifting from above a west Malibu exploding in spasmodic flames, to cast an ominous shadow over Point Dume that fateful Friday afternoon. That image and the view the next day of the smoldering ruins of homes of friends and neighbors, and our house miraculously still intact, will be with me for a long, long time.

And I had been hurting, physically, though I did not mention it my commentaries. But I did document it in support of our insurance claim, which also cited the negligence and culpability of the Southern California Edison Company, whose wires and poles reportedly sparked the blaze at a remote canyon core.

I noted that the Woolsey Fire had erupted on Nov. 8, 2018, the very day I was sent home from the UCLA Medical Center where I been hospitalized recovering from another of my cancer-related surgeries, an emergency laparoscopy cholecystectomy, and subsequent septic shock. The release came with the strict instructions that I confine myself to bed for at least a week, to rest and recover. We first heard of the fire when we arrived home later that day, but reports had it far north. Still, it was a restless night.

We awoke on the morning of Nov. 9, 2018 to an order to evacuate, as the fire was headed directly for Point Dume. We decided to retreat to a nearby beach area and wait to see how the it developed and what direction it would head. But first, we had to decide what keepsakes and valuables should and could be saved. With the fire bearing down upon us, and the evacuation mandate echoing, it was a nightmare. We somehow managed to gather up crucial documents, such as our passports, legal titles and deeds, and family photos, and pack an overnight bag; and with our parrot and two dogs in tow, off we went to shelter nearby on the Zuma Beach parking lot.

Meanwhile, Malibu residents who had tried to escape via the Pacific Coast Highway were caught in a major traffic jam that lasted hours while the fire continued to race towards the ocean. They were threatened, and shortly so were we, for the parking lot where we were sheltering dead-ends at the Point Dume cliffs. If the fire breached the highway we would be engulfed, at water's edge and with no way to drive out.

I watched with increasingly anxiety as the fire marched down the hills of Malibu Park, witnessing homes exploding as the fire progressed, heading directly for where we were sheltering. When a huge cloud of acrid black smoke traveled over our heads, we decided it was time to head away from Malibu. However reluctantly, we joined the bumper-to-bumper traffic inching down the lone route toward Santa Monica. Having ordered us to evacuate, the Malibu municipality did nothing to help.

As a result, the drive with us in separate cars was frightening, dodging oncoming fire engines, weaving down the Pacific Coast Highway constantly looking in the rearview mirror to see if the fire was on our heels, its glow seemingly just over the ridge at our side, the black smoke darkening the sky. To add to motorist anxieties, the City of Santa Monica had closed its borders, refusing to allow any more refugees from the fire to enter by car. We exited further down the freeway, in Culver City, where by following other cars found a restaurant with an outdoor patio. There we sat with our confused pets and struggled to eat, while trying to decide what to do next.

My wife contacted her sister, Katherine Highcove, who lived with her husband, Joe, in Woodland Hills, in the San Fernando Valley and about twenty miles from us over the Santa Monica Mountains' coastal ridgeline. Having watched the disaster unfold on television, and now hearing from us, without hesitation they invited us to come stay for as long as necessary. We gratefully accepted.

The next day we were called by our then-tenant, who had sheltered on Zuma Beach, and told that our house and their apartment above our garage had survived the fire—barely. However relieved, I would spend the next week ailing and restless at my sister-in-law's, going back and forth on the back roads to Malibu, checking on our house, and tending the chickens of our neighbor who had been barred from returning,

Ostensibly because of myriad safety concerns, the county had declared a quarantine, sealing off the Malibu coast and blocking residents from going back, until at least power was restored. I got through daily on my frayed press credentials, ferrying supplies to residents who hadn't evacuated but had instead stayed to fight the fire. Though castigated by the city manager, in many cases they'd saved their homes and those of their neighbors. Heroes all.

It was nearly two weeks and the electric power restored and the fear of looters abated before the barriers came down and residents were allowed to return to their homes, or what was left of them. Because of the fire's fierce winds, blazing embers had alighted seemingly at random, setting some houses on fire, to burn to the ground, while only dusting others.

Though our house was covered in toxic ash, we were happy to be home, as were the animals, ignoring the lingering smell of smoke. I would spend the next month recuperating in our damaged home, then being frustrated for the next two years while repairs proceeded sporadically due to an obstinate, disinclined insurance company and the dearth of workers.

The pain from the Woolsey Fire and aftermath was emotional, physical, and financial. Our community had been wrecked beyond repair. Numerous neighbors who, having fled Malibu, were either unwilling or unable to rebuild. Included were many longtime residents with an institutional memory of the ambiance and character of Malibu. They were gone, to be replaced over time by tourists and wealthy part-timers with no vested interest in recreating the neighborly closeness of a small town.

Five years later, swaths of Point Dume that had been burned remained under construction, with backhoes and trucks still clogging the streets and disrupting the rural quiet that had pervaded the peninsula in the past. But for many the problems were worse. If the possible sale of their homes had been an option, it was being adversely affected because many insurance companies were no longer offering reasonable coverage in fire areas. Buyer weren't interested. As for our home insurance, it was not renewed, sending us scurrying to find another carrier and end up paying more for less coverage.

"So so lucky," commented my New York learned lawyer daughter, Alison. My deceased father would have added, as he did to me once after a personal misfortune: "Get over it, you still got your health, so enjoy it." It was a gruff attitude borne of surviving as a youth in an ominous Europe. And no doubt my mother would caution: "Survivors shouldn't look back."

Nonetheless, the memory of the worst Malibu fire in history still weighed on my consciousness months after, as I considered what to write for my commentaries, while growing increasingly perturbed about how too many fire victims were being treated by miserly insurance companies and, worse, city apparatchiks and covetous consultants feeding off the flood of post-fire rebuild funds.

And then there was an unapologetic city manager who, behind closed doors, was presumably counting the post-fire state and federal disaster grants, proclaiming how despite the fire she had balanced the city's budget and books. Echoing resident complaints is what got me dropped from the local public radio station, which courted the goodwill of city hall. But if anything the responses to my social media commentaries increased, with "eyeball" counts on several local websites that generally attracted an estimated ten thousand views, in the parlance of the internet, depending on the issues broached.

Heartrending were the very personal stories of victims that I heard in the coffee shops, on lines at Costco, and gossiping at the Trancas Canyon Dog Park, now that it was finally open after being closed for a year.

Most plaintive were the candid comments posted on social media in response to my commentaries. My writing was considered essential reading for anyone remotely involved in the rebuild effort and who wanted to know what victims and others were thinking and, most importantly, feeling. This made me the recipient of much of the residents' pent-up frustration with the city. Admittedly, a lot of these people had seldom heard the word "no" in their privileged lives. But they had reason to be mad this time: local government was being tested and found failing.

Exposed by the fumbling of the rebuild effort, the willful ignorance of Malibu's governance was exasperating, so I tried to put what I saw happening into a larger perspective. I wrote, dramatically:

> The muddle in Malibu can be sadly considered a local manifestation of what certain pundits have described as a rupture of the link between the governing and the governed globally that has exacerbated no less than the crisis of climate change, the continued deterioration of the environment and the dispiriting economic disparity.

The more pointed my commentaries, the more pointed and political were the reactions. "What the city government really owes us is to make it possible for Malibu to return to its old self," declared a resident, continuing that

> we all know what Malibu used to be and the only way to return to that Aloha feeling is to allow rebuilding by those who have been forced out. Part of that is for the City Council to tackle rent gouging with strict enforcement of the laws, lower the rebuild fees and stop the takeover of Malibu by short-term rentals. Our locals need to live in Malibu.

This renewed my plea made prior to the Woolsey Fire for some sort of affordable housing for the people who serve Malibu. I added that the fire victims needed somewhere to live during rebuilding, as did those who were selling their barren and charred sites but still wanted to live in Malibu. These were hard choices for persons who professed their love of Malibu as a seaside rural village with a distinct sense of place, for when ultimately deciding what to do they also had to consider age, feelings, and finances.

In one of my many commentaries in the wake of the disaster, I expressed concern whether there be a hollowing out of Malibu, from a community of congenial households with a local history "to a more anonymous tourist town and trophy luxury houses for the off-putting one percenters, people who can afford the costlier rebuilds." And if so, I asked, how would Malibu change in the coming years?

Those informally questioned were hesitant to reveal their plans because they truly hadn't decided yet or had nagging concerns about insurance, the rebuild process, escalating construction costs, and the time everything would take. Seniors were most concerned. Without prompting, they all expressed anger about how the city and first responders had failed them, and how this had exacerbated their concerns over the future of the city, as it had mine.

They noted with varying emphasis and anguished adverbs the pathetic preparations, the woeful and frustrating mandatory evacuation, and, most of all, the botched deployment of firefighters and equipment. If they blamed anyone, it was City Manager Reva Feldman, who was further reviled for being self-aggrandizing.

This was angrily sounded at the several post-fire forums and echoed in my continuing commentaries "lest we forget who failed us, and who might fail us again in the future fires, sure to come, to a changed Malibu, sure to be."

DEMOCRACY'S SOFT UNDERBELLY

Then came the Covid-19 pandemic, which if anything heightened my concerns for Malibu. The visual and performing arts that had so diverted me crashed, and consequently my reviewing them. I now confined myself to my house, making masked forays to the neighborhood dog park, shops for essentials, and the nursery to buy plants.

My commentaries on local planning and politics that previously had been pointed became more so, and with the 2020 election pending, provocative. No longer mildly nonpartisan as I had been on public radio, I could now vent, so I riled, for example, against the tragic farce of President Trump. But I seldom did in print or broadcast, for having no national exposure, and so many other similarly incensed commentators did, I instead focused on the upcoming local elections and post-Woolsey Malibu.

"If you care about the future of Malibu and the value and enjoyment of your home," I wrote in a social media commentary,

> you have to be concerned about the local election now in its formative stage. By any personal or popular measure, the conceit of Malibu as a distinctive community known the world over as a prestigious, if not pricey, address has been on the wane for its permanent neighborly residents.

I identified these residents as those who might walk the neighborhood streets and beaches, who'd raised children or currently had them in the public schools, and who maybe shopped in the local stores and farmer's market: "these are the residents who lived through the Woolsey disaster, witnessed the abdication of our first responders, and the continued, unapologetic feigned efforts of a mostly inept bureaucracy, to be sure with a few exceptions."

And I added, drawing a line in the sand of an increasing divided Malibu, "This is in contrast to those who have second and trophy houses here, with or without resident caretakers, secluded behind security gates: the hedge and trust fund supercilious, the haughty weekend one percenters, then there are the partying short term renters and the noisy neighbors from hell."

Identify them as you will, these aliens were on the increase in Malibu, to the detriment of school enrollment and the death of locally owned stores and affordable eateries. "Indeed, are there any left?" I asked, and then added it was my hunch that "these aliens also are the riffraff speeding and trashing our streets, and . . . these pandemic days, not wearing masks in public. I continued:

> As for the present and past Councils who I've chastised for being in effect toadies, to be fair they never signed up for having to steward a city through the rough times of the last several years, while being scammed by a wily staff and special interests, but rather to enjoy the prestige and perks, and not necessarily govern. A few should not be there on the dais. I sadly state this, for it's time to reform City Hall, to

> drain the swamp and put local government on high ground to pursue the city's noble vision, and to serve the true residents of Malibu. . . . [W]e don't need apologists or acquiescing, if amiable, councilpersons, and we don't need novices, but rather creditable professionals and the passionate locals who will join to take back Malibu, for those who live here. Let us therefore welcome the election season, with caution.

With three seats of the five up for grabs in the election, it was vital to win them all to gain the needed reform majority. But only two of the three reform slate candidates won, prompting the two identified pro-development incumbents to embrace the third, who squeaked in thanks to the avid support of the city's formidable realtor community—and with dire consequences. Forming a perverse majority, they castigated the outspoken reformer who had garnered the most votes, Bruce Silverstein, and conversely praised and rewarded the city manager. I labeled their action, "willful ignorance."

> Beyond the City Council majority's self-serving public relations, I asked, "what of the planning and advocacy Malibu needs to prepare for the next disaster that is sure to come, let alone the daily demands of a fragile city deluged with tourists and part-time residents?" I noted that valued perspectives had been suggested on a simmering social media, "but sadly it seems the Council majority doesn't listen, dismissing them as a vocal minority, as if they didn't have valid observations and rights."

And to add a professorial touch to my commentary, I quoted Machiavelli: 'those who themselves are not wise cannot be well advised.'" What was apt for Florence under the Medicis in the sixteenth century was apt for Malibu in 2020. I continued: "Debatable is whether Malibu's governance needs to suffer the time and trouble of a remake empowering a strong mayor as has been proposed, who just may have his or her own predispositions. Especially, if the local real estate lobby had it sway," and added, "It seems simpler if the council would do its job and usher Reva and her parasitic personnel out the door."

The complaints by residents of favoritism, as well as ineptness, were directed primarily at the city's rebuild project. And this despite it being heralded as Malibu's number one priority, with scripted promises by past mayors. But after the self-congratulations and staged photo op, it was back to the in-and-out basket pantomime shading city hall's prime priorities of payroll, perks, and pensions.

If anything, the commentaries laid bare the inadequacies of the city council, which I contended for too long had been relegated to a ceremonial role, orchestrated by a self-serving, bloated bureaucracy and select consultants.

For this sad state of affairs, I blamed the majority councilpersons for allowing themselves to be manipulated, "be it out of vanity, being lazy or just frankly not being particularly qualified or smart." And I suggested the blame also "must be borne by the naïve neighbors who voted for them and put their signs up on their lawns, and that has on occasion included me, and willingly played to Malibu's cult of amiability, seductive, yes, though also subversive."

But there was light at the end of the dark tunnel that Malibu's city hall had become. The continued requests by Councilperson Silverstein of the city manager's office for accountability and transparency apparently nettled Feldman, who retained a lawyer, and proffered an offer to resign. This she did in time, but not before extracting from the neophyte council majority a $350,000 parachute and proviso it would not investigate or sue, and from the local sycophants and businesses a fawning farewell luncheon.

This prompted me to comment on social media that in the four years of her concocted incumbency as Malibu's overpaid and underachieving city manager, you did have to be impressed by Reva Feldman's chutzpah. "If only she had served Malibu with that shameless spirit instead of herself and her entourage of staff and special interests," I commented ruefully, "she just could have persevered despite her fumbles in the Woolsey Fire and the aftermath."

Feldman left leaving a cloud of questionable governance over city hall and successive city council majorities in the continued sway of rapacious local real estate interests. And I continued to comment wherever possible on the tribulations of my Malibu and the quest for livability in a most beguiling, though precarious, environment.

But I did so wary and weary of its smalltown politics, which I feared because of local greed, ignorance, and indifference, had become the soft underbelly of democracy, and the quest for a sense of place, and its promise of livability, an increasing challenge.

GOING FORWARD

The Covid-19 pandemic easing in late 2022, I gradually ventured out of my cocoon in Malibu, to return to the world of cities and culture beyond. I was of course vaccinated and taking precautions, having already survived a bout with the virus, while also frankly bored of the consuming parochial politics and provincial governance of Malibu and its mercenary realtors.

Though I was not tired of tending my landscaping and bird and butterfly refuges, and continuing my social media commentaries, in which I hopefully had raised in the community consciousness of Malibu's vision of a "unique land and marine environment" and the need for its protection, if not for the fragile seacoast ecology, then for its livability and value.

And still I kept involved locally, harboring the continuing hope for an enlightened planning effort to rejuvenate the city's forlorn civic center with housing for the burnout victims, seniors, teachers, and the local workforce, and create a real village neighborhood. I continued, then, to inundate the local social media with redundant pleas to make public safety a top priority, preventing and fighting wildfires not by giving consultants pamphlets to hand out, but by organizing and supplying local fire brigades and shaming the fire department into doing its job.

Then there was my repeated clarion call to revitalize the city's rebuilding project to prioritize the Woolsey burnout victims, fast-tracking a practical permit process. I was now also urging the support of the new city manager, Steve McClary, in shaking up the city hall bureaucracy, starting with planning, then code enforcement. And I continued to argue that short-term rentals and Airbnbs be curbed while land use policies be refined to serve Malibu residents, with the hope the city become more family-oriented.

For questioning the council majority I and several other outspoken residents were subsequently accused of "inexplicable" extremist views by the twice-serving mayor Karen Farrer in a legal deposition in an investigation of favoritism in city hall. The irony was that we, the accused extremists, were among the group of reformers who, however naïvely, had encouraged the "investigation." Unfortunately, it had turned into a costly whitewash by an arbitrarily selected local law firm that dutifully recorded the charges of the sitting majority that had hired it and bluntly ignored all the other substantiated charges, including mine.

The hope of streamlining and fast-tracking the approval process turned out to be a public relations sham, as was a promise to hire knowledgeable staff who hopefully would actively advocate for the city's forlorn residents.

Persisting was the question of whether Malibu as a fabled address could somehow survive as a livable community with a sense of place and not just as a trough for avaricious real estate interests and a bloated bureaucracy. Will hope for Malibu's noble mission statement to maintain its unique rural character prevail over its history of poorly planned development and an undiscerning, self-aggrandizing local leadership? Will Malibu's residents, still reeling from the Woolsey disaster ever get the requisite transparency and accountability required for good governance?

Yes, I wrote wishfully, echoing the residents who had long battled to preserve what is special about Malibu. Hopefully they, we, would prevail, instead of the well-connected and deep-pocketed, along with the sinecurists at city hall, who had tenaciously clung to their malpractices, hiding behind a baleful status quo.

To be sure, like the looming raucous national election of 2022, the local election in Malibu was not neighborly. Taking a cue from the Trump playbook were several residents defending the feckless council majority, spewing a steady stream of falsifications and personal insults.

Indeed, with their twisted logic and blatant lies written in bursts of bad grammar and spelling I thought they might undermine their perverted polemic and expose themselves as petulant, if greedy, juveniles in their attacks on individual private residents. I believed that this would favor the two reform-minded candidates and spell victory for the slow-growth crowd.

It did not, as Malibu split its vote, going overwhelming for the state slate of decidedly progressive Democrats and nationally for Biden-blessed candidates. But locally, narrowly, it chose the two nondenominational conservative candidates, and the city's woebegone majority prevailed. It was a sad commentary on the traction of the city's realtors and development community.

I was disappointed, but not surprised. My faith in the democratic process in a privileged community like Malibu where property rights are paramount had been on the wane for some time. The greed in the private sector was palpable and insidious, and in wanting to keep the dialogue among neighbors civil, I avoided commenting on it publicly. But if asked, I was always ready to grumble.

The local vote, in concert with the indifference of those who did not vote, also could be seen as a scathing riposte to the flagrant failures of government during and after the fire when Malibu residents were left to fend for themselves. In my view this was a breach of Jeffersonian democracy's hallowed social contract between public institutions and ordinary citizens, between the governing and the governed, the fire department and homeowners, city hall and residents.

"Where are the institutions worthy of our trust?" I asked on social media. As we could see in our bubble of Malibu, its newspapers were fading, just like its public radio, which was good for weather and traffic but unreliable for reporting or editorials. All continued to defer to the status quo of city hall, while seemingly awaiting to cash in their Malibu chips to a deep-pocketed buyer, regardless of their dumb or dumber politics.

The institutional link between the governing and the governed was being irrefutably strained internationally and nationally. But also obviously locally, making one doubt we would ever achieve a consensus protecting Malibu's fragile environment, certainly not when there was a buck to be made by gaming the system.

Or maybe I was just getting tired of arguing for a modicum of civic responsibility in a Malibu growing greedier and more self-serving, and beyond, the helplessness I felt witnessing a suffering Los Angeles, its homelessness shameful and rife.

Whatever the case, it fed my desire to return, or some would say escape, to my experiencing the visual and cultural arts and entertainment venues. They were once again beckoning, however hesitantly, and were not as crowded as in the past. They were strangely quieter, too, I discovered on several trips to New York City and Philadelphia to catch up with family and friends and to venture into the subdued central cities.

But when once again happily traveling abroad, especially to familiar France and Paris, life seemed as vibrant as ever, if pricier. It appeared all just wanted to forget or ignore the pandemic, the war in Ukraine, the seismic political shifts, or they did in public places, at least. Being swept up in a bustling city can do that.

As in my maverick critic past, I ricocheted through different cities, a flaneur, attending with wife Peggy an orchestrated schedule of cultural events and architectural viewings, going to ethnic eateries, revisiting historic landmarks, and returning to remembered neighborhoods.

Beyond Paris in the fall of 2022—and the latest art exhibits, leisurely meals, and a bout with Covid in a depressing Dijon—were side trips to the wine country and Provence. Then on another excursion in spring 2023 we went to familiar Amsterdam and its resplendent Rijksmuseum for a heralded, consummate Vermeer exhibit, and from there to singular Venice. The step was slower, but the heart beat faster and the soul soared.

Having had to suppress my cultural curiosity for two years due to the pandemic, I now celebrated its return, while also prodding my now fewer editorial connections in the hope of structuring some sort of critical presence on social media and the waning world of print. This while cutting back on my local commentaries, their impact obviously being minimal other than to praise the stalwarts and shame the malfeasants.

I didn't think about creative strategic planning and development in some sort of public or private consultant association or as an adjunct academic. I was convinced that those days were gone forever. Then came a call from a friend I once served as a planning consultant, asking me if I'd take a meeting with an aspiring developer whom he thought I could possibly help, in Malibu and perhaps beyond.

As is my wont, I said yes, of course, and joined him and the touted developer for a discreet lunch in Malibu. The developer said he wanted to pursue humanistic projects, environmentally sensitive, contextual, user-oriented. In a word, "livable." My type of projects.

Maybe, I thought, this could include my long wished for housing in a residential enclave to serve those who serve Malibu: teachers and first responders, in addition to the still suffering Woolsey Fire rootless burnout victims, and maybe some work-live artist lofts. Hopefully it could be imaginatively designed, featuring communal stoops, well-landscaped public spaces, and a community garden. So for me, it was "once more unto the breach." I signed on as his strategic creative consultant. At eighty-seven years, I felt young again.

After several months, however, I came to the sad realization that my local stature and exalted plans were just being used as a ruse by the covetous developer to wrest approval for a luxury hotel. I quit, my dream of the needed housing and its promise of a sense of community and place, lending Malibu a soul, rattled, my ego bruised. Is this sadly to be my future, I pondered?

But the dream persists.

It not incidentally also gave this book what I felt was an appropriate ending, consistent with my mother's echoing maxims, to never look back, only forward, for as she did, I consider myself immortal, until not.

AFTERTHOUGHTS

Prospects of immortality aside, my urban odyssey coming to an end, still moot is the inherent search for a sense of place, the soul of cities, as a fount of civilization, if not more modestly, livability.

To be sure, over the nearly ninety years as I have jumped rock to rock in the turbulent urban waters, there has been a welcomed rising design consciousness and environmental awareness, site specific and everywhere, in theory and practice, academic and empirical.

Be it by sitting on a stoop, or meandering through neighborhoods, surveying cities and the suburbs beyond, you can see that there is much redevelopment and reimagining to celebrate. This includes innovative design, inspired landscaping, resourceful recycling, assiduous rehabilitation, and—particularly pleasing—an increasing sensitivity to the user, a wish to serve human endeavor.

At the same time, at present, there also is much to be alarmed about: climate change imperiling the environment and life, insidious racial prejudices poisoning populations, income disparity fomenting vulgar private opulence and public squalor, homelessness and hunger, ignorance and harm, greed and fear stoking hurtful hate, seriously threatening democracy. Humankind doesn't seem to be getting any better.

What indeed of the future?

INDEX

A

A Theory of Good City Form, by Kevin Lynch, *128*
Abe, Rosenthal, 20, 54–57, 93–94, 96
Abel, David, 226–27
Adams, Frank S., 17–20, 22, 54
Aerospace Museum, LA's Exposition Park, 159
After The Planners, by Robert Goodman, 139
Alaska, xiv
Albers, Josef and Anni, 253
Alden, Bob, 56
Alison, 84, 101, 181, 286
"All The Pap That's Fit to Print," *Village Voice*, 55
America, xv, xvii–xix, 24, 59, 71, 79, 88, 107, 134, 168, 277
Amsterdam, 2, 299
An Architectural Guidebook to Los Angeles, by David Gebhard and Robert Winter, 262–65
Angeleno, 130, 214
Angelenos, 126, 243
Asia, 93–94
Aspen, 86, 90
Architect's Newspaper, 231
Architecture Unbound, by Joseph Giovannini. 258–62
Archnewsnow.com, 231
Art Center, College of Design, Pasadena, 214–16
Australia, 36

B

Babyn Yar, xvii
Baldwin, James, 37
Banta, Sara, 181
Baxter House, 80, 136–37
BBC, 171
Beavers, Rhett, 217, 219–20
Bedford-Stuyvesant, 25, 31
Bellow, Saul, 29
Berkshires, 49
Berlin, 256
Bernheimer, Martin, 139
Bernstein, Ken, 134
Beverly Hills, 9, 119, 255
Bilbao, 166, 172, 260–61
Bing, Xu, 250–51
Bloomberg, Mayor, 201, 203, 205
Bogaard, Claire and Bill, 155
Boston, 2, 120, 127
Boyle Heights, 112, 163
Bradlee, Ben, 93, 102–3
Bradley, Tom, Mayor, 129
Brandes Gratz, Roberta, 97
Brentwood, 119
Broad, Eli, 170, 179
Broadway, i, 28, 38, 120, 169, 199, 255
Bronx, xvi, 5, 46, 54, 212
Brooklyn, xviii, 1–2, 10–12, 16, 21, 25, 55, 113, 138, 156, 188, 196–97, 209, 265
Brownson, Omar, 244
Bryant Park, 15
Bunker Hill, 165
Byzantium, 63

Index

C

Cabrillo Museum, 159
Calder, 174
California, 2, 105–6, 116, 118, 121, 126, 129, 132–33, 135, 140, 145, 147, 151–52, 165, 180–81, 184, 189, 197, 213, 221, 225, 228–29, 233, 237, 253, 263, 267–68, 270, 277, 283
California Planning and Development Report, 147
Cambodia, 93
Canada, 39, 47
Canadian Broadcasting Company, 86
Cape Canaveral, 162
Caplanski clan, 156
Carey, Hugh, Governor, 100
Carlson, Ann, 254
Carnegie Hall, 176
Carter, Jimmy, President, 100
Catledge, Turner, 57–59, 61
CBS TV *Sunday Morning*, 53
Center for the Study of Los Angeles, 126
Central Park, 5, 9, 28, 111–12
Chagal, Bella, 255
Chagal, Marc, 255
Challenger, 162
Chandler, Raymond, 108
Checkpoint Charley, 256
Chelsea, 10, 202–5
Cheuse, Alan, xvi, xviii, 107
Chicago, 108
China, 250–51
Chinatown, 119
Cities in the Race for Time, by Jeanne Lowe, 70
City University of New York, 167, 196
Civic Center Urban Design Task Force, Malibu, 276
Chula, Vista, 220
Cliffside Drive, 272, 274
Cloward, Richard A., 88
Coffey, Shelby, 103
Collie, Border, 254
Columbus Circle, 31
Coney Island, xviii, 1
Constance, 84
Copenhagen, 108
Copland, Aaron, 183
Cork, xvii
Cornell, 13–14, 18, 66, 70, 104, 201
Cornell Daily Sun, 15
Crown publishers, 133
Culver, city, 284
CUNY, School of Architecture, 211
Cuomo, Mario, 36

D

Dada, 251
Danube, xvii
Day of the Locust, by Nathanael West, 108
Defensible Space, by Oscar Newman
Denver ,110
DeSapio, Carmine, 35
Detroit, 66
Dewey, John, 252
Dexin, Gu, 250
Didion, Joan, 92
Dijon, 299
Disney Imagineering, 7, 167
Disneyland, 125, 215
Donleavy, Steve, 99
"Do Real Planning," guidelines, 238
Doubleday Books, 15
Downtown News, 173, 175, 179, 190, 195
Dreyfuss, John, 121, 139, 149, 156
Dublin, xvii
DuBrul, Paul, 92

Duke University, 250
Dunne, John Gregory, 106

E

East Harlem, 7, 20, 26, 40, 52, 198
East Harlem Independent, 26, 51
Edwards, Steve, 190
Eichhorn, David Max, 128
Elements of Style, The, Strunk and White, 17, 249
El Mercado, East LA, 112
Emmy, 67, 168, 171–72, 184–85, 256
Ennis House, LA, 137
Empire State Building, 9, 201
Epstein, Bob, 120

F

Farmer's Market, L.A., 119
Farrer, Karen, Mayor, 296
Feldman, Reva, 289, 294
Fishel, uncle, xvi, xviii–xix
Fitzgerald, F. Scott, 108
Flatbush, 1, 3, 9, 199
Florence, 293
Forbes, 48
Fort Bliss, 14
Fort Dix, 14
Fox Television News, 177, 190
France, xvi, xviii, 166, 299
Franklin, Benjamin Houses, 26
Franklin Plaza, 27,
Fremont-Smith, Eliot, 21, 104, 128
Freund, Wini, 75
Fried, Joseph P., 77
Fuller, Buckminster, 88

G

Garcetti, Eric, Mayor, 145, 245
Garcia, Margaret, 219

Gebhard, David, 262–63
Gehry, Frank, 155–61, 163, 165–66, 168–69, 171–72, 174–77, 179, 184, 187, 245–47, 260
Gelb, Arthur, 56
Germany, 166, 256
Getty Center, 135, 223–31
Gill, Irving, 224
Giovannini, Joseph, 258–62
Glaser, Milton, 90
Glassell Park, 191
Glenwood Springs, 90
Goldin, Greg, 231, 233
Goldwyn Library, 160
Goodman, Robert, 139
Govan, Michael, 229
Graham, Martha, 255
Grand Central Market, L.A., 112
Grazer, Brian, 123
Great Society, 52
Greenfield, Jeff, 78
Greenwich Village, 4, 35, 39–40, 200, 208
Guerra, Fernando J., 126, 188
Guggenheim Museum, 166, 177, 260

H

Habitat, UN Conference on Human Settlement, 86
Hall family, 23
Hall, Margaret Mary (Peggy), 106, 141, 269–70
Hamilton, Calvin, 145
Hammer Museum, 252–53
Harlem, 5, 7, 20, 25–27, 31, 35, 37–38, 40, 50–52, 60, 63, 66, 68, 74, 112, 138, 198, 212
Harrington, Michael, 88
Hausman, Baron, 46

Hawthorne, Christopher, 223
Hecht, J. Randolph, 221
Hefner, Hugh, 29
Heimann, John, 100
Henningsen, Nancy, 101
Herkimer, 13
Highcove, Katherine, 285
Highland Park, 218–219
Historic Preservation magazine, 133
Hitler, Adolf, xvi
Hollywood, xiv, 119, 124, 141, 144–45, 160, 236–37
Hong Kong, 264
HOPE, NYC housing program, 27
Hough, Michael, 279
Housing Crisis U.S.A., by Joseph P Fried, 77
Houston, 19, 162
Howard, Jane, 92–93, 111
Hudson, river, 39, 99, 202, 240
Hughes, Langston, 73
Huxtable, Ada Louise, 28, 139

I
Idyllwild Arts foundation, 181
Imagine Entertainment, 123
Inman, Robert, 262, 264
Italy, 2
Ithaca, 13
Ivy League, 16, 18

J
Jacobs, Allan B. 141–42
Jacobs, Jane, 39–40, 42–48, 50, 52, 75, 92–93, 97, 105–6, 111, 113, 130, 141–42, 241
Javits, Jacob, 25, 40–42
"Jew Card," 157
Jewish Journal, xv

J. Paul Getty Trust, 135
Joe, 196, 258, 262, 285
Johns, Jasper, 251–52
Johnson, Philip, 28
Jones, Quincy, 230, 242

K
Kaplan, Alison 181
Kaplan, Fanny, xvii
Kaplan, Josef 181
Kaplan, Kyle, 181–83
Kappe, Ray, 213, 224
KCRW, City Observed, 173, 175, 178, 184, 249
Kennedy, Bobby, 22–26, 28–32, 50, 254
Kennedy, John, 30, 32
Kiley, Dan, 5, 276
Killefer Flammang, 195, 226
Kirk, Bill, 26, 50–52, 91–93, 101–6, 155
Knoxville, 107
Koch, Ed, 35–36, 98
KPCC, "Off Ramp," 178–79, 184–87, 249
Kyiv, xvii
Kyle, 106, 179, 181–83, 273

L
LA Lost & Found, 47, 133, 263
LA Follies: Design and Other Diversions in a Fractured Metropolis, 161
Lance, Burt, 100
Landregan, Stephanie, 216–18
Lautner, John, 153
Leapman, Michael, 99
Lee, Dick, Mayor, 34, 63–64, 66–67, 212
Lehrer, Ruthanne, 130
Lenin, Vladimir, xvii

Les Halles, 112
"Lessons of L.A.," *Oculus*, 122
Levin, Brenda, 226
Lewis, Anthony, 24
Liang, Shaoji, 251
Lichtenstein, Roy, 253
Limbaugh, Rush, 248
Lincoln Center, 240
Lipsyte, Robert, 95, 99
Lloyd, Frank, 137, 159, 224
London, 34
Long Day's Journey into Night, by Eugene O'Neill, 255
Looking At Cities, by Allan B. Jacobs, 141
Los Angeles Conservancy, 127, 130, 134
Los Angeles County Museum of Art, 136, 250
Los Angeles Review of Books, 134, 258
Long Island Daily Press, xiii, 12, 16
Los Angeles Times, xii, xiv, 7, 47, 79, 103–5, 107, 111, 116, 129, 138, 140–41, 147, 151, 155, 167–68, 184–85, 187, 193, 223–24, 227, 234, 256, 258, 261, 267, 279, 302
Lowe, Jeanne, 70
Loyola Marymount University, 126
Lubell, Sam, 231, 233
Lynch, Kevin, 128

M

MacAdams, Lewis, 245, 247
MacArthur Fellowship, 43
Machiavelli, 293
McMansions, 279
Maddux, John, 192
Mailer, Norman, 56, 104
Malcolm X, 37–38

Malcom, 37–38
Malibu, 9, 196, 200, 210, 252, 257, 266, 268–98, 300
Maitin, Samuel, 16
Malkin, Carol, 128
Malko, George, 108
Manhasset Bay, 68
Manhattan, 5, 9–10, 14, 34, 46, 48–49, 69, 99, 111, 119, 196, 198, 201–2, 209–210, 240, 242, 263
Mayne, Thom, 264
McClary, Steve, 296
McGill University, 195
McGovern, 77
McMansions, 279
McPherson, Bill, 91, 101, 128
Mead, Margaret, 88, 93
Meruelo, Richard, 189, 191–92
Miami, 77
Mike, 84, 101
Mikesh, Robert, 128
Mitchell, John, 33
Model Cities, 52
Mohawk Valley, 13
Moley, Raymond, 239
Montreal, 196
Morphosis, 264
Moscow, xvi
Moses, Robert, 42, 44–46, 52, 65, 239–42, 245
Moss, Eric Owens, 213–14
Moss, Jeremiah, 206–9, 213–14
Mother Theresa, 88
Murdoch, Rupert, 36, 95–101

N

Napoleon, xvi
NASA, 162–63
National Register of Historic Places, 131

Index | 307

Nelson, Daniel, 69, 80–81
Neutra, Richard, 153, 224
Never Built Los Angeles, by Greg Goldin and Sam Lubell, 231-32
New Babylon, 108–9, 133
New Haven, 5, 34, 62–63, 65–67, 69, 91, 138, 189, 276
New Jersey, 6, 14, 67–69, 138
New Jerusalem, 108–9
New Republic, 86, 88
New York City Educational Construction Fund, ECF, 33, 68-69,118, 167, 193
New York Herald Tribune, 27
New York Post, xiv, 36, 47, 95, 104, 111, 302
New York Times, xii–xiii, 5, 16–16, 20, 23, 32, 49, 55, 57, 77, 79, 92–93, 99, 104, 111, 128, 139–41, 148, 155, 162, 167, 184, 198, 202, 208, 212–13, 249, 302
New Zealand, 87
Newark, 66–68
Newfield, Jack, 78, 92
Newman, Oscar, 77
Newsday, 76–77, 95
Newspaper Strike, NYC, 1962, 53
Nicholas, Frederick, 170
Nixon, Richard, 32–34, 77
North Carolina, 34, 252
North Hempstead, 74

O

Oculus magazine, 81–83, 122
O'Donnell, Michael, 26
Office of the Comptroller of the Currency, U.S. Treasury Dept., 148
Office of Historic Resources, City of L.A., 134
O'Keefe, Georgia, 110

Olmsted Brothers and Bartholomew, 232
O'Neill, Eugene, 255
Oculus, 81, 122, 200
Olmsted, Frederick Law, 42, 232, 240–41, 245
Oregon, 270
Ouroussoff, Nicolai, 187

P

Pacific Standard Times, 228–30
Pan Pacific Auditorium, L.A.,131
Paris, xvi, xviii, 2, 9, 112, 120, 299
Pasadena, 113, 132, 141, 154–55, 214
Pasadena Redlining, 132
PBS, 171
Peace Corp, 26, 51–52
Peg, 270, 272
Peggy, xii, 181, 269, 299
Pennsylvania Avenue, 149
Pennsylvania Avenue Development Corporation (PADC), 91,
Pereira, William, 229
Pereira&Luckman, 232
Perin, Constance, 84
Philadelphia, XV, 299
Philbin, Ann, 252
Piven, Frances Fox, 88
Planetizen, 42, 147, 200, 202, 235
Planning Report, the, 147, 191, 195, 223-31, 235, 240, 242, 262
Point Dume, 272, 283–84, 286
Poland, xviii
Pomeroy, Lee Harris, 212
Pompeii, 9
Poor People's Movement, by Frances Fox Piven and Richard A. Cloward, 88
Port Washington, 68–69, 72, 74–78, 80, 85, 87, 130, 137, 198
Portage Bay, 89

Preserving Los Angeles, by Ken Bernstein, 134-136
Princeton, 18, 20, 54, 67–70, 212
Pritzker Prize, 166, 229, 245, 264
Public Works: A Dangerous Trade, by Robert Moses, 239
Pulitzer Prize, 54, 93

Q
Quatro Design Group, 193
Quebec, 47
Queens, xv, 11–13, 196
Quinn, Sally, 103

R
Rabe, John, 184
Railroad Perishable Inspection Agency, 10, 14
Reaganomics, 149
Rebecca's Restaurant, 161
Richards, Kristen, 122
Rijksmuseum, 299
Rikers Island, xvii
Rios, Jose, 172, 185
Riveredge, 193–94, 244
Rockefeller Foundation, 44
Roloff, Michael, 73
Romania, 105
Rome, 6
Rosenthal, A. M., 20, 54, 56, 93
RTKL Design Group, 193, 244
Rudofsky, Bernard, 71–72
Russia, 156

S
Saar, xviii
Sacramento, 248
Sadie, xv, 11, 87, 156
Sadik-Kahn, 202

Salem, 270
Salisbury, Harrison S., 31–32
San Bernardino, 178
San Diego, 220
San Fernando, 191, 268, 285
San Francisco, 127, 135
San Gabriel Valley, 155
San Jacinto, 181
San Pedro, 159, 163
Santa Ana, 280
Santa Fe, 110
Santa Monica, 9, 58, 109, 120, 149, 156, 158–59, 184, 216, 248, 262, 269–70, 279, 282, 284–85
Sargasso, 105
Sayo, 196
Schanberg, Syd, 93–94
Schindler, Rudolph M., 153, 224
Schindler, Suzanne, 212
Schulberg, Budd, 108
Seattle, 89–90
Seymour, Ruth, 178
Shakespeare, William, 10, 40
Shanghai, xix
Shapiro, Harvey, 20, 51, 75
Sharron, Walther, 50–51, 66, 69, 84
Shulman, Julius, 133, 224
Shuster, Simon, 43, 75, 88, 105, 139
Sidenbaum, Art, 105, 127
Sikeston, 107
Silver Lake, 119, 152–53
Silverstein, Bruce, 292, 294
Simi Valley, 280
Skirball Cultural Center, 253
Smith, Eliot Fremont, 21, 128
Solovitz, Sammy, 17–19
"Son of Sam," NYC Serial Murders, 97
Southern California Edison Company, 283
Spain, 166, 172

Sparks, Frank, 170
Spitz, Sarah, 178
Spring, Bernard, 6, 70
Stalin, Josef, xvi–xvii
Staats-Zeitung un Herold, 16
Steinem, Gloria, 28–29
Stewart, Potter, 279
Streets For People, by Bernard Rudosky, 71–72
Sulzbergers, 56, 59
Sunland, 163
Sunset Blvd., L.A., 119.

T
Talese, Gay, 28, 58–59
Tauber, Gilbert, 21, 53
Taylor, Jean Sharley, 104–5, 139, 148–49, 192
Thailand, 2
The Abuse of Power, by Jack Newfield and Paul DuBrul, 92
The Dream Deferred: People, Politics and Planning in Suburbia, 73, 84, 105, 141
The Last Landscape, by William H. Whyte, 71
The Long Goodbye, by Raymond Chandler, 108
The New York City Handbook, 21, 49
The Other America, by Michael Harrington, 88
The Private Lives of Public Schools, by Suzanne Schindler, 212
The Vast Majority, by Michael Harrington, 88
The World at Ten, PBS TV, 84
Thomas, Dylan, 40
Tilburg, Jan Van, 226
Tinseltown, 125

Toback, David, 128
Tolkien, John Ronald Reuel, 78
To the Sargasso Sea, by Bill McPherson, 105
Toronto, 46–47, 156
Trancas Canyon Dog Park, 287
Trastevere, 6
True Confessions, by John Gregory Dunne, 106
Truman, Harry S., 34
Trump, Donald, xviii, 290, 297
Turpin, Dick, 126

U
UCLA Center for the Art of Performance, 254
UCLA Extension Graduate Department of Landscape Architecture, 216–20
Udall, Morris, 23–25, 30
Ukraine, xvi–xix, 299
Upper Nyack, 196
Ur, City of, 9
Urban Design Studio, City of L.A, 134
U.S. Office of the Comptroller of the Currency, 104

V
Vancouver, 86–87
Vanishing New York; How a Great City Lost Its Soul, by Jeremiah Moss, 206–209
Vaughan, Sam, 75
Vecsey, George, 80
Venice, 9, 156, 159–61, 163, 229, 299
Vermeer, 299
Vietnam War, xiv, 46, 77
Village Voice, 55, 239
Virginia, 28

W

Wagner, Mayor, 25
Wall Street, NY, 118
Walt Disney Concert Hall, 165-166, 168-177,
Walther, Dwaine, 69
Walther, Sharron, 26, 50–51, 66, 69, 84, 137
War on Poverty, by Michael Harrington, 52
Warwick, 12
Washington Heights, "Upstate Manhattan," 198
Washington Market, West Village 121
Washington Post. 77–78, 91–93, 101–103
WNBC *Late Afternoon News*, 53
Wechsler, James, 98
Weeks, Bridgitte, 103
West, Nathanael, 108
Westwood, 216, 252
Whitney, Linda, 220–21
Whyte, William H., 43–44, 50, 71, 75, 79
Wikipedia, 279
Williamsburg, 196
Will Rogers State Historic Park, 253-54
"Will The Real Port Washington Stand Up"? *Newsday*, 76
With Man in Mind, by Constance Perin, 84
Wolfe, Dan, 54, 56, 104
Wolsey Fire, 278, 280, 282–83, 286, 288, 291, 294–96, 300
Woodbridge, John, 91
Woodland Hills, 285
World War II, xvii, xix, 83
WQXR, 31, 249
Wright, Eric Lloyd, 137
Wright, Frank Lloyd, 137, 159, 224, 232

Y

Yale University, 21, 35, 63, 66, 241, 279
Ylvisaker, Paul, 67–68

Z

Zalman, uncle, xviii
Zuma Beach, 282, 284–85
Zumthor, Peter, 229

ABOUT THE AUTHOR

SAM HALL KAPLAN is a renowned multimedia journalist, author, and teacher, with a parallel career in planning, design, and development. He has been a metropolitan reporter for the *New York Times*, design critic for the *LA Times*, and Emmy Award winning reporter/producer for local television news. He further has worked as an editor of the *New York Post*, a public radio commentator, and a contributor to many popular and professional publications and websites.

The peripatetic Kaplan also has served as a strategic consultant to Disney Imagineering, the Milken Institute, Howard Hughes Properties, and several planning and architecture firms, and has held public service posts. These have included directing the design and construction of innovative mixed-use air rights developments in New York City and acting as a special assistant to the US Comptroller of the Currency. Books include *The Dream Deferred, L.A Lost & Found*, and *L.A. Follies*.

He has taught and lectured at the Art Center College of Design, UCLA, SCIARC, USC, Yale, Princeton, and the City University of New York, and has received grants from the Ford Foundation and the National Endowment for the Arts, and awards from the AIA, APA, AFTRA, and the Sierra Club, among others. He is married to Margaret Mary Hall, and is the (proud) father of four and grandfather of three.

www.ingramcontent.com/pod-product-compliance
Lightning Source LLC
Chambersburg PA
CBHW020326240426
43665CB00044B/720